A Living Revolution

Anarchism in the Kibbutz Movement

A Living Revolution

Anarchism in the Kibbutz Movement

By James Horrox

AK
PRESS
EDINBURGH · OAKLAND · BALTIMORE

AK Press
674-A 23rd Street
Oakland, CA 94612
USA
www.akpress.org
akpress@akpress.org

AK Press
PO Box 12766
Edinburgh, EH8 9YE
Scotland
www.akuk.com
ak@akedin.demon.co.uk

The above addresses would be delighted to provide you with the latest AK Press distribution catalog, which features the several thousand books, pamphlets, zines, audio and video products, and stylish apparel published and/or distributed by AK Press. Alternatively, visit our web site for the complete catalog, latest news, and secure ordering.

The production of this book was made possible in part by a generous donation from the Anarchist Archives Project.

Printed in Canada on 100% recycled, acid-free paper with union labour.

Cover design by Chris Wright | seldomwright.com
Interior by Kate Khatib

Table of Contents

Foreword

Fierce opposition to Zionism, and to the capitalist-military machine oppressing millions under its flag, is only emboldened by the encounter with the betrayed dreams of liberation and solidarity that lie shattered in its dustbin. For there is no question that things could have turned out very differently in this land, had the designs of the young Jewish men and women who landed on these shores during the first decades of the twentieth century come to fruition.

The communards of the early kibbutz settlements in Palestine hardly shared what Emma Goldman called "the dream of capitalist Jewry the world over for a Jewish state machinery to protect the privileges of the few against the many." What carried them to Palestine was the desire to build a classless society, a "commune of communes" based on self-management, equality, and Jewish-Arab cooperation. At stake was nothing less than the opportunity to transform the Jewish mobilization around Palestine into a project for the social liberation of all peoples, a project that could only be achieved under the banner of *stateless socialism*.

Yet the defining influence of anarchist currents in the early kibbutz movement has been one of official Zionist historiography's best-kept secrets. In the retroactive absorption of the communards' experience into Israel's nation-building myth, only a few selective manoeuvres were necessary in order to obliviate its aspects that would have proved too subversive for the new state's unifying republican ethos. Thus, the first kibbutzniks' personal sacrifices, the emotional intensity of their relationships and their revival of Hebrew as a spoken language were all played up as paragons of dedication, and mobilised to generate a sense of historical debt. But other elements—especially their antagonism towards private capital, their calls for binationalism, and the feminist struggles of women in the communes—were all left out of the historical accounts, school textbooks and public rituals, and excluded from the packaged narrative served up to subsequent generations.

It is against this background of induced collective amnesia that *A Living Revolution* makes its vital contribution. James Horrox has drawn on archival research, interviews, and political analysis to thread together the story of a period all but gone from living memory, presenting it for the first time to an English-reading audience. These pages bring to life the most radical and passionate voices that shaped the second and third waves of Jewish immigration to Palestine, and also encounter those contemporary projects working to revive the spirit of the kibbutz as it was intended to be, despite, and because of, their predecessors' fate.

The early kibbutz experience is of special interest to anarchists today, since the early twentieth-century communes were the first large-scale movement emphasizing the constructive, creative and spiritual aspects of anarchism—aspects that have become central to the movement in recent decades. Class antagonism was certainly present between the bourgeois Jewish owners of the first-wave colonies and the young new immigrants who initially sought work there. But the first communes were founded precisely in an attempt to carve out autonomous spaces of production that would subvert the initial stages of capitalist accumulation in Palestine. Rather than building up to an insurrection or a general strike—a strategy relevant to revolutionizing existing, mature capitalist societies—the communards sought to nip capitalism's emergence in the bud by constructing alternatives that would snatch the ground from under capitalist Jewry and take the lead in shaping the new society's economic and social structure. The period between 1904 and 1924 marked a unique historical crossroads in which such a manoeuvre made perfect sense.

With this perspective in mind, there is a point to be made concerning the ambivalent response that *A Living Revolution*, by its very premise, may raise among those who (like ourselves) are committed to ending all occupation, militarism and social injustice in Israel/Palestine today. Unfortunately, the Zionist account has become so pervasive that the early kibbutzim are almost universally seen as nothing but predecessors of the Israeli state, and therefore as fully partaking in responsibility for its eventual crimes against Palestinians and Jews alike. According to such a view, the idea of holding them up to the light of Kropotkin and Landauer takes on an incongruous, even disingenuous air.

Yet this view only makes sense if one accepts the premises of black-and-white political correctness that pervade the contemporary Left. There is certainly room to question the validity of applying anti-colonial hindsight to people that any progressive would otherwise consider economic migrants or refugees. Why is the search for anarchism in the early kibbutz movement any more objectionable than, say, pointing to the New England town meeting as a source of anarchist inspiration—as if those meetings did not take place on indigenous peoples' colonized lands? In the same way, resistance to the premise of *A Living Revolution* seems to have nothing to do with historical impartiality, and everything to do with the fear of tarnishing anarchism's good name (an oxymoron if there ever was one) through its association with early Zionism.

Yet it is a grave mistake to interpret, let alone pass judgment on, the efforts of the past in light of the injustices of the present. Such an approach partakes of a retroactive historical fatalism, one that has no place in the analysis of a movement that declares that "Anything can happen." Historical movement is never deterministic. There is never a single, linear and inevitable course of affairs charted out in advance. What would have happened in Palestine had the October Revolution been more successful in spreading to central Europe? Or if Jewish workers had more effectively resisted the British-sponsored takeover of their institutions by Ben-Gurion and his men? Or, for that matter, if Hitler had been killed in the Great War? Anything could have happened, just as it can today.

Acknowledging this is crucial if we are to encounter and assess the early kibbutz movement on its own terms, from the perspective of its own protagonists, as *A Living Revolution* so successfully does. Let their story and the sense of an open future inspire all those who struggle for freedom and justice on this Earth.

Uri Gordon
Kibbutz Lotan, May Day 2008

Acknowledgements

This book was written on three continents, over the course of two and a half years. The number of people who have contributed their ideas, comments and opinions along the way seems virtually infinite, and my sincere thanks go to everyone who's shared with me their knowledge and experience.

Much of the research that went into *A Living Revolution* was drawn from interviews and conversations with kibbutz members, former members, researchers, scholars and activists in Israel, Europe and North America. Some are directly quoted, but those who are not mentioned also contributed enormously to the development of the ideas in this book, and to them I am extremely grateful. I'm especially indebted to David Walker at the University of Newcastle-upon-Tyne and Mike Tyldesley at Manchester Metropolitan University for their support during the early stages of the project, and to Uri Gordon, Menachem Rosner, Yuval Achouch, Anton Marks, Duncan Riley, James Wake, Yiftach Goldman, Nomika Zion, Yuvi Tashome, Marianne Enckel, Yaacov Oved and Avraham Yassour, each of whom has played their own invaluable role in shaping the subsequent direction of the research. This project, however, could not have happened at all without the unwavering commitment and enthusiasm of my friend Rachel Purvis, who, frankly, never ceases to amaze me.

My editor, Joel Schalit, has devoted an enormous amount of time and energy to this book, painstakingly sifting through successive drafts of the manuscript, correcting my mistakes and supplying me with his valuable comments and suggestions. Without Joel's patience and devotion, *A Living Revolution* would never have seen the light of day, and to him I extend my sincerest gratitude and appreciation.

To all my friends who have been there for me during the difficult and frustrating process of writing this book I also give my heartfelt thanks. My ultimate debt of gratitude, however, is to my parents, Keith and Maureen Horrox, and to my partner, Anna Smith, for their unconditional love and support throughout.

Introduction

"As man seeks justice in equality, so society seeks order in anarchy. Anarchy—the absence of a master, of a sovereign—such is the form of government to which we are every day approximating."
—*Pierre Joseph Proudhon, 1840*

Of all the "utopian" social experiments in recent history, Israel's kibbutz movement is at once the archetype and a unique exception. From an unprepossessing collection of mud huts on the bank of the river Jordan, the simple idea of a communal society, free of exploitation and domination, quickly took root in Palestine and blossomed into a nationwide network of egalitarian communities. Through good times (and unfortunately through bad), these communes have not merely existed, but have persisted in different forms for nearly a century.

Unlike other "utopian" projects, most of which have historically been short-lived, ostracised by their host societies and generally regarded with suspicion and mistrust, the kibbutzim played a pivotal and decisive role in the founding of a nation and the reconstruction of an entire people. From the earliest days of their existence the kibbutzim took on the vast multitude of tasks that the Jewish renaissance demanded: They helped build Israel's infrastructure and lay the foundations for a national economy, took responsibility for the mass absorption of countless thousands of immigrants, created a national trade union incorporating more than three-quarters of the country's total workforce and provided an industrial and agricultural contribution to the country that continues to far outweigh the percentage of the population they house.

In no other state have communes played such a central role in national life. Yet, of the countless academic studies that have been carried out on this most famous of communal movements, few have successfully found a paradigmatic precedent for its unique mode of organisation. Most have tended to settle for ambiguous, catch-all labels like "communism" or "socialism in miniature." The system that has served the kibbutz communities so well for so long, however, is actually a politico-economic model as far removed from state-based forms of socialism as from market capitalism. While only a few mainstream observers have conceded that the kibbutzim embody even "an anarchist element," there is a much stronger case to be made for the kibbutzim being the ideological progeny of the anarchist tradition than the state-socialist one. [1] It is this case that this book intends to examine.

Anarchism's Social Vision

Ever since 1840, when Pierre-Joseph Proudhon used "anarchy" for the first time to denote a positive social doctrine, the term has been so consistently misrepresented that its meaning has been almost completely lost. To most, "anarchism" speaks more of a dystopian nightmare than the utopian philosophy it actually is, and, as a result, the ideology has largely been denied the attention it deserves as a political and economic theory.

Far from being the advocacy of disorder many believe it to be, anarchism is essentially an anti-authoritarian form of socialism. Based on the belief that hierarchical forms of politics are both undesirable and unnecessary, it proposes the dismantling of all authoritarian, coercive and exploitative institutions within society and advocates their replacement with alternative institutions of voluntary, non-governmental cooperation. Whereas state-socialism seeks to impose a traditionally hierarchical social order by means of centralised, top-down political and economic structures and processes, anarchism starts out from the assumption that people are capable of governing themselves without such institutions or the kinds of power relationships they necessarily require. By "ruling from below," anarchists believe, at the level of localised, self-governing communities, society will be able to transform itself into a self-managed, directly democratic and ecologically sustainable system, devoid of the exploitation and inequality intrinsic in the state-socialist model found in the former USSR and contemporary China, to name the most obvious examples.[2]

Peter Kropotkin

Anarchist ideas first began to emerge during the early 1800s, and, throughout that century, they rapidly crystallised into a coherent current of social thought with clearly defined objectives, highly developed not only in its critique of the capitalist state but in its conception of a future, post-capitalist alternative. This book focuses primarily on the political legacy, in the form of Israel's kibbutz movement, of Russian-born philosopher Peter Kropotkin (1842–1921)—one of the most influential anarchist theorists of the nineteenth century, whose theory of anarcho-communism (variously known as anarchist communism, libertarian socialism or communitarian anarchism) has left perhaps the greatest legacy to subsequent anarchist thinking.

Kropotkin's anarchism was based on the conviction that human progress is dependent on mutual aid and cooperation, rather than competition. The vision of a future post-capitalist society he described was one in which the coercive and exploitative institutions of the centralised capitalist state would be replaced by a freely-federated network of voluntary, agro-industrial communes, administered democratically by the members, with no hierarchical authority structures or any framework of legal sanctions.

Within these decentralised communities, people would live in equality as both producers and consumers, with the distribution of goods and resources taking place in accordance with the communistic principle of "from each according to his ability to each according to his need." Property and the means of production would be owned in common, the wage system abandoned and the capitalist division of labour replaced by the integration of manual and white-collar work through systematic rotation of work roles. With self-management and direct democracy taking the place of centralised decision-making structures, this system, Kropotkin believed, would ensure a free, classless society.

According to Kropotkin, the capitalist economic model is only a logical and desirable one if personal gain and surplus value (economic growth created by unpaid, or to put it in Marxist terms, "exploited" labour) are taken as the starting point of our economic activities. Should the needs of the individual be taken as the starting point, on the other hand, we cannot fail to reach "communism," a mode of organisation that, he said, enables us to satisfy all needs in the most thorough and economical way.

Viewing labour as a social activity dependent on collective cooperation rather than solitary effort, Kropotkin held that the wealth produced by this labour should be owned in common and used to promote the collective good. Having been created by the collective efforts of all, property, the means of production and the requisites for the satisfaction of society's needs must be at the disposal of all.

In Kropotkin's future society, all property—including the means of production—would be owned communally by the collective's members. With the means of production owned by all, products manufactured would be at the disposal of all. The abolition of private property, Kropotkin believed, and the passage of the means of production into common ownership would mean that the wage system could not be maintained in any form. As far as possible, all goods and services should be provided free of charge, with goods available in abundance accessible without limit. Anything in short supply would simply be rationed.[3]

For Kropotkin, the integration of manual and white-collar labour was crucial to creating circumstances in which the individual would not be forced to work, either through coercion or the promise of remuneration. Quite apart from the social stratification resulting from the division of labour (where job role determines social status and level of material reward), Kropotkin found the idea that we should spend our lives confined to a single, repetitive activity "a horrible principle, so noxious to society, so brutalising to the individual."[4] By putting an end to the separation of manual and cerebral work, he argued, "work will no longer appear a curse of fate: it will become what it should be—the free exercise of all the faculties of man."[5]

Although remaining a self-governing entity, Kropotkin's "free commune" would exist within a federated network of similarly decentralised organisations, each one a productive unit in an economy built on the specialisation of functions.

The many and varied needs of society would make interdependence between communes inevitable, and they would thus grow together into a complex, fluid, decentralised society, in which voluntary associations within and between the federations of communities would replace the hierarchical and centralised productive centres of the capitalist state. With federal power kept to an absolute minimum and kept strictly under the control of each communities' delegates, the economy would be coordinated through this interwoven network of local, regional, and national groups and federations.

The No-Government System

Like Marx, Kropotkin believed that the way economic activity is organised determines all other aspects of social life; the "non-economic superstructure" of a community—its social, cultural and political norms—reflects the character of the economic base. The particular system of government employed in a given society is thus the expression of the economic regime that exists in that society, and vice versa. In Kropotkin's ideal society, where the antagonism between employer and employee has been replaced with voluntary, cooperative labour, there is no need for government at all. "The no-capitalist system," he wrote, "implies the no-government system."[6]

This does not mean that an anarchist community would not have rules, but rather that the rules and behavioural norms that ensure social harmony would be arrived at collectively, and maintained voluntarily by agreeing parties without mechanisms of coercive authority—no police, courts or penal system—to enforce them. Social cohesion would be ensured as people replaced the competition and antagonism that typify market-driven societies with cooperation, solidarity and mutual aid.

Once the inequalities built into the state-capitalist model have been eliminated, so would the need to redress them, making crime a thing of the past. The threat of legal sanctions imposed by any form of governmental authority would therefore be rendered superfluous, with unwritten social mores perfectly satisfactory to ensure social harmony. Fulfilment of the individual's obligations to society would be assured by one's own social habits and "the necessity, which everyone feels, of finding cooperation, support, and sympathy among his neighbours."[7]

Anarchism and the Kibbutz Movement

Kropotkin's influence on the nineteenth century anarchist Left was so profound that his theory of mutual aid and decentralised, cooperative production has come to underpin most subsequent forms of communitarian anarchism.[8] It is entirely fitting, given his prominence and prolificacy within the European socialist circles of his day, that many of those most influential in shaping both the philosophy and the practical character of early socialist Zionism were not only aware of

Kropotkin's ideas, but viewed them as an important source of inspiration for the new society they hoped to create in Palestine.

Kropotkin himself documented anti-Semitism and identified greatly with Jewish workers during the years he lived in England and the United States. Fluent in Yiddish, he spoke with Jewish workers and met and corresponded with many of those who would go on to be key figures in the plans for cooperative settlement in Palestine, including Franz Oppenheimer, architect of the very first Palestinian-Jewish cooperative at Merhavia.[9]

Kropotkin's books subsequently were some of the first to be translated into Hebrew and distributed in Palestine, and his articles were reprinted in the journals of many of the groups and organisations involved in the early Jewish labour movement. According to historian and kibbutz member Avraham Yassour,

> The idea of building the future through independent communal creation appealed to many of the pioneers… [Kropotkin's] doctrine, which was based primarily on the absolute need for freedom of the individual and consequently on the absolute need for voluntary and non-governmental organisations, was eminently suitable to the reality that came into being with the kibbutz movement.[10]

The young men and women who arrived in Palestine during the first three decades of the twentieth century, finding no state structures except the colonial artifices of the Ottoman Turks, and later the British Mandate, found an unprecedented vacuum, which they attempted to fill with a combination of ideologies. Within this ideological ferment, anarchism exerted a much more dominant influence than is often believed. According to kibbutz historian Yaacov Oved, "anarchist influences were prevalent" among the founding generation of communards, and every strand of the kibbutz movement felt the impact of Kropotkin's anarchism to some degree.[11]

Gustav Landauer

The list of Kropotkin's admirers in the Jewish labour movement at that time includes some of the most famous names in socialist Zionist history. The man perhaps most singularly responsible for introducing Kropotkin's ideas into this milieu was German anarchist intellectual Gustav Landauer (1870–1919). Through Landauer's close friendship with Jewish theologian Martin Buber, his ideas regarding social transformation became central to the thinking of many of the youth movements that came to Palestine and established kibbutzim in the early 1920s, and in particular to Hashomer Hatzair (the Young Guard), whose communities later became the Kibbutz Artzi federation.

Landauer rose to prominence within the European Left during the 1890s with the radical student group, the Berliner Jungen (Berlin Youth). As editor of the group's newspaper, *Der Sozialist* (The Socialist), Landauer became something of a figurehead among the young, middle-class revolutionaries of *fin de siècle* Berlin, and he quickly made a name for himself further afield. By the turn of the century, Landauer had established a Europe-wide reputation as an essayist, lecturer, playwright, novelist, journalist, theatre critic and political theorist. Though his middle-class background and opposition to the class war often put him at odds with the mainstream workers' movement, his contribution to *fin de siècle* German culture was such that his list of admirers included some of Germany's most highly esteemed literary and philosophical figures.

Influenced by the ideas of Friedrich Nietzsche, Peter Kropotkin, Leo Tolstoy and Pierre-Joseph Proudhon, as well as by the German Romantics and English-language literary icons such as Oscar Wilde, Walt Whitman and William Shakespeare, Landauer's political outlook went firmly against the materialist grain of the late-nineteenth and early-twentieth century European anarchist Left. His pacifistic, non-doctrinaire form of anarchism was defined by his belief that the state is not an abstract entity existing beyond the reach of human beings, an entity that could be "smashed" by violent revolution, but an intricate and complex living organism composed of a variegated multiplicity of direct, living, interpersonal relationships between individuals. As Landauer famously wrote in 1910,

> The State is a condition, a certain relationship between human beings, a mode of behaviour; we destroy it by contracting other relationships, by behaving differently toward one another... We are the State and we shall continue to be the State until we have created the institutions that form a real community.[12]

For Landauer, it is the corruption of the human spirit (*Geist*) that keeps human beings locked into the competitive, mutually antagonistic relationships that perpetuate capitalism and the state. Should people step out of this artificial social construct, rejuvenate the communal spirit that had, in premodern times, bound society into a cohesive spiritual whole, and enter into a new set of relationships with each other, then capitalism and the state could not survive.

Revolution must therefore be a process of wholesale regeneration, a spiritual overhaul beginning with the individual and extending to the entire life of society. Rather than aiming for the revolutionary overthrow of bourgeois state-capitalist institutions, Landauer believed that to overcome capitalism and the state individuals must unite into community, "come together, grow into a framework, a sense of belonging, a body with countless organs and sections."[13] If this were to happen, the "creation and renewal of a real organic structure" could begin, and it is this organic structure that in time "'destroys' the State by displacing it."[14] With the growth of individuals into families, families into communities, and communities into associations, an entire alternative infrastructure would rise up within the bosom of the state, eventually to outgrow the existing order and replace it with a voluntaristic, freely-constituted "society of societies."

Landauer argued that the anarchist movement should therefore focus its efforts on restructuring of society from below, on constructive self-emancipation through the establishment of peaceful, self-managed, self-sufficient cooperative ventures as the seeds of a non-alienated future. Ultimately, this future would see interlaced alliances and interalliances of agro-industrial *gemeinschaft* settlements freely woven together into a "society of societies." Within these communes, the artisanal forms of production and rural communal traditions of pre-modern societies would be restored in tandem with small-scale industry, and the organic unity between agriculture, industry and crafts, and between manual and cerebral work, re-established.

With clear echoes of Kropotkin, Landauer described such a community as a "socialist village, with its workshops and village factories, with meadows, fields and gardens, with great and small cattle and fowl—you urban proletarians, get used to this thought, however foreign and strange it may appear at first, for that is the only beginning of true socialism that remains."[15]

The Kibbutz

Landauer's belief that individual self-realisation is the key to human progress, along with his conviction that this could be achieved at any time, means utopia, for him, exists in the eternal presence, rather than at a future stage of human development. This idea was profoundly appealing to the generation of Jewish youth responsible for the foundation of the kibbutz movement. It is no coincidence that much of Landauer's social theory, itself rooted firmly in the ideas of Kropotkin, would end up being put into practice in the kibbutzim.

The kibbutz is a voluntary, self-governing community, administered democratically by its members with neither legal sanction nor any framework of coercive authority to ensure conformity to its collectively-agreed upon behavioural norms. The source of political authority in the community is the general assembly of all members (the *asefa*) in which every member has an equal vote on every matter relating to kibbutz life, with decisions made by majority vote. Until very recently, private property was nonexistent on the kibbutz, with all property, including the means of production, owned communally and with production carried out collectively, without individual remuneration.

Built around a participatory economy, with the principle of job rotation ensuring that no social distinction exists between manual and white-collar labour, "the community's structural arrangements," as one writer puts it, "are unilaterally built for social fellowship, mutual aid, economic cooperation, diffuse power, informational networks and visible, nonexploitative labour."[16] Goods and services within the commune are provided on a basis of the Marxian formula "to each according to their needs."

As a self-contained social and economic entity, the kibbutz is what Martin Buber famously termed a "Full Cooperative." This means that, in contrast to traditional co-ops—organisations within which people came together for some or other specific purpose—the kibbutz embraces the whole life of its society. This being the case, it is more correctly described as a gemeinschaft-type society, a community built on strong primary relationships, norms and social control in which individuals are related to each other in an "all-embracing mutual conditioning."[17] As such, the kibbutz is founded on an amalgamation of production and consumption that requires the community's direct involvement in, and catering for, every sphere of life—political, economic, social and cultural activity alike.

The membership of the settlements today ranges from 50 to 2,000 people per community, with the average population of each standing between 400 and 500.[18] While each kibbutz is an autonomous entity, its general assembly retaining sovereignty and autonomy over its internal affairs and responsibility for its own social, political, cultural and economic development and decision-making, it exists as part of a federated structure of similar communes. The 269 settlements currently in existence are linked in a federative structure with a secretariat in Tel Aviv.[19] Should a decision of the secretariat not be accepted by the general assembly of a given kibbutz, the secretariat has little or no power of coercion to change the outcome.

The Kibbutzim and Zionism

In his postscript to a 1974 edition of Kropotkin's book *Fields, Factories and Workshops*, British anarchist Colin Ward cites the kibbutz as one of the few examples in history where Kropotkin's social theory has found successful practical expression. With this statement however, comes one caveat: "In citing the Jewish collective settlements as an exemplification of Kropotkin's ideal commune," he writes, "we have to consider them without reference to the functions they have performed in the last decades in the service of Israeli nationalism and imperialism."[20]

For some, this will be quite a caveat. The kibbutz movement's post-1948 link to the state of Israel—a country whose name has, to the contemporary global Left, become synonymous with apartheid and contemporary colonialism—including the number of its members who join the security services, the Israel Defense Force (IDF) and the political elite, certainly goes a long way towards explaining why the kibbutzim have generally not been perceived by anarchist movements as partners in their struggles. Many see the kibbutz's very existence as predicated on the forcible displacement and subjugation of the region's native Arab population, and would consider any progressive ideals of equality and social justice that the kibbutzim profess to hold nullified by the massive *inequality* on which the practical manifestation of these ideals has come to be based.

By definition, no commune that is officially loyal to any state can be viewed as an anarchist entity. However, that does not mean that we cannot identify and learn from the political precepts actualised *within* that commune. An article in London's anarchist newspaper *Freedom* in 1962 observed how

> [The kibbutz] is one of the best examples of democracy and certainly the nearest thing to practising anarchism that exists. Every pet theory of anarchism, like decentralisation, minority opinion, "law" without government, freedom and not license, delegation of representation are all part of the daily pattern of existence. Here in microcosm may be seen the beginnings of what might happen in a genuinely free society.[21]

Throughout history, all projects attempting to self-organise have been caught in different types of power networks that have complicated their existence. The kibbutz is no different.

Chapter 1
The Beginnings of the Kibbutz Movement

The foundations of cooperative settlement 1880–1919

"Our community does not *desire* revolution, it *is* revolution."
—*Martin Buber*

The kibbutz movement is the product of an exceptional set of circumstances. At a specific time and a specific place, a host of different factors came together in a chance convergence without which the kibbutzim would not, and could not, have come into being. The uniqueness of the kibbutz experiment cannot be fully appreciated without first coming to terms with the forces that shaped the movement's early development, and the context in which the kibbutzim emerged.

The story of the kibbutz begins in the *shtetls* of Eastern Europe during the late-nineteenth century. Russia's Jewish population had faced anti-Semitic discriminatory policies and state-sanctioned persecution in varying degrees since the 1400s, but, under the rule of Tsar Alexander II in the late 1800s, the country became an increasingly hostile environment for the thousands of Jews who lived there. From the 1850s onwards, the Tsarist regime enacted a string of policies designed to destroy independent Jewish life within the Pale of Settlement (the area of land including Poland, Belorussia, the Crimea, Bessarabia, and the Ukraine to which the country's Jews had been confined since 1791). With anti-government sentiment taking root among Russia's peasantry—and with it radical political doctrines seen by the ruling elite as potentially threatening to the existence of the regime—the Tsarist authorities deliberately popularised anti-Semitism as a political weapon, with the assumption that many of the radicals were of Jewish origin.

Portraying Jews as "Christ-killers" and the oppressors of Slavic Christians, the Tsar and his establishment increasingly stoked the fires of religious and nationalistic xenophobia and encouraged disgruntled peasants to vent their frustrations with the regime on their Jewish compatriots. The last two decades of the century marked the zenith of state-sanctioned persecution. In 1881, a wave of bloody pogroms swept through 166 towns in the southern part of the country, leaving large numbers of Jews dead or injured and thousands more in extreme poverty. In the aftermath of Alexander II's assassination in March that year, Russia's Jews found themselves on the receiving end of a string of state-enforced anti-Semitic legislation designed, according to Alexander III's friend and advisor Konstantin Pobedonostsev, to cause one-third to emigrate, one-third to convert to Christianity and one-third to starve.[22]

A staunch reactionary and firm adherent to the maxim "Autocracy, Orthodoxy and Nationalism," Alexander III placed the blame for the 1881 upheaval squarely on the shoulders of his country's Jews, and, the following year, issued the now-notorious "Temporary Regulations," which further legitimised oppression of Russian Jewry. The Temporary Regulations, or "May Laws" as they became known, included residency restrictions, which prohibited Jews from living in towns of fewer than 10,000 inhabitants—even within the Pale of Settlement—restricted basic rights, made freedom of movement increasingly difficult and systemised Russia's already strict anti-Jewish education quotas, which resulted in thousands being excluded from professions and denied a university education.

The May Laws, which were subject to repeated revisions over the following years, represented the beginning of a string of similarly oppressive legislation that solidified the Jews' legal status as inferior citizens in Russia. In 1892, for example, Jews were banned from voting or standing in local elections, which in many towns with large Jewish populations resulted in reverse proportional representation, the majority forcibly subjugated to openly hostile minority governance. As a result of this, together with ensuing legislation, hundreds of thousands of Jews were driven out of towns and villages across Russia, with many of the country's major urban areas—including Kiev and Moscow—completely cleansed of their Jewish inhabitants.

In addition to the dire humanitarian crisis forced upon Russia's Jewish population, the escalation of persecution had two key effects: First, the country's Jewish intelligentsia began to turn their attention to political activism. The century had given them much to draw on, for Russia had witnessed the domestic emergence of a wide variety of radical left-wing political doctrines, the latter half of the 1800s seeing numerous shades of socialist, anarchist, nihilist, liberal and syndicalist ideologies all beginning to take root. The ideas of Marx, Kropotkin, Tolstoy, Proudhon and Bakunin were entering the political spectrum and these ideologies, together with the rise of the Populist movement and the Tolstoyan agricultural communes, provided inspiration to a generation of persecuted Jews seeking a solution to their own increasingly desperate situation.

Aliya

The second major consequence of the upheaval was mass Jewish emigration. While the vast majority of the 20,000 or so Jews who fled Russia in 1881–1882 emigrated to the United States and Argentina, a few hundred headed for Palestine. Along with a small group of Yemenite Jews who began arriving from

Sanaa in 1881, these immigrants became the first of the six *Aliyot* (waves of immigration) to the country.

At the time, Palestine was a province of the Ottoman Empire under Turkish rule. The few Diaspora Jews who moved there before the advent of Zionist-inspired immigration had typically done so either to study at local *yeshivas*, or to live out the last years of their life and be buried in their ancestral homeland. At the start of the 1880s, Palestine's incumbent Jewish population, concentrated mainly in the religious centres of Jerusalem, Safed, Tiberias and Hebron, numbered somewhere between 13,000 and 20,000. While these Jews devoted their attention to religious activities and lived off the proceeds of charity raised in Europe (the *Halukka*), the new immigrants who began arriving in the early 1880s were the first to do so with aspirations of economic independence, aiming to cultivate the land in order to create the necessary socio-economic conditions for large-scale Jewish national revival in the country.

A small number of these First Aliya Jews (or *Biluim*,[23] as they became known) began to settle in Palestine as early as 1880, founding the first "new" Jewish settlements at Rishon Le-Zion, Rosh Pinah, Zichron Ya'akov, Gedera and Petah Tikva. These newcomers, and the stream of Jews that followed them to Palestine during the next few years, were treated with a certain degree of suspicion by the Turkish authorities. To them, the new immigrants were potential agents of a hostile power that threatened the existence of their country, and the Ottoman government accordingly made Jewish immigration as difficult as possible.

The early Biluim found themselves unable to obtain official permission to establish settlements in Palestine, which would support mass immigration, and in 1883, the Turkish authorities banned Jewish immigration from Russia and Jewish land purchases altogether. Immigration continued, however, and the laws regarding Jewish acquisition of land were circumvented by registering land purchases in the name of Jews from Western Europe and distributing *baksheesh* (bribes) among the local administration. By the early 1890s, upwards of 20,000 more *olim* (immigrants)—the majority of them from southern Russia—had arrived in the country.

The Second Aliya and the Birth of the Kibbutz

Unlike their immediate predecessors, these new *émigrés* explicitly propounded Zionist ideology, exhorting the "encouragement and strengthening of immigration and colonisation in Eretz Yisrael through the establishment of an agricultural colony built on cooperative social foundations" and the "politico-economic and national spiritual revival of the Jewish people in Palestine."[24]

The few communities that were established in Palestine during the 1880s and 1890s, however, were not nearly enough to lay the foundations for the national revival the Zionists were hoping for. According to historian Walter Laqueur, the enthusiasm and industriousness of the Biluim was matched only by their lack of preparedness. "They knew nothing about agriculture," Laqueur writes, "and found the work in unaccustomed climactic conditions almost unbearable. Above all, they had no money to buy land and equipment, and there were no funds for the construction of houses. Since…they had neither horses nor oxen nor agricultural implements, they had to work the stony land with their bare hands."[25] Having headed to Palestine with the intention of being the harbingers of Jewish national revival, within a short time of their arrival, the *Biluim* had become almost entirely dependent on charity. By the turn of the century, their projects were surviving on the financial input of foreign investors such as French Jewish philanthropist Baron Edmond James de Rothschild.[26]

While these First Aliya settlements could be considered the early forerunners of the kibbutzim, it was the immigrants of the Second Aliya who were instrumental in establishing the first *kvutzot*, or "proto-kibbutzim." This wave of immigration was, again, directly linked to events in Russia. Between 1903 and 1906, a second, much more devastating wave of pogroms broke out across parts of the country, leaving around 2,000 dead and resulting in a dramatic escalation in the numbers fleeing the country. With the concurrent rise of the Zionist Organisation, founded by Herzl in 1897, the idea of the permanent settlement of Palestine was beginning to gain popularity among world Jewry, and, as a result, Palestine was rapidly becoming the destination of choice for Jewish refugees.

Although this wave of immigration was far from homogenous, almost all were young, unmarried and came from Russia. The main contingent came from what was then known as White Russia, from eastern Poland and Lithuania. These new immigrants had been raised in a traditional Jewish environment and spoke Yiddish, but all had at least a basic understanding of Hebrew. In addition to these, and a small group from Yemen, there were also substantial numbers from southern Russia. Settlers from largely assimilated, affluent families, they spoke only Russian.[27]

These Second Aliya olim arrived in Palestine only to be shocked by what they found. The harsh climactic conditions that greeted them on their arrival caught them unawares: searing heat, deserts in the south, and swamps and rocky land in the north combined to create an environment that bore little resemblance to the Biblical land of milk and honey that many of them had been led to expect. Diseases such as malaria were widespread and took a heavy toll on the immigrants. However, the inhospitable conditions were not the only source of disappointment for these young, radicalised pioneers. They were equally taken aback by the economic situation of the First Aliya Jews already living and working in the country.

By this point, as noted earlier, the First Aliya settlements were being propped up almost entirely by Zionist philanthropists like France's Rothschild family. But even more distressing to the newcomers was the fact that the First Aliya Jews had resorted to hiring Arab workers to help build their settlements. While cheap, experienced Arab labour was the natural preference of the First Aliya farmers, it had certainly not been the intention of many Second Aliya *halutzim* (pioneers) to establish a class of bourgeois Jewish landowners exploiting the indigenous Arab population.

"This was not the way we hoped to settle the country," wrote one Second Aliya immigrant working at Zichron Ya'akov. "This old way with Jews on top and Arabs working for them."[28] From a nationalistic point of view, stratifying economic life along ethnic lines also threatened to subvert the emergence of a self-sufficient and autonomous Jewish economy, which was seen as a non-negotiable imperative for the reconstruction of the Jewish nation in Palestine.

In any case, First Aliya farms performed badly, with low profitability, and the Diaspora Zionist movement's emissary Arthur Ruppin soon had cause to report that private infrastructure alone would be incapable of supporting large-scale Jewish immigration. In his address to the Jewish Colonisation Society in Vienna following a six-month visit to Palestine in the spring and summer of 1907, Ruppin delivered a grim prognosis of the First Aliya enterprises, underlining the inadequacies of the floundering Rothschild colonies, and instead spoke positively of economic diversification based on cooperative principles.

Although he acknowledged that Rothschild's philanthropy had achieved much during the early period of immigration ("Our position today," he declared, "is very different from what it would have been if we had had to start our colonisation work from the beginning"), Ruppin insisted that it was not enough.[29] The single-crop farming of the First Aliya settlements was too great an economic risk under the circumstances, he reported, and the system of administration employed in the Rothschild colonies "blocked the development of a spirit of independence" among the workers.[30] Rothschild did not trust the abilities of the colonists, and he insisted on direct supervision of workers and complete managerial control by his agents. The commands of the administrators and agricultural experts appointed to oversee every group of colonies were binding, but, from a formal and legal standpoint, the risk was still carried by the worker.

"A situation like this is impossible in the long run," Ruppin declared. "It is hard for me to imagine a system under which the farmer must bear the responsibility while [merely] following the instructions of the administrator."[31] As Ruppin saw it, workers in the capitalist enterprises simply did not feel the same sense of personal responsibility as the farmer who takes the risk for his own decisions, and this feeling of alienation he viewed as a significant contributory factor to the inefficiency of the First Aliya farms.

Ruppin was not alone in recognising the impotence of the First Aliya enterprises. During the first few years of the twentieth century, the idea of cooperative settlement had become a widely respected one among world Jewry, thanks, in part, to the First Zionist Congress in August 1897, and the emergence of influential treatises such as Nachman Syrkin's *The Jewish Problem and the Jewish*

Socialist State, which was published the following year. Active in revolutionary circles in Russia, Syrkin fiercely opposed "bourgeois" elements within the Zionist Organisation and propounded the notion that Zionism should be achieved through the cooperative settlement of the Jewish working classes in Palestine. By 1898 he had put forward a systematic analysis of the needs of the Jewish immigrants, the proposed character of a cooperative settlement, and the essential infrastructural foundations necessary to synthesise the two.

As the influence of the Zionist Organisation mushroomed during the early years of the twentieth century, a broad consensus developed within the organisation that the way forward in Palestine lay in the establishment of collectivist structures, cooperative settlements and collaborative economic institutions, rather than in injecting private capital. By the time of the Second Aliya, Syrkin, Ruppin and other prominent Zionists had reached a general agreement that "the answer to the problem of Jewish labour lies in cooperation," concluding that

> Future settlements must entirely eliminate the antagonism between employer and employee, between the rich colonist farmer and his slaves, exploiter and exploited. In the cooperative settlement the worker owns the capital, and the cooperative character of the work sweetens the drudgery of toil and lifts the age-old curse and stigma it bears everywhere. In the planned cooperative settlement, the question of Jewish labour will find a solution, because the main problem, that of labour and capital, will be solved.[32]

The early years of the century, therefore, saw mainstream Zionist bodies busying themselves raising the necessary funds to finance of cooperative socio-economic institutions capable of settling large numbers of immigrants, rather than turning to capitalist investors like Rothschild. Ruppin himself would become an important advocate of collective settlement, and, in 1908, established "The Palestine Office" in Jaffa, which administered and coordinated all settlement projects in Palestine on behalf of the Zionist movement.

Degania

It was within this context that the first *kvutza* (communal settlement) emerged. But unlike the other cooperative structures and agricultural training farms being set up in Palestine at the time, its emergence was not down to any premeditated social or economic planning on the part of the Zionist Organisation.

The first kvutza was founded in 1910 by a group of young immigrants from the Romni Commune in Russia, who had been traveling around Palestine working in the various collective and quasi-collective settlements established throughout the country. On their arrival, members of the Romni had found employment at one of the First Aliya enterprises, Rishon LeZion, and had been "morally appalled" by what they saw in the Jewish settlers there, disgusted by the way it and other farms like it were run "with their Jewish overseers, Arab peasant labourers, and Bedouin guards."[33] Instead of the beginnings of an egalitarian society, founded on principles of equality and self-sufficiency, the group felt that the First Aliya Jews had succeeded merely in replicating the exploitative socio-economic structure of the Pale of Settlement, where Jews worked in clean jobs, far from the point of production, and relied on other groups to do the so-called dirty work.

Their subsequent experiences in the other First Aliya enterprises did little to alleviate their initial disillusionment. One member of the group, Joseph Baratz, wrote of his time working at the settlement of Zichron Ya'akov: "We knew more and more certainly that the ways of the old settlements were not for us... We thought that there shouldn't be employers and employed at all. There must be a better way."[34] The group eventually ended up at the Kinneret Farm at the foot of the Sea of Galilee (also called Lake Tiberias and Lake Kinneret), a large settlement comprising numerous different groups engaged in the process of land cultivation. Run by an appointed manager and functioning by means of a hierarchical-managerial structure, the farm's system did not sit comfortably with the egalitarian aspirations of many of the immigrants who worked there.

One of the workers' major complaints—both at Kinneret and other farms across the country—was that they were under constant supervision and scrutiny from managers and overseers. This resulted in endless squabbles and even strike action. However, the workers of the Romni group were also reluctant to accept the obvious alternative offered by the existing system, which was that they should accept promotions and become managers themselves. Many workers did find a way out through such channels, but Baratz and his comrades saw this as a betrayal of the most fundamental conviction underpinning all their values and ideas: "The belief in the moral superiority of a life of work" records kibbutz historian Henry Near, "and in their own obligation (and desire) to continue in this way of life."[35]

Baratz and his associates considered the alternative to be synonymous with their original ideological vision: the creation of a new social system built on the principle of voluntary cooperation. It would not be long before they would have the opportunity to test their conviction. In October 1909, a strike broke out when Kinneret's Jewish workers decided they could no longer put up with the oppressive, arbitrary administration and the use of hired Arab labour. Following a fiery dispute with the settlement's authorities, the Romni group, ten men and two women still in their teens, left the farm with the intention of settling their own piece of land according to their own principles.

Like many of the other immigrants, the Romni group had lived communally for some time in their pre-Aliya life back in Russia. Since their arrival in Palestine, the idea of establishing a permanent commune had begun to develop within the group. As Joseph Baratz recalls,

Thanks to our communal life, a feeling of intimacy between the members grew up. We talked a great deal about the "commune"; for a certain time, this was the main idea [which was discussed]: communal life not just for a chosen few, but as a permanent social system, at any rate for the bulk of the pioneers who were immigrating to Palestine.[36]

Having made the decision to stop travelling and establish a permanent settlement, the Romni communards were approached by Arthur Ruppin. According to Baratz, Ruppin "saw that the administrative methods at Kinnereth [sic] were unsatisfactory and he decided that a tract of land should be handed over to the halutzim to develop on their own responsibility."[37] Ruppin proposed that they start work on a piece of land on the bank of the Jordan River called Umm Juni, which had recently been bought by the Palestine Land Development Company from the Jewish National Fund (JNF).[38]

So, in October 1910 the first kvutza was born. The settlement, which they named Degania (Cornflower) after the crops they grew there, would come to represent a turning point in the Jewish settlement of Palestine. As kibbutz historian Avraham Yassour puts it, Degania represented "the founding of a permanent social system in which the group assumed complete responsibility for the farm and developed it according to its own principles."[39]

These principles can be summarised succinctly in the words of the group's 1910 letter to Ruppin, as "a cooperative community without exploiters or exploited."[40] Degania's founders went to great lengths to ensure that their new farm operated in a manner as far removed as possible from that of the First Aliya settlements. They decided on mixed-crop farming and intensive cultivation, as this was more labour-efficient and promised a more sustainable economic existence than the single-crop farming of the First Aliya settlements, which largely depended on global market prices and seasonal/weather conditions. The lifestyle they created was based on political and material equality, freedom and democracy, the cardinal principle of the community being the elimination of all forms of hierarchy and rank. It was, in their own words, to be an exemplary society with "no managers and no underlings."[41]

At Degania, private property was nonexistent, with everything from livestock and agricultural machinery to the contents of members' rooms owned by the collective. Such a society, the kibbutz's founders felt, would "increase the dignity of the individual and would free energy and independence for spiritual creation."[42] The group was adamant that no kind of work should be considered more important than any other, nor any kind of work looked down on as inferior. Its members organised the farm's production and consumption on a communal basis, with all managerial decisions taken collectively, management based purely on direct democracy and informal debate. The members' meeting was seen as the "supreme institution," and in it "every matter was to be discussed and every decision was to be taken according to the majority opinion."[43]

Each kibbutz member received a monthly income of fifty francs from the Zionist Organisation, and the group pooled these wages, maintaining a common household and a communal purse. Believing firmly in equality in the fulfilment of needs, they thus succeeded in eliminating any connection between contribution and reward, with each giving according to his ability and receiving according to his needs.

In marked contrast to the ailing farms of the First Aliya immigrants, less than a year after its establishment, Degania was already showing a fiscal profit.[44] The concept of communal groups of workers cultivating publicly-owned land was one that evidently caused a certain amount of excitement throughout the country. Following the success of Degania, the idea began to spread throughout the Yishuv[45] and among Socialist Zionist youth movements abroad, and soon other groups began trying to farm the land in a similar way. Before long, kvutzot were being set up wherever land could be bought, more often than not during this early stage on desolate wasteland or swamps, which the pioneers quickly set about cultivating.

Conditions were not easy; malaria, typhoid and other diseases were commonplace among the settlers, and many had difficulty adjusting to a life of hard physical labour. Throughout the Second Aliya, the development of these settlements was sporadic, atomistic and based largely on trial and error, but before long, the structure of the kibbutz had begun to coalesce at Degania.[46] By the end of the Second Aliya in 1914, 28 kvutzot with a combined total of 380 permanent members had been set up, each community running on principles broadly similar to the Degania farm.[47]

Although Ruppin et al. were not without their misgivings, there was general agreement from an early stage that this was a project that should be pursued on a wider scale. Every one of the kvutza settlements provided a better return on capital invested than the market-driven farms of the First Aliya immigrants, and, as a result, what started out being viewed as little more than an interesting experiment rapidly became an important and respected element of the Jewish labour movement in Palestine, and a project whose success quickly garnered the attention of onlookers abroad.[48]

Cooperative Settlement: Variations on a Theme

Throughout the Second Aliya there existed a wide range of different social, cooperative and communal organisations throughout Palestine. There were already numerous cooperative enterprises, a variety of collective labour groups worked the countryside and communal-living associations operated throughout the Yishuv.

The extent to which immigrants had been living communally and pooling resources, before the establishment of the first kvutzot, is often forgotten in discussions of the origins of the kibbutz movement. Jewish communes had existed in Palestine from 1904 onwards, and egalitarian ideals had been actualised in varying degrees in the other models of cooperative agricultural settlement that existed prior to, and eventually alongside, the kvutzot. The cooperative settlement at Merhavia was a second model, although not as collective in nature as the kvutza communes (the settlement functioned by means of a more hierarchical managerial structure and differential payment according to individual contribution). Less organic in its origins and based on rigid theoretical plans drawn up years before its foundation (see Chapter 2), Merhavia would serve as the prototype for the *moshav* settlements.

A third social model can be seen in the Kinneret farm where the Degania members, trained along with many who would go on to set up Ottoman Palestine's other kvutzot. As is clear from the origins of Degania, Kinneret's hierarchical management structure and oppressive administrative methods collided with the egalitarian principles of many of its workers, and this would eventually contribute to Kinneret's later evolution into a collective-style kvutza. A fourth model, and another major source for collective settlement during the earliest years, was the Bar Giora organisation. This group grew out of an organisation known as the Hashomer (the Watchmen), whose members were, from an early stage, "motivated by a conviction that the commune was the best way of life for themselves and their families."[49]

This group developed an "alternative model based on cooperative settlement, having in mind the elimination of exploitation and bourgeois relationships."[50] Its members would later become instrumental in the establishment of the many new collective settlements set up following the success of the earliest kvutzot, including Tel Adashim, Kfar Gila'adi, Ayelet HaShachar, and the kvutzot Haroim and Tel Hai.

Thus, the Second Aliya immigrant groups developed into a wide variety of different collective and quasi-collective economic organisations. However, on the political front, there existed just two main groups, Hapoel Hatzair (the Young Worker), to which the Romni group were affiliated, and the more orthodox Marxist Poalei Zion (Workers of Zion). The two groups would later combine to form Ahdut HaAvoda (Unity of Labour). At this stage, these organisations deliberately kept their distance from mainstream party politics, distrustful of political parties' ability (or even inclination) to promote the interests of the workers on the ground. Instead they supported what Israeli historian Avraham Yassour terms "innovative social organisation,"[51] which, in practice, involved organising at a grassroots level, setting up various trade and cultural associations as "mutual aid societies," whose goal was "supplying basic necessities in times of need."[52]

In an article published in the journal *HaAhdut* in 1914, the final year of the Second Aliya, Nachman Syrkin saw fit to assert that "colonies established in the country without regard to social concepts and based on the domination of one person by another, exploitation of the many for the benefit of the few, will continue to stew in squalor and iniquity."[53] While differences existed between the various groups of settlers during this early period, there is little doubt that leftist ideas were the dominant force in shaping the political landscape of the Yishuv. Ultimately though, it would be the kvutzot that emerged as the pre-eminent mode of organisation from that period, and, as the idea gained a foothold in Palestine, they gradually began to absorb increasing numbers of workers from the other collective-style settlements of the Second Aliya.

Chapter 2

Diggers and Dreamers

Ideology in the Second Aliya

"As we now come to re-establish our path among the ways of living nations of the earth, we must make sure that we find the right path. We must create a new people, a human people whose attitude toward other peoples is informed with the sense of human brotherhood and whose attitude toward nature and all within it is inspired by noble urges of life-loving creativity. All the forces of our history, all the pain that has accumulated in our national soul, seem to impel us in that direction... we are engaged in a creative endeavour the like of which is itself not to be found in the whole history of mankind: the rebirth and rehabilitation of a people that has been uprooted and scattered to the winds."
—*A.D. Gordon, 1920*

Most historians believe that the immigrants responsible for the kibbutz movement's foundation did not arrive in Palestine with any preconceived ideas for the settlement of the country. Martin Buber himself wrote that the kibbutz "owes its existence not to a doctrine, but to a situation, to the needs, the stress, and the demands of the situation" and his analysis has tended to be accepted virtually at face value.[54] The early years of the movement's development, according to Buber, merely show the Jewish immigrants "responding to circumstances as they met them, without clearly defined practical plans or established principles."[55] For members of the earliest kvutzot, he claims,

> The point was to solve certain problems of work and construction which the Palestinian reality forced on the settlers, by collaborating. What a loose conglomeration of individuals could not...hope to overcome, or even try to overcome, things being what they were, the collective could try to do and actually succeeded in doing.[56]

The writings of many of the earliest settlers underline the organic way the first kvutzot came into being; the point *was* to solve immediate problems, and the efficacy of cooperative labour in solving these problems was quickly proven. "The *Kommuna*, per se, was not a doctrine," wrote Degania's Joseph Baratz. "It did not come to us from the outside, from other people, from strange countries. We did not read any books about the kvutza; it is a local creation of Eretz Israel. Its source and root is the national and moral ideology."[57] Elsewhere, Baratz recalls how the Romni group "did not arrive at [the kibbutz] idea by a process of objective thought and consideration. It was more a matter of natural feeling: 'What is the difference between me and my comrade, and why should each of us have a separate account?'"[58] His wife Miriam later recorded a similar sentiment: "It is not a theoretical approach," she wrote. "We had not read about *Kommunas* in action. We had no examples."[59]

But to leave it there and attribute the kvutzot's emergence purely to circumstantial necessity is to underestimate the extent of the ideological factors involved in the movement's inception. We know that a wide range of social and political ideas were in circulation among the Zionist youth in Russia who would arrive in Palestine during the Second Aliya. As noted in Chapter 1, this wave of immigration was directly linked to events in Russia between 1903 and 1908, a time when the country was a hotbed of ideological ferment and a fertile breeding ground for radical political doctrines. Most of the rank-and-file newcomers already had some knowledge of the basics of alternative ways of life, and many brought with them direct experience of various different political subcultures. Some had also taken an active part in the abortive revolution of 1905, and had arrived in Palestine hoping to synthesise their aspirations of social justice with those of building a Jewish homeland in Palestine.

While Baratz may have had no concrete examples on which to draw, the early development of the kvutzot also saw many of the communards paying close attention to other experiments abroad. Important templates were found in the religious communes in the United States, the Russian artels, and the agricultural communities set up by followers of Tolstoy in the Northern Caucasus of Russia, of which some of the earliest settlers had had direct experience prior to emigrating.[60] Kibbutz historian Henry Near describes how the generation instrumental in the formation of the kibbutz was, in fact, "subject to the conflicting claims of almost every doctrine and dogma, from extreme orthodoxy in a variety of forms, through half a dozen variants of Zionism, to enlightenment and assimilation." According to Near,

> Virtually every variety of social doctrine…struggled for ascendancy among the Russian intelligentsia [in Palestine]: populism and Tolstoyan thought, every type of anarchism from nihilism to the communalism of Kropotkin, social democracy of the Bolshevik and Menshevik varieties, liberalism and more.[61]

The notion that the emergence of the kvutzot was the accidental result of "ideal motives join[ing] hands with the dictates of the hour," downplays the extent to which these "ideal motives" actually came into play during this time.[62] Though the kvutzot founders certainly came to understand what Buber calls the "needs, stress, and the demands of the situation," they did so only through the prism of the theories and values that they had absorbed in their youth. In seeking holistic solutions to both their own immediate problems, and to those of the Jewish nation as a whole, the young men and women of the Second Aliya attempted to put into practice the various socialist and anarchist ideals that they had acquired, and incorporate them into a new, permanent social model.

In an environment where so many conflicting shades of socialist ideology struggled for pre-eminence, the one accepted ideal was the concept of revolution. But this was a unique kind of revolution, in that it did not have an antagonist. Class differences were essentially nonexistent among the *émigrés* of the Second Aliya in Palestine, and this meant that it was not a question of proletariat versus bourgeoisie, but, instead, the building of a completely new kind of society from scratch—a society free of the evils the young Jewish immigrants had seen around them in their Diaspora countries.

Central to this revolution was the idea of inverting the Jewish social pyramid of the Diaspora, the regeneration of their selves, and the creation of a new kind of human being. As one veteran of the Second Aliya put it, those who arrived in Palestine between 1904 and 1905 "directed their actions to changing existing reality... They attempted behavioural norms directly opposed to those in existence,"[63] their intent being to "determine both the political agenda in Palestine and the Jewish condition world-wide."[64]

A.D. Gordon

Even at this early stage, the Second Aliya kvutza pioneers had their intellectual mentors in whom we can see embodied precisely the kind of ideological convictions from which the kvutzot were born. Nowhere has the philosophy of the early halutzim found fuller expression than in the figure of Hapoel Hatzair leader Aaron David Gordon, whose influence in the formative years of the movement gives lie to the idea that the way of life at Degania and its contemporaries was purely the result of accident or circumstantial necessity. In Gordon's work, both the ideological and practical objectives of the pioneers came together, and it is clear not only from the content of his writings, but from the esteem in which he was held by the Palestinian Jewish workers' movement, that the ideological convictions with which the early halutzim approached the kibbutz went far beyond the practicalities of land settlement.

Born into a middle-class, orthodox Jewish family in Podolia in 1856, Gordon had been brought up in the heart of the Ukrainian countryside where his father worked in the management of agrarian estates. An early member of the Hibbat Tziyon (Love of Zion) movement, Gordon had proven himself a charismatic teacher and local community activist. By the time he arrived in Palestine in 1904, at the age of forty-eight, thanks to his father's profession he had a knowledge of agriculture and the natural world unusual among the immigrants at that time, most of whom came from sedentary, urban lifestyles.

Upon his arrival in Palestine, Gordon worked at the First Aliya settlements at Petah Tikvah and Rishon Le-Zion before eventually settling at Degania. Although he was never actually a permanent member of the community, his name has today become firmly entwined with Degania. He spent much of his life in Palestine working there, and he was fondly described by Joseph Baratz as "the most strange and wonderful figure in our kvutza."[65] In his memoirs Baratz tells how Gordon

> had a great love of manual labour, and he thought everybody should work with his hands—teachers, writers, administrators. One day, he was explaining this to [Chaim] Arlosoroff, the President of the National Fund, who had come to see him. He was spreading manure with a pitchfork in a field. "You see," he said, "when you stand in a field and you use your pitchfork like this...and this...you feel well and you feel you have a right to live." He used to say that by work a man is healed.[66]

This love of manual labour and the natural world became a distinguishing feature of Gordon's writings, and it was to be an important influence on the generation of young, middle-class, urban Jewish youth attempting to metamorphose into hardened, rural labourers in Palestine. Influenced particularly by Kabbalistic and Hassidic mysticism, as well as by the existentialism of Nietzsche and the agrarian anarchism of Tolstoy, Gordon believed that manual labour was not only essential for the regeneration of the Jewish people (it is through labour, he argued, that "a people becomes rooted in its soil and culture"), but also that it held a more holistic value.[67] Gordon believed that physical and, in particular, agricultural work enabled human beings to connect with nature through creativity, and that it was through a return to nature that individuals, peoples and humanity as a whole would be able to find spiritual succour and a more meaningful way of life:

> Man's life has been cut away from its source. Naturally, it has become narrowed, impoverished, meagre, hollow, empty, uninteresting, vain. On the one hand, this results in a feverish pursuit of a life of pleasure, of sickly passion, of grasping at anything in the dregs of life that still has pungency... On the other hand, there follow perplexities, barren spiritual confusion, sterile scepticism, aimless wandering, vacillation, mystic fancies, useless despair. The light in life has been lost; its zest has gone; the talent for understanding life is wasted; in short, the talent to live has been destroyed.[68]

Gordon's outlook echoed the Tolstoyan belief that humans, themselves basically natural beings, are best when and if they reject the mechanical artifices of civilisation and live their life in an organic relationship with other people and nature. In contrast to modern urban culture, Gordon perceived no hierarchy in the natural world. To him, the cyclical characteristics of nature provided a replicable model for human society, and it was largely through his influence that physical, agricultural labour and closeness to nature came to be seen by the settlers not just as a means for the satisfaction of human needs, but as an end in its own right. It has been suggested that this so-called "religion of labour" that Gordon preached acted as a "surrogate moral code"[69] for the kibbutz pioneers, akin to Tolstoy's secular religiosity, the notion of "seeking the Kingdom of God not without, but within ourselves."[70]

Gordon certainly saw himself as part of the Zionist movement, but his Zionism was staunchly pacifistic and anti-militarist, and the idea of creating a Jewish state is never mentioned once in his entire body of work. While he believed in the Jews' historical right to live in Palestine, Gordon viewed the Arabs as an example of an organic nation living in harmony with the land, from which the Jews should take an example. At the same time, he was anything but naïve about Arab resistance to Zionism, which he viewed as a perfectly understandable reaction to Jews' westernised and rootless lifestyle. He thus envisaged the future of Jewish-Arab relations as one of peaceful competition at best—at least until the Jews fully reconnected with the land and earned the respect and cooperation of their neighbours.

While strongly opposed to capitalist forms of labour exploitation, Gordon also rejected "socialism"—by which he always meant Marxism—with its emphasis on the class struggle for different economic relationships as the key to overcoming capitalism and alienation. In Marxism, Gordon saw a continuation of the reigning mechanistic conception of the human being and society, an expression of alienated thought rather than a response to it. Since class was itself an artificial organisation of human beings, the proletariat could not be expected to serve as an agent of human transformation. Instead, he believed that the nation—an organic collection of individuals based on the principles of kinship and shared cultural values—was the only agent capable of heralding such change.

Furthermore, Gordon viewed the Marxist emphasis on changes in economic organisation as a privileging of form over content. The understanding that society would not change unless the individual changed was as central for Gordon as it was for Landauer and Tolstoy. It was therefore through the self-improvement of each and every individual, within the context of a revival of organic national life, by which mankind—and in this setting Diaspora Jewry—would be able to achieve national renewal.

It is in this context that Gordon emphasises the spiritual value of labour. Since human beings were deteriorating in proportion to the degree that they became alienated from the natural world, and since the Jewish people in the Diaspora had been affected more than any other in this respect (doubly detached from what

Gordon saw as the cosmic flow of creativity, by being both away from their land and occupied primarily in trade and liberal professions, rather than in agriculture), Gordon viewed a return to nature and a life of physical, and especially agricultural, work as essential. This reconnection between man and land through agricultural labour was, for him, the *sine qua non* of the spiritual and political reawakening of humanity.[71]

Due in part to his refusal to discuss his own philosophy in terms of labels like socialism or anarchism ("or any other isms"),[72] Gordon has been the subject of varying and often radically conflicting interpretations. On the one hand, he has come to occupy a central place in modern leftist historians' explanation of why Zionism, irrespective of its secular claims, is indeed religious, and even a classically nationalist concept. According to British academic Jacqueline Rose, it was para-religious spiritual socialisms like Gordon's that laid the ideological groundwork for the reconciliation of Judaism and Zionism, and ultimately for the contemporary right-wing national-religious ideology espoused by Israel's settlement movement.

Israeli political scientist Ze'ev Sternhell similarly argues that naturalism of the kind Gordon espoused, European romanticism and hostility towards modern industrial capitalism, converge in a Zionist context to become compatible with a classical nationalist outlook. Attempting to debunk the idea that a synthesis of socialism and nationalism was ever even on the agenda for the kibbutz pioneers, Sternhell suggests that the ideologues of Labour Zionism realised early on that the two objectives were incompatible. The pursuit of egalitarianism, he argues, was only ever a "mobilising myth…a convenient alibi that sometimes permitted the movement to avoid grappling with the contradiction between socialism and nationalism."[73] In Gordon, Sternhell sees the archetypal embodiment of this contradiction, and he draws on the particular form of nationalism Gordon preached to portray him as an almost fascistic figure: "In his rejection of the materialism of socialism," Sternhell writes, "[Gordon] employed the classic terminology of romantic, *volkisch* nationalism."[74]

For Sternhell, as for Rose, the religious component to Gordon's organic, cultural conception of nationhood is indicative of the way that Zionism expressed its religious character, undermining its portrayal of itself as a secular endeavour opposed to the "slave morality" of Diaspora Judaism. Gordon's positive attitude towards "the traditional requirements of religion: its beliefs, its rituals [and] its commandments,"[75] speaks to Sternhell of the consonance between his worldview and European integral nationalism, which also regarded religion, tradition and ritual as essential components of national identity. Gordon's "religiosity without belief in God"[76] is thus deemed confirmation of his consistency with integral nationalism's "affirmation of religion as a source of identity [which] had no connection with metaphysics."[77]

There is little doubt that Gordon's nationalism, with its volkisch and cosmic, spiritual complexion, flew in the face of the fundamental values of materialist, Marxist socialism. Less well examined in mainstream historiography, however, is its clear congruity with certain forms of anarchism prevalent within the libertarian romantic-revolutionary circles of fin de siècle Central- and Eastern Europe. An alternative interpretation of Gordon to that proffered by his latter-day detractors holds that it is, in fact, the left-wing, democratic and humanitarian school of volkisch romanticism—the same school that informed the kind of nationalist outlooks endorsed by figures like Rudolf Rocker, Mikhail Bakunin and Gustav Landauer—to which Gordon actually belongs.[78] The imbrication of romanticism, volkisch nationalism, anti-capitalism, secular spiritualism and mystical emphasis on land as the source of creativity embodied in Gordon's thought was central to Landauer's anarchism in particular, an overlap that was acknowledged by Gordon himself. In 1920, he returned to Palestine from a conference in Prague excitedly claiming to have "found his ideas" in Landauer's writings.[79]

Gordon's pacifism, communitarianism and silence on the question of a Jewish state have led those contemporary Israeli radicals familiar with his work to view him as one of the first and most influential anarchists in the early kibbutzim. The anti-authoritarian, anti-Marxist critique of bourgeois capitalist modernity Gordon introduced to the founding generation of communards has often singled him out as an early ideological forerunner of contemporary eco-anarchism in particular. Not only did he promote many of the key themes that are today encompassed within the eco-anarchist school (primitivism, bioregional democracy, pacifism, secession, intentional community and so on), Gordon was among the most prominent and prolific ideologues of a project that, for a time, actually translated these values into a working social model. For this reason, some see him as an especially important figure within the ideological heritage of eco-anarchism: "Gordon's kibbutz," writes Hune Margulies of The Martin Buber Institute for Dialogical Ecology, was "founded on strong anarcho-socialist and ecological principles… He was close to Buber in his espousal of anarcho-socialist communitarianism, and he was close to Spinoza in his secular spirituality. Current ecological thought will be best served by re-examining Gordon."[80]

Gordon and the Kibbutz

In 1905, along with Yosef Ahronowitz and Yosef Sprinzakand, Gordon founded Hapoel Hatzair (The Young Worker), a pacifistic, anti-militarist Zionist group dedicated to the idea of communal land settlement. His writings were published regularly in Hapoel Hatzair's magazine, alongside articles by and about other well-known anarchists of the time, including Kropotkin, Proudhon and Hapoel Hatzair theoretician Chaim Arlosoroff. Among the Jewish pioneers at that time there was abroad agreement that attempting to create a new kind of polity meant the creation of a new kind of person, and it is not hard to see why the young idealists of the Second Aliya had little difficulty in identifying with the Nietzschean/Tolstoyan ideas of spiritual renaissance Gordon preached.

But as well as laying the philosophical groundwork for the movement, even at this early stage, Gordon and his followers evidently had very clear ideas about the practical dimensions of the kibbutz and its role in the regeneration of the Jewish people. According to Gordon,

> the basic idea of the kvutza is to arrange its communal life through the strength of the communal idea, through aspiration and the spiritual life, and through communal work so that the members will be interdependent and will influence each other along their positive qualities... The kvutza...can and must work on two fronts. On one side—that of work and nature, the person must be free and must reform him or herself through work and through nature. The individual must associate with the very work and the very nature wherein he or she labours and lives. On the other front, there is the life of the family in the kvutza. The kvutza must serve as a family in the finest meaning of the term. It must develop its members through the strength of their mutual, positive influence... As soon as [individuals] draw together and begin to associate with one another, they become a family as though they had already passed through the sacred rites of marriage.[81]

This passage contains two important ideas: First, the emphasis on the individual having a direct relationship with the work s/he undertakes reiterates that the kvutzot, from the outset, explicitly sought to avoid the alienation inherent in the capitalistic production process. Second, and perhaps more significant at this stage, is Gordon's allusion to the idea of family, reminiscent of Tolstoy's belief in the importance of universal brotherhood, the hope that familial bonds could be extended into the wider fraternity of mankind as a whole, which is also found in Landauer's anarchism. Gordon is essentially introducing the anarchist argument that humanity's natural bonds of empathy and fraternity, corrupted by the influence of the capitalist state and the trappings of modernity, need to be restored in order to create a new kind of society.

Gordon's is a philosophy that would continue to underpin the ideas and actions of certain sections of the movement for many years to come. Hapoel Hatzair continued to look to him as their spiritual leader, and the early groupings of Hashomer Hatzair that arrived in the country from 1919 (and subsequently evolved into the Kibbutz Artzi federation) initially expressed a great affinity to his ideas. In 1923–24, the year after Gordon's death, Hapoel Hatzair supporters in Galicia, led by Pinhas Lubianker, set up the Gordonia youth movement, which adopted Gordon's existential philosophy and acted as a counterbalance to the Marxist influences that were, by then, beginning to appear in the politics of other pioneering groups. However, in the decades following his death, Gordon's subversive ideas would be muddled and eventually forgotten in the process of Zionist mythmaking, retaining only his personal example of dedication to agricultural labour and Jewish renewal for the Israeli historical narrative.

Franz Oppenheimer

While Degania and its immediate successors originated spontaneously and organically as anarchical settlements, they were certainly not without their principles. Moreover, some of those early immigrants also actually came to Palestine armed with "clearly defined practical plans." There, in fact, existed in the Diaspora a variety of highly detailed, codified blueprints for cooperative settlement pre-dating the establishment of Degania by many years, some of which drew directly on Kropotkin's ideas. Ironically, some of the earliest evidence of the Russian anarchist's influence on such plans is found in the work of Franz Oppenheimer, who collaborated with Theodor Herzl in the economic planning of the World Zionist movement and was the principal architect of the cooperative at Merhavia in the Jezreel Valley (prototype of the moshav model).

Despite how well known they were, Oppenheimer's plans for the settlement of Palestine still often tend to be overlooked by the popular tendency to ascribe the emergence of the early communal settlements merely to prevalent conditions and hardships. Although it represents the beginning of a form of social organisation distinct from the kibbutz, the Merhavia cooperative's background can be identified as among the first signs of Kropotkinite ideology amongst Palestine's Jewish settlers.

The theoretical foundations of the model Oppenheimer proposed were published in his 1896 book, *The Cooperative Settlement: A Positive Attempt to Overcome Communism by Solving the Social and Agrarian Problems*, in which he drew heavily on the ideas of Robert Owen, Charles Fourier, and also of Kropotkin (with whom he met and corresponded). Oppenheimer's social theory centred on principles of mutual aid, the abolition of private land ownership and the peaceful subversion of capitalism as part of an attempt to "change the very economic basis of society and its 'government.'"[82] The future he envisaged for the Jewish nation was one "free of oppression and private ownership,"[83] and it is broadly in such terms that he describes the foundation on which the Jewish homeland was to be based: "Self reliance and mutual aid as perceived by socialist cooperative thought. Agriculture (because a nation that is not rooted in its land cannot exist). Land as common property (to foster cooperative settlements that provide all needs honourably and justly)."[84]

In his subsequent work, *The State*, published in 1907, Oppenheimer characterised the capitalist state as "an organisation of one class domination over the other classes. Such class organisation can come about in one way only," he wrote, "namely through conquest and subjugation of ethnic groups by the dominating group."[85] He was, according to one writer, firmly committed to voluntarism, individualism and mutualism, and "projected a systematic program of anti-statism, peaceful land appropriation and 'reassignment,' abolition of ground rents...[and] cooperative colonisation and settlement."[86]

Oppenheimer's proposals were peppered with Tolstoyan and Gordonite themes, and, like Gordon, he would later profess a deep affinity with the ideas of Gustav Landauer.[87] While obvious anarchistic traits permeated his thinking, however, Oppenheimer's ultimate goal was "a mixed community composed of farmers, artisans—even of persons of independent means—indistinguishable from any other community, except that the land doesn't belong to individuals, but is possessed by the community."[88] His blueprint also involved differential payment according to work performed, and administrative management, albeit as a "transitional stage."[89]

Oppenheimer's plans were treated positively by Zionist leaders and actualised to a certain degree in the short-lived Merhavia cooperative. Yet they met with wholehearted opposition from the Jewish workers' movement in the kvutzot, and in the context of this discussion it is important to note why this was so. On November 11, 1911, Degania made plain its reasons:

> The workers [at Degania] perceive utter freedom of work and initiative as an imperative to their existence as a group and reject any form of coercion from above. They also reject two of Oppenheimer's principles: different pay levels, and the appointment of an administrator to supervise a group of experienced workers.[90]

Degania's Joseph Bussel wrote at the time:

> Only free and collective work will revive the workers as well as the country... We reject any form of government... Once we begin to believe that children are private property, that gardens are private property, that talent is private property, what will follow?... The idea of a kvutza is a new one; our way of life presents a big revolution... We have set out to establish a new collective way of life for everyone.[91]

A council of agricultural workers from Hapoel Hatzair, which convened at Kinneret Bussel in 1919, furthered opposition to Oppenheimer's moshav concept in much the same terms:

> We have seen how the moshavot [sic] exist by exploiting others. We are determined to create a way of life that forces us to perform our own work without any external administration. We must conquer work and do it without supervisors. The kvutza should provide modern forms of work. We must create economic equality, a life of social equality between men and women.[92]

While Oppenheimer's plans clearly bear the hallmarks of Kropotkin's influence, of more interest within the context of this study are the terms in which they were opposed here by the workers at Degania. From these early exchanges, we can see that a virulent anti-authoritarian ideology did play a central role in the Jewish workers' movement in Palestine, even among Degania's founders. If we can identify proto-anarchistic elements in Oppenheimer's thinking, they were evidently not radical enough for Degania's members. The terms in which Degania and Hapoel Hatzair opposed Oppenheimer's ideas further highlight just how close the ideology that motivated the rank and file workers in the kvutzot was to anarchism. As early as 1911, the Degania pioneers were already consciously seeing their settlement as a revolutionary one, and one that they "set out" to establish as a blueprint for a future collective society.

Josef Trumpeldor

Franz Oppenheimer was by no means the only one to draw up plans for the settlement of the country. His ideas, of course, ultimately had nothing directly to do with the foundation of the kvutzot themselves, but codified programs for the establishment of anarchistic communes in Palestine, programs that consciously pointed to Kropotkin's influence, played a part even in the establishment of the earliest Second Aliya kvutza communes.

Of particular interest is the figure of the Russian war hero Josef Trumpeldor. Remembered today as a hero of the Israeli right in connection to Revisionist Zionism, Trumpeldor is a complex figure, and some would say paragon of a uniquely Zionist paradox: an anarchist-influenced right-winger involved in the creation of an anarchist-socialist project. Having achieved recognition for his military service after being drafted into the Russian army in 1902, Trumpeldor was decorated by the Tsar for bravery in the Russo-Japanese war. He was friends with Revisionist Zionist Ze'ev Jabotinsky, and, together, the two founded the first Jewish military organisation, the Jewish Legion (also known as the Zionist Mule Corps), which fought with British forces in World War I. Unfortunately, history has seen Trumpeldor's having become synonymous with fascist elements in the Zionist project; following his death in an armed skirmish at Tel Hai in 1920, his name was taken by Jabotinsky for the Revisionist youth movement Beitar—an acronym for "The Josef Trumpeldor Alliance."

However, during the early part of his life, Trumpeldor was not only voraciously anti-capitalist, but very close in his ideas to anarcho-syndicalism. He was educated in Kropotkin's anarcho-communism while a student at the University of St. Petersburg, and was heavily influenced by the Tolstoyan communal anarchism practised by settlers near his hometown of Piatigorsk in the Northern Caucasus of Russia. During the early 1900s, he began to connect the activities of the Tolstoyan settlements with his own ambitions of moving to Palestine, and this synthesis would later find expression in his declaring himself "an anarcho-communist and a Zionist."[93]

By 1908, Trumpeldor had drawn up a detailed program for the settlement of communal groups in Palestine. Predating the establishment of the Degania farm by at least half a decade, Trumpeldor's programme is outlined in a series of letters, the first written to his parents while he was being held as a prisoner of war during the 1904 Russo-Japanese war, and following his repatriation in 1906, to his friends in Russia and to those who had already moved to Palestine. Many of the recipients of his letters, including figures like Zvi Schatz, would become major players in the early kibbutz movement. Trumpeldor's letters outline his idea of establishing an anarchistic commune, first in Russia, and then Palestine, and lay out the beginnings of a highly detailed theoretical programmatic plan for settlement.

In developing this social program, Trumpeldor attempted to combine a strategy for the development of these communes with an ideology designed to overcome the inherent weaknesses of Zionism, Jewish youth and socialism, and in doing so, he refers repeatedly Kropotkin and Tolstoy's ideas, and encourages his friends to draw their inspiration from such thinkers.[94]

As well as his direct experience of the Tolstoyan communes in Russia, Trumpeldor had thoroughly studied the theoretical basis of socialism and anarchism and the practical communal experiments launched by proponents of each. The reading lists he drew up for his friends span virtually every form of socialism through populism and anarchism, including works like Kropotkin's *Conquest of Bread* ("written in very easy language," Trumpeldor observes, "suitable for everyone").[95]

The kind of communist community Trumpeldor described was essentially a collectively-organised agro-industrial commune. "Life in the settlement is founded on agriculture," he wrote, "but will be impossible without industry since otherwise it will be badly exploited by the capitalist world."[96] Built around a participatory economic system, the commune would be capable of providing "everything necessary for a comfortable life";[97] all property would be owned communally and profits distributed "according to the needs of the members."[98]

Job rotation and combined, integrated labour would allow for a full and balanced existence, circumventing the problems encountered by previous experiments. "The earlier settlements," Trumpeldor wrote in 1908, "could not have succeeded because of 1) lack of substantial material base, 2) too much physical work, 3) the absence of adequate intellectual satisfaction, 4) a lack of conditions for cultural progress, 5) a lack of practical skills, 6) the fact that members would have found no satisfaction in their work."[99]

Trumpeldor would become one of the most prominent figures in the early Jewish workers' movement in Palestine. In 1913, he brought a group of Russian Jews to Palestine and worked in various locations throughout the country, including the Degania settlement. "He himself never really stayed in one place long enough to live the collective life," writes Avraham Yassour, whose translations of Trumpeldor's letters were published in 1995, "[but his] writings identified many issues which were later to confront the kibbutz movements, such as urban versus rural, industry versus agriculture, white collar versus blue collar, progress versus simplicity, an ideological motivation centred on individual self-realisation versus sacrifice for the nation."[100]

Trumpeldor's thinking would be influential in the establishment of the Gedud HaAvoda (Labour Brigade), the organisation that would evolve into the Kibbutz Hameuhad stream of the movement. "Like Kropotkin," he wrote in 1908, "I believe that only a very large, territorially extensive commune leads to anarchy."[101] As will be shown in Chapter 3, it was on this basis that Hameuhad would later evolve. Moreover, the path Trumpeldor was plotting was not just for a handful of idealists, but was to be a permanent and all-embracing social system—"We want to find a solution to the problem that faces all Jews," he wrote, "and also—at least to some extent—all humankind."[102] When Trumpeldor returned to Petrograd, Russia in 1918, he established the HeHalutz, an organisation designed to prepare Jewish immigrants for emigration to Palestine. He later returned to Palestine himself.

Community-building in the Second Aliya

While Trumpeldor's ideas would have a lasting influence on the thinking of the Jewish labour movement in Palestine, it has been argued that the plans drawn up by individuals like him were of little practical relevance in the early years. Henry Near suggests that it was the groups that arrived in the country with *less* clearly defined plans who were more readily able to reconcile their practical actions with their principles. What the founders of the successful kvutzot shared, Near believes, was simply a positive attitude to the idea of community. "Within this framework of basic values," he suggests, "they could approach the actual details of community building with a high degree of flexibility."[103]

We know that many of the Second Aliya olim arrived in Palestine with clear ideas concerning socialist Zionism and the reconstruction of their lives. Near is right in saying that the range of ideologies that abounded during the early years typically centred on a positive attitude to communal living. However, integral to their particular conception of "community," to the "basic values" of which Near speaks, were an opposition to centralised power structures, private property, the wage system, hierarchical managerial structures and state authority. While the ideas of anarchist theoreticians like Kropotkin were being incorporated into the programmatic proposals for the settlement of Palestine that were being drawn up abroad, many of these same ideas were also already finding expression spontaneously in the kvutzot.

The first kvutza communities arose organically as anarchical grassroots organisations, the products of "sociological and political imagination wielded through transformative actions," rather than from a thought-out blueprint labelled "anarchism" (or "socialism," or anything else for that matter) by the founders.[104] But although their communities would clearly not have come into being had it not been for the peculiarities of the situation, as we have seen in this chapter, Palestinian Jews already had a clearly defined philosophy that went far beyond dealing with the practical problems of land settlement.

Sure, not all the early supporters of the kvutza idea had such far-reaching ambitions as Gordon and his followers, although the latter did constitute a sizable and important part of the movement and would set the tone for the subsequent development of the kibbutzim. For many in the upper echelons of global Zionism, the pattern of organisation employed in the kvutza was simply the most expedient way of organising agricultural production. But even a cursory glance at the historical testimonies of those responsible for establishing the earliest communities reveals the popular assumption that "no clear social program had evolved, other than to transplant life to another land" to be highly questionable.[105] No *one* single social program had evolved, but the goal of the kvutza pioneers was certainly not simply to transplant life to another land.

The kibbutz founders had clearly-defined ideological objectives, and the communities they established began, and survived, on the strength of their ideological convictions.[106] Anarchism's role in shaping these convictions may have been more of a "subideational" or subconscious one, but that broad philosophical framework, woven from the values and theories that the communards had absorbed during their youth, laid out the ethical foundations of the kibbutz. The early development of the movement cannot realistically be understood separately from those values and theories.

Examining the conversations that took place at Degania during those early years—its members' opposition to Oppenheimer's proposals, for example—it becomes clear that the group's ideological convictions had much greater importance than is often assumed in the key decisions that assured the community's survival. Minutes from Degania's General Assembly meetings support this, showing that decisions were made not just on the basis of expediency, but often on the basis of what members thought they *should* be doing on principle.[107] Often, it seems, ideological factors exercised the dominant influence.

The debates and ideologies outlined in this chapter demonstrate that, regardless of whatever other ideas the upper echelons of the Zionist Organisation or the Western colonialist powers had in mind, the workers on the ground were deliberately viewing their settlements as cells of a new, anarchistic society built around a participatory economy, free from government and external administration. While it has been suggested that anarchism was the "prevalent" ideology during this early period, at this point these ambitions were finding expression in practice more that in the pioneers' rhetoric.[108] The founders of Degania and their contemporaries did not go around proclaiming themselves anarchists—they lived it.

Chapter 3

Realising the Revolution

The Pioneering Groups of the Third Aliya

"We are at present undergoing two great efforts at human renaissance: one in Russia where they wish to change human existence through the state, the machine, status, terror and organisation, and the other, here, in this country where the effort is qualitative, small, and difficult. It is the path to the natural cooperation of small human units towards a new community... There in Russia, everything is determined through norms. Here we are guided by real life and freedom. There a state, here a community."
—*Meir Yaari, 1920*

The Polish-Soviet War and the Russian Civil War brought with them a fresh outbreak of pogroms in Russia between 1918 and 1920, far more devastating than those that preceded them in the 1880s and early 1900s. This new wave of ethnic cleansing left an estimated 70,000 to 250,000 Jews dead, and more than half a million homeless. This period of upheaval, coupled with the Balfour Declaration in 1917, which promised the Jews their own homeland in Palestine, resulted in a dramatic increase in immigration to Palestine.

Between 1919 and 1923, about 35,000 new immigrants arrived as part of the Third Aliya, the majority of them from Russia and Poland with a smaller contingent from Lithuania, Romania and Germany. With this influx of settlers, the development of the kibbutz movement entered a new phase. During the 1920s, the kibbutzim underwent a process of institutionalisation as new communities were built, federations were formed, ideas, structures and practices began to crystallise, and the settlements of each group strengthened ties with their neighbours.

The pioneers at the forefront of this process arrived in Palestine much better prepared than their Second Aliya predecessors. Many had received some agricultural training prior to their arrival, they spoke better Hebrew and, generally, they came in organised groups rather than as individuals. As well as Hapoel Hatzair and the Gedud HaAvoda, several European halutzo-Zionist youth movements would contribute significantly to the kibbutzim of this period. From Poland, Hashomer Hatzair was of particular importance, as were a number of youth groups from Germany—including Blau-Weiß, the Jung-Jüdischer Wanderbund (JJWB), the

Brith Olim, the Werkleute and later the Habonim.[109]/[110] Members of these and other organisations arrived in Palestine familiar with the progress of the earliest kvutzot and aimed to further what their forerunners had created. Throughout the 1920s and 1930s, they took the kvutza concept, built on it and turned what had previously been a loose, experimental network of communal agricultural settlements into larger, more permanent institutions that we now recognise as kibbutzim.

Already having the example of the Second Aliya kvutzot to draw upon, the kibbutz pioneers of the post-Great War period were also significantly more radicalised than their Second Aliya predecessors. The years immediately following the First World War had seen a wave of revolutionary activity across Europe with widespread social and political upheaval altering the complexion of much of the continent. During this period, radical left-wing doctrines experienced a rapid upsurge in popularity among a generation of disenfranchised Jewish youth. Many of those who headed for Palestine in the wake of the First World War did so with the memory of the various European revolutions fresh in their minds. Some had been directly involved in the various uprisings in Europe and most brought with them highly detailed conceptions of the kind of society they wanted to create in their new homeland.

Among this new generation of kibbutz pioneers there was a "great interest"[111] in anarchism, and, according to Avraham Yassour, many who arrived in Palestine as part of the Third Aliya did so with their one "major aspiration [being] to establish an anarchistic community."[112] Kropotkin's article, "Anarchist Communism," was published in the Hapoel Hatzair anthology *Maabarot 3* in 1920, alongside an essay about him by Hapoel Hatzair's leading intellectual, Chaim Arlosoroff. In 1923, Kropotkin's *Mutual Aid* became one of the first books translated into Hebrew and distributed among the immigrants in Palestine, and *The Great French Revolution* followed soon after.[113]

Gustav Landauer

The man most responsible for introducing anarchist ideas into the kibbutz of the 1920s and 1930s was Gustav Landauer, a figure today largely forgotten outside the German- and Hebrew-speaking world, but whose "anarchist form of Jewish messianism" was central to the thinking of many Jewish groups involved in the building of kibbutzim during this period.[114] Landauer's anarchism was brought to Socialist Zionist circles by Jewish scholar and theologian Martin Buber, with whom he had been close friends since they met at an early gathering of the Berlin-based bohemian group Neue Gemeinschaft (New Community) in 1900.

Although Buber's vision of future society was more concerned with the state being reduced to its "proper function" than its wholesale elimination, he was nevertheless close in his ideas to Landauer, envisaging an ideal society composed of a decentralised pattern of federally-connected associations, a "*communitas communitatum*, the union of communities into community, within which 'the proper and autonomous common life' of all the members can unfold."[115] The chapters on Landauer, Kropotkin and Proudhon in Buber's seminal work, *Paths in Utopia*, illustrate the degree to which his own utopian social theory was informed by the ideas of these figures.

Landauer himself had broken with the Jewish community at a young age and had little exposure to Judaism during the early part of his life. His early works tend to refer to the Christian-mystical tradition, and very few references to Judaism are found in any of his writings or letters prior to 1908. When he met Martin Buber, however, this changed. In Buber's work, particularly *The Legend of the Baal-Schem* (1908), Landauer discovered a conception of Jewish spirituality with which he quickly expressed a clear affinity. The Hasidic legends to which Buber introduced him appeared to fulfil Landauer's messianic vision of an egalitarian society, representing to him "the collective work of a *Volk* signifying 'living growth, the future within the present, the spirit within history, the whole within the individual... The liberating and unifying God within imprisoned and lacerated man; the heavenly within the earthly.'"[116]

In a 1908 review of *The Legend of the Baal-Schem*, Landauer noted that "Judaism is not an external accident, but a lasting internal quality, and identification with it unites a number of individuals within a *gemeinschaft*. In this way, a common ground is established between the person writing this article and the author of the book."[117]

Landauer and Socialist Zionism

Although his friendship with Buber led to his developing a close attachment to Judaism, Landauer remained deeply suspicious of political Zionism. While never explicitly "anti-Zionist," he saw attempts at the territorial concentration of the Jewish nation in Palestine as missing the true purpose of Judaism. In his essay, "Are These the Ideas of a Heretic?," which appeared in a collection published by a Zionist student organisation in Prague in 1913, he chastised the factions within Zionism that were more concerned with creating a Jewish state than embracing what he felt to be the true calling presented to them by the unique circumstances of their Diaspora existence.

While other nations are contained within the stifling artificial restrictions of state boundaries, Landauer believed that the Jews' dispersal across the world put them in a unique position inasmuch as they, as a nation, already transcend state divisions. In a speech to a socialist Zionist group in Berlin in 1913, he argued that, being "less addicted to the cult of the state" than other nations, the Jews' historical calling—and particularly that of Eastern European Jews, who were generally less assimilated than their Central- and Western European brethren—was to help construct socialist communities separate from the state.[118]

His views on the Zionist project notwithstanding, Landauer, through Buber, became extremely interested in the progress of the earliest kvutzot in Palestine. Buber had been active in European Zionist circles since 1898, and, during the first decade of the century, he noted how much of the anarchist philosophy Landauer had tried to introduce to the European workers' movement had been actualised in the early Jewish settlements. Recognising that the absence of permanent power structures in Palestine at that time meant that the kvutzot were of great importance in building this new kind of society, Buber came to see these Jewish communities as potentially heralding a socio-political structure patterned along the lines of his friend's anarchism.

Unlike Buber, Landauer's own interest in the movement was almost certainly more for its potential as a radical new form of social organisation than for its particularly Jewish character. Within the fertile ideological climate that contributed to the kibbutz of the 1920s and 1930s, his anarchism carried considerable intellectual clout. By 1913, his influence was being strongly felt within Zionist circles, and over the following years he delivered numerous lectures to Europe's Jewish youth groups, many of whose members would immigrate to Palestine as part of the Third Aliya.

We can tell something of the importance and influence of Landauer's ideas from an exchange of letters—republished as an appendix to this book—that took place in the spring of 1919 between Landauer and Dr. Nachum Goldman. In March that year, Germany's socialist Zionist organisations called a conference in Munich to "clarify their relation to socialist settlement in Palestine,"[119] and Goldman, who later rose to prominence as president of the World Zionist Organisation, invited Landauer to present a paper on several issues relating to the development of the kibbutz movement.

One of Landauer's biographers, Ruth Link-Salinger, identifies this correspondence as "an indication of the seriousness with which Landauer's 'utopianism' as *a program and a blueprint* was treated by those in Jewish socialist circles of the time, who were attempting to build in modern Palestine a voluntaristic, mutualistic, 'free' society" [my italics].[120] As Link-Salinger remarks,

> When…one reads closely in the letter—and between the lines of the letter—inviting Landauer, one realises that the very "utopia" about which these intellectuals were dreaming had a close affinity to the social constructs with which Landauer's name had been associated both in Germany and abroad as a result of his writings and his political activities.[121]

As significant as the fact that Goldman sought his advice in the first place (Landauer's own position on Zionism might make him seem an unusual choice for the conference), is the topic assigned to Landauer for discussion. The subject matter of his lecture was to include the problem of centralised and decentralised society, the nationalisation of land and natural resources, the nature of industry and the question of international exchange in the new society the Socialist Zionist groups hoped to create in Palestine. As Link-Salinger observes, the points Goldman raises in his letter provide a valuable insight into just how closely their plans for the kibbutzim related to Landauer's future anarchist order. Those who were drawing up plans for the new society wanted it to be based on exactly the kind of "decentralised community system" that Landauer had been advocating, with the emphasis on the community as a unit "in which the people have a direct relationship with one another." Economic and political centralisation was to be avoided at all costs.

Particularly interesting, considering the timing of this exchange, is the insight Goldman's letter gives us into the debates regarding the industrialisation of the settlements that had evidently been taking place among the groups. Until this stage, the kvutzot had been farming communities, their primary aim being to invert the Jewish socio-economic structure of the Diaspora by turning to agriculture. However, within Europe there was already talk of consolidating the movement into a permanent agro-industrial social system. Reading between the lines of Goldman's letter, he was essentially asking Landauer how to build a functioning participatory economy and a socio-economic model that would subvert the emergence of a "new, petit-bourgeois, capitalistic working class." "Only a few amongst us are Marxists in the sense that we demand socialisation of the means of production," Goldman wrote. "Before our eyes is the image of a factory organised on the basis of association in which the workers participate as owners and have equal rights concerning all problems of distribution of profits, administration, etc."[122]

Landauer never made it to the meeting. At the time of their letter exchange, he found himself at the epicentre of the Bavarian Revolution. In the final days of April 1919, the Bavarian Soviet was overthrown by counterrevolutionary troops from the right-wing Freikorps militia, and on May 1, Landauer was arrested. The following morning, as he was being transferred to Stadelheim Prison, he was beaten and shot to death by a mob of soldiers.

Landauer's untimely demise would do nothing to lessen the continued impact of his ideas, however. By the end of his life, according to Link-Salinger, Landauer's unique form of anarchism had become "the most suggestive 'blueprint' for utopia since Hertzka's *Freiland* of the nineteenth century."[123] In a speech to a Hapoel Hatzair conference in Prague in 1920, Buber referred to him as "the secret spiritus rector" and "the designated leader of the new Judaism." According to Buber,

> Landauer's idea was our idea. This is recognition of the fact that the main thing
> is not a change of order and institutions, but a revolution in Man's life and
> the relations between Man and his fellow...and in accordance with this idea,

Landauer was to have participated in the building of a new land and a new society as a guide and mentor.[124]

Active in Palestine and central Europe, and in Berlin and Prague in particular, Hapoel Hatzair taught a program of Jewish rejuvenation based on community, self-labour, religiosity and spiritual nationalism, and its outlook contained much of the populism and anti-statism that was central to Landauer's anarchism. The June 1920 edition of *Die Arbeit*, the organ of Hapoel Hatzair published in Berlin, was entitled *Gustav Landauer Gedenkheft*, and carried republications of some of Landauer's essays concerning the Jewish experience and the need for communal land settlements.

In addition to their impact on organisations like Hapoel Hatzair, as part of a counterculture that swept across the continent in the years immediately following World War I, Landauer's ideas exerted a near-programmatic influence on many of the youth groups that arose from the ideological crises of post-war Europe. The left wing of the Wandervögel, a neo-Romantic youth movement, at that time contained important Jewish, Zionist and socialist groups whose members identified with Landauer's neo-Romantic communitarian anarchism, and a number of groups originating from the Wandervögel and the German youth movement would be important in kibbutz-building during the inter-war years.

The early grouping of Blau-Weiß, the JJWB, the Brith Olim, the Werkleute and the Habonim would all contribute to the kibbutz of the 1920s and 1930s. Poland was also significant in that it would produce the Gordonia youth movement, and also, perhaps most importantly of all, Hashomer Hatzair.

Hashomer Hatzair

All of the groups mentioned here felt Landauer's influence in some way or another, but it was felt particularly strongly within the ranks of Hashomer Hatzair.[125] Members of this group (*shomrim*, as they were known) would be at the forefront of the process of kibbutz-building during this period, and the federation they established, Kibbutz Artzi, would subsequently become the ideological backbone of the kibbutz movement. By the end of the century, Artzi would comprise 85 kibbutzim, numbering around 20,000 permanent members, with a total population of approximately 35,000. This equates to around 32 percent of the entire contemporary kibbutz movement.

Hashomer Hatzair formed in the Polish province of Galicia in 1913 from a merger of two earlier groups—Hashomer (The Guard), a Zionist scouting organisation, and a majority faction of the ideological study circle Ze'irei Zion (The Youth of Zion).[126] The group's early inspirations came from the likes of Baden Powell, Gustav Wyneken and the philosophies of Nietzsche, Buber, A.D. Gordon and the Wandervögel. They also had close ties with the German youth movement.

From the earliest days of its existence, the organisation expressed itself in the same kind of quasi-religious, ethical-idealist language as Landauer, and would be deeply influenced by his ideas when it came to the question of kibbutz-building.

In a recent interview, kibbutz veteran and former Habonim member Haim Seeligman commented that, of all the groups arriving in Palestine during the Third Aliya, it was Hashomer Hatzair who did the most careful reading of Landauer.[127] In his memoirs, *From Berlin to Jerusalem*, Gershom Scholem recounts how

> Gustav Landauer's book, *Aufruf zum Sozialismus* (*A Call for Socialism*), left a deep impression not only on me, but also on no small number of young Zionists... The social and moral perception of anarchists like Tolstoy and Landauer was of inestimable importance in the building of the new life in Eretz Israel.[128]

As the first groups of shomrim began to arrive in Palestine in 1919 in the wake of the Balfour Declaration, they did so with highly developed conceptions of the direction that the country should take in terms of its social, economic and political dimensions, and the role they wanted the kibbutz to play in this new society. Although their revolutionary aspirations were given impetus by the October Revolution in 1917, and by the creation of the Soviet Union, it would be some years before Marxism would become a serious influence on the group.

For the first decade or so of the organisation's existence, it was the anarchisms of Landauer and Kropotkin that formed the basis of its members' social and political ambitions. Manes Sperber, who was a member of Hashomer Hatzair at the time, recalls how the Russian Revolution "nurtured our interest in the Social Revolutionaries...and in the anarcho-communist theory of Kropotkin, the revolutionary prince, far more than in Marxism."[129]

Regardless of what may have been discussed in the upper echelons of the Zionist Organisation at the time, the early groupings of Hashomer Hatzair certainly did not arrive in Palestine to lay the foundations for a state—Jewish, socialist or any other kind. On the contrary, they "dreamt of a state that was not a state, but rather a large confederation of communes."[130] In 1940, one of the early leaders of the organisation, Meir Yaari, put it slightly more bluntly when he affirmed that "the Hashomer Hatzair road to the kibbutz was anarchistic."[131]

> [In the movement's early years] we were what is known as anarchists; we believed in the establishment of a new society in Eretz Israel, we lived in a time of big hopes and dreams... We believed in a prototype of future society in which the individual's life would be free of coercion, while being autonomous.[132]

Central to this prototype for the future society was the kibbutz. The shomrim were openly hostile to the political parties already in existence in the Jewish settlement in Palestine, and Sperber recounts how the group "did not want to exert power within the State, but rather to make the State and power superfluous."[133]

The shomrim saw their own role as an almost messianic one: "What stirred them was a deep sense of historical mission," writes Yassour, "of returning to a homeland which waited to be replenished and to a culture which waited to be revived. At the same time, they envisioned their revitalised homeland as a society shaped in the spirit of [the] anarchist ideals then widespread in Europe."[134]

Betanya

For some, including Yaari, this road began at Betanya Illit, one of several small, tented encampments in the hills above Lake Galilee where the new immigrants began to settle when they arrived in Palestine in 1919. The Betanya members saw themselves as a "prophetic elite,"[135] arriving in the country to lay the groundwork for the revival of the Jewish people. In a letter to his comrades in 1920, Yaari wrote that the shomrim's main ambition at that time was to establish "an anarchic community" in the country.

"Our communities," Yaari argued in an article published in the Hapoel Hatzair newspaper in January 1921, "do not tolerate government; they are forming an anarchic tissue by their free joining together."[136] According to one historian,

> The kibbutz was to be an integral unit in which the link between the individual and the group would not only be economic. The main objective...was the establishment of a network of autonomous groups bound together by economic, educational and social ties. The focus of this concept was to be the human and his or her intrinsic value.[137]

The shomrim's camp at Betanya would become legendary not just within the Hashomer Hatzair kibbutzim, but throughout the entire movement, for the collection of its members' diaries, *Kehillatenu* (Our Community), which was published and distributed in Palestine during the Third Aliya. *Kehillatenu* would have a great impact on the subsequent development of the kibbutz movement, and the sentiments recorded within its pages show that Landauer's advocacy of "not state, but society, i.e. a union which is not the result of coercion but emerges from the spirit of free, self-determined individuals" was fresh in the minds of Betanya's members.[138]

Having seen the various revolutions in Europe fall short of success, and having watched with interest the progress of the Second Aliya kvutzot from abroad, the group at Betanya evidently shared Landauer and Buber's optimism about the kvutza as a prototype for this communal, post-capitalist order.[139] It was in Palestine that the young idealists at Betanya believed the revolution would come about.

Are not the kvutzot...[the] very frames in which the revolution will realise itself?
The kvutza is like the shallow pit dug around the tree in which rainwater is
gathered during the storm; and there, discreetly, drop by drop, the process of
renewal comes about... The thousands of individuals who will come down like
plentiful rain from the clouds of the world-storm will realise revolution in life.
The ancient ways of life shall be forged white-hot, and out of the fire shall come
a new formation.[140]

For the Betanya members, as for Landauer, the foundations of this "new
formation" lay in the spiritual dimensions of community. Landauer held that "the
main thing is not a change of order and institutions, but a revolution in Man's life
and the relations between Man and his fellow," as Buber put it, and this belief was
the central pillar of Betanya. In many respects, this was at the heart of Landauer's
appeal to this generation of pioneers. For them, as for Landauer, the creation of a
new society must be rooted in the creation of a new human being.

The conversations that took place at the camp were meandering philosophical
discussions of the cosmos and metaphysics. Instead of having a formal meeting
in a dining room, confined in content strictly to practical matters, Betanya's
meetings took the form of animated discussions around campfires, and in them
the members would attempt to break down what they felt to be the false values
imbued in them by their upbringing in bourgeois capitalist society. As one
member wrote,

> Each individual within our circle who had filled his or her mind with all sorts of
> spiritual values arose and denounced these values...as illusions having no basis
> in the soul of the essential person. There was only one real value which gave
> weight and real content to the individual and the cosmos and in society. Love
> could shake the spirit unto its foundations. We knew then that no idea could
> be realised before that positive moment when the past is negated and the whole
> person, not just a part, is rebuilt.[141]

According to one member of the settlement, "the idea of renewal was
crystallised within us on the very first day of our arrival";[142] the diary entries
intimate that the Betanya members viewed a "direct relationship between people
[as] the first condition in forming a community":

> In order that one understand his or her fellows, and forgive, one must know
> them. This is a psychological rule that cannot be erased from the human soul.
> If the social life is to be beautiful, profound and pure, in order that a new
> society can be created, then it is necessary that people understand their daily
> lives, their petty deeds, and their own primitive nature. The society which lives a
> complete, full life cannot ignore this daily existence...even if it should so desire.

You must first understand, for only then can you believe, forgive, and love your brothers and sisters. It was here that we found our new way! We drew it up from the depths of our souls. Each of us revealed his or her true self to the others, including that which was ugly, or venomous. In this way, we won the hearts and understanding of our fellow members.[143]

It is perhaps only when seen through the prism of Landauer's anarchism that one realises how crucial this period of "spiritual" regeneration was in the anarchistic vision of the early shomrim. It was this breaking down of interpersonal barriers and nurturing of a spiritual connection between individuals that provided the bedrock on which the kibbutzim would be built. Yaari would later describe the camp at Betanya as "the well-spring of collective life in our movement,"[144] emphasising how "Betanya emanated the spiritual content that shaped the kibbutzim."[145] Out of the small nucleus of anarchists at Betanya who arrived in Palestine with dreams of self-realisation and spiritual revolution, there would develop, within the next half century, a network of more than eighty kibbutzim.

The first Hashomer Hatzair kibbutz from the Kehillatenu group was set up at Beit Alpha in 1922, and, over the course of the decade, the organisation would establish four more settlements—Mishmar Ha'Emeq, Merhavia, Gan Shmuel and Ein Shemer. In April 1927, the Council of Hashomer Hatzair collectives unified the settlements established by the group into a nationwide federative structure, the Kibbutz Artzi Hashomer Hatzair Federation (National Kibbutz Movement of the Young Guard), and laid down a number of principles by which they envisaged the kibbutzim of their federation functioning. The kind of community described at the 1927 meeting, codified in the "Program of the National Kibbutz Movement," was an integral community embracing the economic, social and cultural spheres of life, a community they saw as "pioneer nuclei of the new society":

> Each kibbutz within the Kibbutz Artzi is an organic unit… It is an autonomous way of life, serving both as a prototype for the…society of the future and as an independent political and ideological collective. The nature of the kibbutz stems from its very social life, which aims at integrating the individual with the community for vital communal tasks. It creates the conditions for a free unfolding and development of the personality. It establishes a new social morality, and tries to find liberating solutions to the problems of the family, women and childrearing.[146]

Within each Artzi kibbutz, great emphasis was placed on tight social cohesion and "ideological collectivism." As Near explains, this ideological collectivism was seen as "a framework for continuous ideological action and discussion: a constant search for consensus, a reluctance to reach decisions opposed by a substantial minority, and a readiness to defer the resolution of conflicts or to reach compromises for the sake of movement unity—all this backed by unanimous support for the general movement line once a decision had been made."[147]

According to one insider, "since our lives were collective in every way, it seemed quite natural to hold common ideological beliefs which strengthened our social, economic and cultural cohesion."[148] Throughout the 1920s, this emphasis on a tight cohesion in all areas of kibbutz life can be seen to permeate Hashomer Hatzair's activities; direct individual involvement in the social, economic, cultural, and political arenas, the strengthening of inter-kibbutz activities, mutual aid and the development of joint enterprises were all seen as basic imperatives of the Hashomer Hatzair communities.

Emphasis was placed on egalitarianism and the belief in the organisation as a revolutionary body, on the importance of the active participation of kibbutz members in matters affecting internal social problems and the overall social, economic and political direction of the kibbutz, and on the exercise of direct democracy. The anarchist idea of a neighbourhood community—a group of neighbouring settlements practising mutual aid with each other, in order to ensure equality and cooperation—would continue to be a pervasive motif of the Hashomer Hatzair settlements' way of life, as well as of the kibbutz movement in general.

As a youth movement, the organisation remained active in the Diaspora as well, and, by the late 1920s, had, in addition to its four kibbutzim, around 38,000 members in Eastern Europe. The foundation of Kibbutz Artzi in 1927 led to expansion into new territories, including Hungary, France and the United States, and by 1939 the movement numbered 70,000 members worldwide. The Diaspora youth movement continued to serve as a reservoir from which the kibbutzim of Kibbutz Artzi gained a fresh influx of immigrants every year. Educational ideas continued to play a key role in the Hashomer Hatzair and Kibbutz Artzi groups' activities, and it is important to note that Landauer and Kropotkin remained on the syllabus.

As for the groups' national intentions, Artzi saw the kibbutz achieving the "historical and constructive aims of the Jewish working class by founding economic enterprises in the country and in town, extending its activities as much as possible into all branches of production, and preparing the working class for economic self-management":

> Constructive activities of the working class should not be regarded as the main avenue for resolving class antagonism. The organisation of production and of the economy as a whole by the working people based upon the principles of justice and equality, can only be achieved with the extinction of the present regime through social revolution.[149]

Changing Direction

At the Hashomer Hatzair conference held at Kibbutz Beit Alpha in 1924—three years before the establishment of Artzi—Yaari argued that Landauer and Kropotkin's ideas were "no longer suitable" for the developing kibbutz movement. He argued against the proposal to call the federation of Hashomer Hatzair settlements "communal anarchism," and instead spoke positively about Marxist ideas.[150]

The fact that this proposal was made at all is obviously significant in itself, but this conference has been identified as the turning point at which a "shift from the spirit of anarchism to movement institutionalisation" occurred.[151] Certainly Hashomer Hatzair's rhetoric began to take on a Marxist complexion around that time—the passages quoted above, from the 1927 meeting, hint at an incipient notion of "class antagonism" that Landauer, for one, would doubtless have been uncomfortable with.

Even after Hashomer Hatzair adopted its supposedly "Marxist" stance, however, members of the organisation still studied the works of Landauer and Kropotkin closely, and would regularly attend lectures by Landauer's friend and executor, Martin Buber. Conversations with former Hashomer Hatzair members and their contemporaries in other youth movements active in the kibbutzim suggest that, while the rhetoric became Marxist, it was the anarchistic ideas of Landauer and Kropotkin that formed the bedrock of their thinking for some years to come.[152]

Hashomer Hatzair remained politically unaffiliated to any of the existing socialist-Zionist parties in Palestine until the mid-1930s, when it officially aligned itself with the left-wing socialist international, the International Revolutionary Marxist Centre (as opposed to the more mainstream Labour and Socialist International). Beginning in 1936, it found an urban political ally in the Socialist League of Palestine, and, after a lengthy process of debate, the Hashomer Hatzair party was officially formed in 1946. Nevertheless, while the official Hashomer Hatzair stance had taken on a Marxist complexion by the mid-1920s, other pioneering groups involved in the establishment of the Third Aliya kibbutzim still rejected Marxist-socialist theories. Many within the kibbutzim at that time argued that the Marxist, class-based concepts of socialism, which were beginning to characterise Hashomer Hatzair rhetoric, were inappropriate to the reality of the reconstruction of the Jewish people in Palestine, and instead continued to align themselves with anarchistic ideologies.

Arlosoroff and Hapoel Hatzair

One of the other major organisations of the era for whom this continued endorsement of anarchistic ideas is certainly true is the Hapoel Hatzair workers' party. Hapoel Hatzair existed in Palestine since 1905 and, following the teachings of A.D. Gordon, had provided the libertarian alternative to the more orthodox Marxist Poalei Zion during the early years of settlement. Significant elements within Hapoel Hatzair retained this anti-Marxist stance well after Hashomer Hatzair had officially turned to Marxism, and as an organisation, it generally remained much closer in its outlook to the ideas of Gordon, Landauer and Russian populism throughout the 1920s. Kropotkin himself was also a significant influence on the group. As noted earlier, his "Anarchist Communism" article had appeared in the Hapoel Hatzair anthology *Maabarot 3* in 1920, alongside an essay about him by one of the party's main ideologues, Chaim Arlosoroff.

Arlosoroff was very much a disciple of Kropotkin and had been since his time studying economics at Berlin University. Before moving to Palestine, he was acquainted with Martin Buber, who was active in Jewish circles in Berlin at the time, and through Buber, Arlosoroff became familiar with the writings of Gordon and Landauer.

By the time he reached university, Arlosoroff was already one of the main leaders of Hapoel Hatzair in Germany. As editor of the movement's journal, *Die Arbeit*, Arlosoroff published his first political articles as well as essays on, and excerpts from, the likes of Proudhon and Kropotkin. The social program he introduced to Hapoel Hatzair was closely modelled on the ideas of these thinkers—a humanistic, communitarian brand of anarchism based on "a return to nature and agriculture as the only alternative to the violence of modern, industrial and bureaucratised life."[153]

Arlosoroff's 1920 essay on Kropotkin, often described as one of the best-written articles on the Russian prince from within the international socialist movement, leaves little doubt as to where its author's allegiances lay. Kropotkin's impact was also plain to see in Arlosoroff's first major piece of work, *Der Jüdische Volkssozialismus* (Jewish People's Socialism), which was published in 1919. The voluntaristic, non-statist socialism he advocates for in the Jewish settlement of Palestine can be seen as a non-doctrinaire amalgamation of anarchist and social-democratic ideas, and, as well as showing clear parallels with Kropotkin, bears all the hallmarks of Landauer's influence. In fact, as one historian put it,

> *Der Jüdische Volkssozialismus* is so full of such Landauer chestnuts as return to nature, the land as a source of creativity, the importance of producer-consumer collectives, the importance of "Gemeinschaftsgesinnung" over class-hate or class rule, the importance of spiritual and cultural creativity for the Jewish masses in Palestine, the importance of an inner sense of socialism which transforms the work of all into the work for all, that one can only marvel at the common core of their thinking.[154]

Arlosoroff's belief in the possibility of social renaissance of modern culture through a back-to-the-land, back-to-nature movement certainly united him with the same aspirations of ideologues like Gordon and Landauer, and his plan for the Jewish settlement of Palestine bears testimony to the impact of these thinkers. In his own words, socialism "will have to be a socialism of freedom, an anti-etatist socialism, an anarchist socialism—or the socialist idea will never succeed."[155]

Arlosoroff was close to the kibbutz movement, for although never a kibbutz member himself, the kibbutz was central to this "anarchist socialism." He viewed it as playing a key role in the creation of this new society. During the early Mandate period he proposed a vision of "the nation as a great federation of free, communist associations"[156] of which settlements like the kibbutz would be the basic social units. In the vision of the future Arlosoroff envisaged,

> One commune will freely join another, or a group of communes…if it sees
> it as necessary for its own existence. In such a free league of communes, the
> communes will regulate their joint affairs through cooperation. Out of this a
> harmonious associated future society will emerge.[157]

Arlosoroff's vision of the kibbutz in the context of socialist Zionism sees the settlements "within the wider horizon of a communitarian, voluntaristic society where state power is supplanted by the free association of human groups."[158]

> This is the new and free society of universal welfare; a society without
> government, a society of communist anarchism… [This] society is not founded
> on power, neither is it a dictatorship of a minority or a majority, nor is it seen
> as an external necessity, whether appearing as a title to property or a policeman's
> baton, whether it is a military command or a government regulation. The basis
> of society is founded on free will, on an association without government, on the
> *élan vital* which anarchist terminology calls *Libre Entente*.[159]

Arlosoroff's own vision for the kibbutz movement was thus rooted very much in the Kropotkinite idea of free association and voluntarism. Since his student days, and well after his arrival in Palestine, Arlosoroff consistently rejected Marxist, class-struggle-based theories of socialism and spent most of the 1920s attempting to steer the Jewish workers' movement away from these kinds of ideas, which had begun to creep into socialist Zionist discourse.

In a speech to the 1926 conference of Hapoel Hatzair in Palestine, Arlosoroff hammered home the message that class struggle simply had no relevance to the Palestinian Jews' situation. As the "state" in Palestine was the British Mandatory authority, he argued, its political character was a reflection of the class forces of British society rather than of indigenous class forces and relations. As a binational society, the horizontal cleavages of class, such as they were, were cross-cut and undercut by the vertical national cleavage between Jews and Arabs.[160] More importantly though, this wasn't even a capitalist society—the *Yishuv* was still a society-in-the-making, and its economy was still very much in the process of self-creation. With "no normal cycle of production or division of national income within a cycle,"[161] and with "no struggling classes within the Jewish people as a whole and among the Jews in the Land of Israel, in particular,"[162] there was simply no place for Marxist theories of class warfare.

> The public standing of the worker in our culture is without parallel: the organised labour movement in Eretz Israel is not a movement of "the proletariat." The Histadrut is the aristocracy... The organised worker is the hegemonic group in society—in the first Representative Assembly [of Palestinian Jews], 48 percent of the delegates were workers.[163]

This speech, entitled "Class War in the Reality of the Land of Israel," was, according to Arlosoroff's biographer, "as much a polemic against the attempts by Zionist Marxists to transfer to Eretz Israel the materialistic class concepts of Marxism, as his essay on Kropotkin was similarly an attempt to present an alternative to a rigid, class-ridden view of socialism."[164] Arlosoroff's notion that this was a society unsuited to Marxist class-war theories was one to which Hapoel Hatzair, on the whole, continued to adhere.

Many believe that whatever anarchist ideologies existed during the early years were dead in the water by this point, but Arlosoroff's writings, influential throughout the Yishuv, deliberately present anarchism as an alternative to the emergent Marxist influences which were based on the kind of rigid class polarisation that many viewed as irrelevant in the context of Palestinian reality. Arlosoroff's voice was by no means a marginal one at this stage. Oved records how his ideas "gave expression to the spirit of the times,"[165] and Shlomo Avineri eulogises him as "very much a star—a *Wunderkind* in his movement."[166]

According to Avineri, "Arlosoroff's writings...made him one of the major thinkers of the modern Jewish national renaissance and its social reconstruction, combining theory and practice in a synthesis rarely found in either theoreticians or practitioners. Probably only in the formative years of the Russian Revolution can one find his counterparts."

In 1930, Arlosoroff was instrumental in bringing about the unification of Poalei Zion and Hapoel Hatzair to form the Mapai Labour Party, and he subsequently edited the party's intellectual journal *Achdut Ha'avoda*. At the 1931 Zionist Congress he was elected to the Zionist executive and was later appointed Head of the Political Department of the Jewish Agency for Palestine, a position he held until his assassination in 1933.[167]

Gordonia

It is worth noting at this point that the influence of A.D. Gordon was still strongly felt within the earlier kvutzot too. While the man himself may have been dubious about tightening "ideological definitions," by 1923, the Congress of kvutza members had decided that:

> The basic principles of the kvutza pattern of life, the purpose of which is to change the pattern of society, can be made effective by the implementation of principles of equality, mutual aid and mutual responsibility.[168]

Gordon died in 1922, but his influence lived on within the movement. As noted above, the early Hashomer Hatzair groups looked to him for inspiration, and he, in turn, admired them for their enthusiasm, sincerity and idealism. In 1923–24, Hapoel Hatzair supporters in Galicia established the Gordonia youth movement in an attempt to keep alive the philosophy A.D. Gordon had brought to the early kvutzot.

Gordonia would come to be characterised by its adoption of its namesake's Tolstoyan, back-to-the-land anarchism and its rejection of the Marxist programs being taken up by other movements at the time. Dismissing abstract social blueprints, Gordonia further distinguished itself from the other movements with its decision not to have anything to do with party-political activities.

It is also significant, considering the increasing level of hostility between Jews and Arabs during the late 1920s, that Gordonia continued to follow Gordon's pacifist outlook, refusing to have anything to do with any groups or movements whose outlook smacked, however faintly, of militarism. Gordonia continued to promote Gordon's emphasis on the agricultural commune, and tended to align itself with the smaller, Degania-inspired kvutza settlements that, in 1925, unified to form the first cohesive federation, Hever Hakvutzot.

Gedud HaAvoda

So far we have seen how anarchistic ideas and mindsets were common fare at the roots of two out of the three early kibbutz federations—Hever Hakvutzot and Kibbutz Artzi. The third major political force in the formation of the kibbutzim during this period was Gedud HaAvoda, the organisation that grew out of the ideas of self-identified "anarcho-communist" Josef Trumpeldor.

As noted in Chapter 1, Trumpeldor had been drawing up plans for the establishment of anarchistic communes in Palestine as early as 1904, and his group of pioneers arrived in Palestine in 1913. During the early 1920s, the Gedud evolved into a major force in the settlement of the country, later becoming the third (and, in the pre-state years, largest) kibbutz stream, Kibbutz Hameuhad. Alongside Trumpeldor, who was killed in March 1920 at Tel Hai, the man most responsible for introducing Kropotkin's ideas to the group was Yitzhak Tabenkin, the "spiritual leader"[169] of Hameuhad.

It is testament either to the complexity of Trumpeldor's politics, or perhaps just to the selective memory of the Israeli establishment, that Trumpeldor is today a hero of Israel's right more than its left. In many respects, Tabenkin is no more straightforward a figure. Although he repeatedly insisted he was not an anarchist *per se*, Tabenkin was close in his ideas to anarcho-communism and acknowledged his admiration for anarchism's contribution to socialist thought: "I am sympathetic towards anarchism," he wrote. "I am conscious of what is revolutionary in anarchism and what is ethical in it."[170]

While Tabenkin recognised the danger of political government, however, he also believed that the workers' movement needed to use state institutions to achieve their ends, and, according to Oved, he doubted whether the state was simply a stage that could (or should) be "leapfrogged or negated in a one-time action."[171] Nevertheless, he saw that the particular conditions of the Jewish workers' movement in Palestine provided an opportunity to create a society without the need for government, and recognised that this was an opportunity that should not be ignored. Stressing the importance of anarchist ideologies in the context of the settlement of Palestine, Tabenkin thus argued that the kibbutz pioneers "must become familiar with the main points of anarchist thought," for its "social morals, and its critical approach to bureaucracy and political rule."[172]

Building on Trumpeldor's idea of a communal labour force ("metal that can be molded to whatever is needed"),[173] the Gedud HaAvoda was conceived with the idea of moving people quickly according to economic necessity, and so took the form of small units that could be sent anywhere they were needed in the Yishuv. The idea was ultimately to create a "general commune of workers," a nationwide, continuously expanding commune with a communal treasury to satisfy the needs of all its members, rather than a federated alliance of smaller, intimate settlements like the early kvutzot and the Hashomer Hatzair communities.

Despite continual squabbles over structure, ideology and so on, the vision of a communal, egalitarian society was unanimously seen as a paramount commitment, and as time wore on, the basic aims and general framework of the Gedud began to take shape, institutionalised in the form of the Brigade's main camp at Migdal.

The Migdal camp served as "living proof to other settlers that a large group of people could indeed live in a communal society with a common treasury."[174] In terms of its actual work assignments, the organisation and groups affiliated to it branched out into a number of different areas. Within a year of its inception it had units of workers engaged in communally-run construction projects all over the country, building roads, railways and infrastructure and draining swamps. Living in tented camps, they shared everything on a communal basis, and although representing the beginning of another tradition distinct from the small kvutza, the two models held many basic ideas and ideals in common.

Unlike both the Hever Hakvutzot and Hashomer Hatzair groups, the Gedud rejected any sort of selective approach in terms of taking on new members, its ultimate objective essentially being the transformation of the entire Yishuv into one big kibbutz whose only limit in terms of size would be economic viability. Not as concerned with personal suitability and ideological solidarity as Hashomer Hatzair—which placed heavy emphasis on shared cultural values and ideals as a means of achieving a maximal degree cohesion[175]—the idea behind the big kibbutz was that the framework they created would cause the members' different viewpoints to "melt" within it, and thus create an exemplary society.[176]

While this notion of a "general commune of workers' may be seen as the Gedud's general approach, within the organisation there existed a broad range of political opinions and differing ideas as to how to settle the land. The diversity of views led to the Gedud being plagued, throughout its nine-year life, by a series of arguments and splits, one of the main struggles being between this centralist conception and an autonomous, independent conception inspired by the smaller kvutzot.

By the time of Gedud's demise (which was inevitable after the second major rift in 1926), the organisation had formed 44 sub-units scattered throughout the country, and trained over 3,000 immigrants. Gedud's major legacy to the kibbutz movement came in the form of the Kibbutz Hameuhad federation. One of the key figures in the organisation, Shlomo Lavi, and a small group of his adherents, had worked in several of the kvutzot communes and reached the conclusion that the kvutza was too small and too introverted in its nature to be either desirable, useful or practicable as a viable tool in the project of nation-building. Lavi doubted whether the kvutza model was economically feasible and proposed the notion of a larger framework that would incorporate a synthesis of industry and agriculture—in essence, extending the principles of the Gedud into a more permanent way of settling the land.

In 1921, Lavi and Tabenkin established a model of the large, open kibbutz community along these principles at Ein Harod in the Jezreel Valley. Ein Harod, as well as Kibbutz Tel Yosef, which was established soon afterwards, would become the paradigm for Hameuhad, which has historically sought to establish the large and continually growing type of kibbutz advocated by Lavi and Tabenkin, intended for thousands and based on an amalgamation of agriculture and industry. Irrespective of Tabenkin's complex attitudes towards anarchism, Hameuhad, according to its founders, regarded Kropotkin as "the closest to us of them all,"[177] recognising the absolute need for voluntary, non-governmental organisations as "eminently suitable to the reality that came into being with the kibbutz movement."[178] According to Oved,

> At the time there was a certain appeal in Kropotkin's ideas on the dominance of mutual aid, the combination of village and city, agriculture and industry and the establishment of a network of new, federatively-connected communities, all of which found solid expression in the theories of "the big kvutza" which was to

replace the small, intimate kvutza with the onset of the big wave of immigration that came in the wake of World War I.[179]

In reality the big kibbutz did not immediately "replace" the small kvutza, but it did represent the beginnings of a new kibbutz stream. HaKibbutz Hameuhad existed alongside the kvutzot until a series of mergers that began in the early 1950s.

State-Building

As Jewish settlement in Palestine gathered pace during the 1920s and 1930s, so too did recognition among sections of the global Jewish community of the moral and political quandaries raised by the creation of a Jewish state.[180] In March 1919, United States Congressman Julius Kahn delivered a petition to President Woodrow Wilson, shortly before his departure for the Paris Peace Conference, in which concerns about the idea of statehood were voiced. Signed by a long list of prominent American Jews, the petition protested "the re-establishment in Palestine of a distinctively Jewish State as utterly opposed to the principles of democracy which it is the avowed purpose of the World's Peace Conference to establish."[181]

Albert Einstein was among the countless Jewish luminaries who voiced similar sentiments. In January 1946, he made a presentation to the Anglo-American Committee of Inquiry, which was examining the Palestine issue, in which he articulated his concerns about the prospect of the monopolisation of power by the Palestinian Jewish community. Four years later he expressed his preference to "see reasonable agreement with the Arabs on the basis of living together in peace [rather] than the creation of a Jewish state."[182]

The Zionism of the early kibbutz communards had never imagined a national revival taking the form of a state-building enterprise. For them, the Balfour Declaration in 1917, promising a "national home" for the Jews, meant an opportunity to establish a completely new form of society and a chance to put their dreams and visions into practice. Collective settlement was not seen simply as the most efficient way of colonising the land in order to create a Jewish state and install a market-capitalist economy, as some have since argued.[183] Though the later centrality of the movement to the creation and defence of Israel is clear, the notion that the pioneers resorted to collectivism simply in order to create suitable conditions for the institution of that state is largely a myth. Even the founders of Degania were strictly opposed to the notions of government and state, and by the time the Third Aliya groups arrived, the idea of building a stateless society on the back of the new social model they had created was one that was widely embraced. The idea held in common by many of the groups arriving in Palestine during the

1920s was to transform the Yishuv into a stateless commonwealth of autonomous communities that would include few, if any, non-collective alternatives.

Anarchism in the Kibbutzim

The rhetoric of Palestinian Jewish anarchism did not simply die out after the initial stages of development. Although it became less of a force, anarchism has continued to appear sporadically as an intellectual current within the kibbutzim throughout the movement's history. During the Spanish Civil War, there was great interest from within the kibbutz movement in the activities of the anarchist militias in Spain. In the late 1930s, a group of youngsters, including some from the movement and some from outside it, formed under the spiritual leadership of Yitzhak Tavori from Kibbutz Afikim in the Jordan Valley. Under the moniker of "The Free Socialists," they published a newspaper in which they reprinted excerpts from the works of classical anarchist thinkers, alongside articles on the Spanish anarchist groups fighting Franco's fascists. Tavori also published articles in Afikim's newsletter on the history of anarchism.[184] During the 1930s, many anarchists from within the kibbutz movement travelled to Spain themselves to join the CNT-FAI militia.

Around the time the state of Israel was founded, the country experienced an influx of western European survivors of Nazism, among whom anarchism had a "specific and visible presence."[185] Many of these new immigrants joined the existing kibbutz settlements, some established new ones, while others began to sow the seeds of the antiauthoritarian organisations that were beginning to take root in the country, unconnected to the kibbutz movement (see Chapter 6). Later, in the years immediately following 1967's Six Day War, groups within the kibbutz movement began a period of ideological questioning that saw a renewed affinity with Buber and Landauer developing among the kibbutzim's intellectual circles.

During that period there was a significant difference between what was happening in intellectual echelons and wider trends across the rest of the movement, and this shift in orientation was not necessarily emblematic of change within the kibbutz movement as a whole. Nonetheless, as disillusionment with Marxist socialism grew (due to experience of its perceived realisation in totalitarian regimes abroad), so too did a renewed affinity with anarchism. Although, by this time, it was too late to turn back the clock, figures like Landauer once again came to provide intellectual inspiration for many kibbutzniks, and the kibbutzim gradually began to acknowledge the historical debt owed by their movement to its anarchist forebears.

Chapter 4

The Kibbutz

The Dynamics of a Free Commune

"We are communists. But our communism is not that of the authoritarian school: it is anarchist communism, communism without government, free communism. It is the synthesis of the two chief aims pursued by humanity since the dawn of its history—economic freedom and political freedom."
—*Peter Kropotkin*

The previous three chapters aim to give some idea of how anarchist ideologies filtered into the thinking of those responsible for establishing the kibbutz movement. We know that the works of Kropotkin, Proudhon, Gordon, Tolstoy and Landauer were widely read and respected among the kibbutz pioneers, and we can be sure too that many figures influential in shaping the direction of the movement embraced the ideas of these thinkers and actively promoted the realisation of their ideology in Palestine. The wealth of documentary evidence leaves little room for doubt as to the extent to which anarchist ideas were in circulation among the founding generation of kibbutzniks. The question of whether or not the theoretical influence of anarchism translated into the practical development of the communities, however, necessitates an examination of the day-to-day running of the settlements, in order to establish the points of convergence between the kibbutz model and the various streams of anarchist ideology circulating among Palestine's Jewish settlers.

Before going on to discuss how the kibbutz works in more detail, we might first want to consider some of the main features of the movement and look at what would constitute a typical kibbutz settlement. But first, we need to ask whether one can even speak of a "typical" kibbutz? The previous chapters explain how ideologically diverse Palestine was during the first three waves of Jewish immigration and indicate how this diversity translated into the praxis of the first settlements. While the political motivations of the founding generation of kibbutz communards were arrived at from common ideological and historical sources—with the ideals of egalitarianism, communitarianism, direct democracy and self-labour widely shared—the movement's subsequent pattern of development was characterised by a constant pattern of squabbles, disagreements, schisms and mergers, with every merger leading to a split, and every split to the formation of a new union.

The ideological disputes that punctuated the movement during the years leading up to independence from Great Britain in 1948 frequently amounted to the splitting of terminological hairs, and took place in spite of a general consensus about how to build the kibbutz and establish its way of life. During the early years of the kibbutz movement, factional infighting resulted in the development of the different federations, each of which came to be distinguished by certain unique qualities.

While some groups proposed a micro-utopian strategy, aiming to create a network of small communes within the Yishuv, as the most efficient way of institutionalising their ideology, others like Hameuhad, proposed an approach that would transform the entire Yishuv itself into one big, all-embracing commune. Hever Hakvutzot—which formed the Ihud Hakvutzot Vehakibbutzim (the Union of Collective Settlements) with a section of Hameuhad in the 1950s, which would later combine with the rest of Hameuhad to form TAKAM (the United Kibbutz Movement)—adhered to the idea of a small, intimate, primarily agriculturally-orientated group. Kibbutz Artzi was guided by its principles of organic growth and selective absorption, and continued to insist that its members subscribe to a collectivist ethos and a common ideology.

But as the century wore on, these gaps began to narrow, and historical processes meant the ideological and structural differences between the kibbutzim of the different movements became less and less distinct. When it became clear that statehood was imminent, rapid and sustained acceleration of the country's economic development became an urgent imperative for the movement. The late 1930s and early 1940s saw the necessity of building an economy capable of coping with the technological demands of industry and agriculture, in practice, resulting in a uniformisation of ideas and practices throughout the movement.[186] The union of Ihud Hakvutzot Vehakibbutzim and Hameuhad as TAKAM, in 1973, is seen as illustrative of an almost complete evanescence of whatever conflicting concepts remained, and of a "narrowing of ideological points of conflict in the socio-economic and political spheres."[187]

The Kibbutz

While the structure and culture of the kibbutz has always been fluid and dynamic, it is still feasible to talk about "the kibbutz" in broadly generic terms and identify features and practices common to all the settlements.

As noted in the first chapter, the Romni group's 1910 letter to Ruppin described the kibbutz as "a cooperative community without exploiters or exploited."[188] This remains the most concise definition of the pre-1948 kibbutzim. Based on ideals of political and material equality, freedom and direct democracy, the kibbutz began as a social unit predicated on the elimination of all hierarchical, exploitative and authoritarian political structures. Private property was nonexistent, and all property, including the means of production, was owned in common. Production and consumption were organised on a communal basis with all managerial decisions arrived at collectively, via a process of direct democracy and informal debate, and systematic rotation of work roles ensured that members shared in every kind of work and that every job carried equal social status.

The supreme institution of collective governance was the general assembly, a meeting of all the community's members in which every matter pertaining to the kibbutz's life was discussed and where decisions were made by majority vote. All income was pooled into a communal purse from which all members were free to take as much as they saw fit. Thus, the founders succeeded in eliminating any connection between contribution and reward, with each giving according to his ability and receiving according to his needs.

It was from this kernel that the kibbutz model would take shape, evolving within a very short space of time into a permanent social system built on the alliance of similar communes in confederation, thus overcoming the problems of isolation. The definition of what constitutes a kibbutz presented in the *Kibbutz Society Regulations* gives some idea of how these original ideals crystallised:

> The Kibbutz is a free association of persons for the purposes of settlement, absorption, maintenance of a collective society organised on the principles of joint ownership of property, self labour and cooperation in all areas of production, consumption and education... The Kibbutz shall provide all the material, social and cultural needs of its members... The satisfaction of these needs shall be implemented in an attempt at realising the principles of cooperative consumption and equal rights under equal conditions, in accordance with the rules and procedures for implementation determined by the kibbutz.[189]

The values and practices underlying the kibbutz as it would develop over the course of the century therefore include communal ownership of all property, including the means of production and consumption, mutual responsibility and mutual aid, communal production and consumption, and directly democratic self-management, both in the economic and socio-political spheres. With the distribution of goods, services and resources taking place strictly according to need, all members benefited from (or suffered) the accumulation of the full product of surplus labour.[190]

The collective, i.e. the entire kibbutz community, had ultimate authority over every aspect its own running, including the settlement's economic/industrial activity, and decision-making power rested with the general assembly of all members. The fact that the collective formed the basis of all social, economic and political activity meant that political and economic decision-making overlapped significantly, with the settlement's economic base (its means of production) and non-economic superstructure (the remaining cultural and political aspects of society) in the hands of the same individuals and groups.

For most of the movement's lifetime, the kibbutz's economy has been based on an amalgamation of industry and agriculture. Although the settlements are still often referred to as "communal farms"—which is what they were during their very early years—today, industry has long since replaced agriculture as the primary mode of production. Almost all of Israel's kibbutzim have now established industrial projects of one kind or another, partly to vary and increase occupational opportunities within the movement (providing suitable jobs for older members and those with disabilities, or for those for whom agricultural work is too strenuous), but also because of the impossibility of making a living purely from agriculture, thanks to increased competition from world markets.

While the contemporary movement's industrial projects are often connected to agriculture (they remain at the forefront of Israel's research and production in irrigation methods, food processing, plastic crop coverings, wine-making and so on), the kibbutzim lead the field in high-tech enterprises as diverse as they are numerous, including production of health products, diamond-tipped tools, printing, television sets, quality glass, furniture, toys, musical instruments and defence products.[191]

Though only around 15 percent of the contemporary kibbutz movement's adult population still works in agriculture (the kibbutzim still provide around 40 percent of the gross added value of Israel's agricultural output),[192] at the outset of the twenty-first century there were 327 kibbutz industrial plants across Israel, and 11 regional corporations comprising about 50 industrial units. These currently make up around 8.5 percent of Israel's total industrial income, with production concentrated in three main areas—plastic and rubber products (37 percent), metals and machines (17 percent) and food (15 percent). Today, industry accounts for roughly 70 percent of total kibbutz production and comprises around 25 percent of the kibbutz adult population.[193]

A Participatory Economy

At its most elemental level, the economic model of the kibbutz can be seen as being built on several interrelated ethical imperatives: the abolition of private property, the absence of a wage system, the integration of manual and cerebral work, and a belief in the fundamental value of labour. In many ways, these basic ideals are intrinsically interdependent, and cannot realistically be disentangled from each another, in terms of both their ideological origins and their practical ramifications for the kibbutz way of life.

Communal ownership was seen as a priority from day one, primarily on the grounds that it promotes solidarity and social cohesion, precluding the emergence of anti-social instincts of selfishness, greed, possessiveness and competition which, it was felt, would rupture the bonds of fraternity that the kibbutz pioneers nurtured in their new society.[194] Within the commune, the individual had nothing other than small personal effects. Everything—from housing and agricultural/industrial machinery to clothes and food—was owned communally by kibbutz members. The land on which each kibbutz is built is owned by the Jewish National Fund (Keren Kayemet)—a national agency, founded in 1901, that rents the land to the kibbutz on a ninety-nine-year renewable lease, with a (nominal) annual rent of 2 percent of the original cost of the land plus improvements, paid after its fifth year. Until 2007, legislation existed to prevent the legal possibility of a kibbutz selling off its assets and liquidating itself, which ensured that if a kibbutz did disintegrate, its assets would be distributed among other movement settlements, thus further preventing the possibility of individual accumulation.

The first principle of the kibbutz's economic model is therefore that all property used and produced by the kibbutz belongs to the entire community as a communal asset. The second is that all work in the kibbutz takes place voluntarily and without remuneration. At the time of writing this is still the case for the majority of the kibbutzim, but it is changing. The introduction of differential payments into kibbutz praxis in the early 1990s marked the beginning of one of the most controversial issues in the recent history of the movement, and it represents an important turning point for the kibbutzim. Until that point, there had existed no wage system in any of the settlements. Dissociation between contribution and effort and the distribution of rewards resulted in an economic culture in which position and status had no bearing on material rewards—with an egalitarian distribution of resources and services regardless of individual labour contribution meaning a total divorce between remuneration and effort.[195]

The third principle on which the kibbutz's economy and value system rests is the concept of the moral value of labour. As discussed in previous chapters, this has its roots in a very specific historical source peculiar to Labour Zionism. The Gordonite elevation of manual labour meant that work was seen by the early halutzim not only as a means to an end, but as an end in itself, and this has been an elemental part of kibbutz life since the very earliest settlements. As one member of the Betanya commune commented during the 1920s:

> Work is a part of [our] life and [our] common creation. Through love for society, a positive attitude towards work is formed, a moment of communality between the workers. In work, the individual realises all of his or her abilities and strengths and sees him or herself independently of creating a community. All work, even the most basic, is then a sacred means for establishing and fortifying the community. This gives it its full content, and it ceases being attached or inferior.[196]

This ethos of labour is perhaps the most enduring legacy of the founding members, remaining dominant in the kibbutzim even to this day. Although derived from a very specific ideological source, bound up with the peculiarly Jewish character of the kibbutz settlements, this ethos also clearly has a pragmatic dimension—albeit perhaps a rather more pedestrian one than the cosmic qualities attributed to it by A.D. Gordon. Communal ownership of property, equal distribution of resources and services irrespective of individual contribution, and equal consumption of goods can only exist based on the willingness of each and every member of that society to work voluntarily. Without universal commitment to this way of thinking, no economic model based on voluntary participation would be able to function. The motivation of each and every individual to do his or her best at every economic branch is the *sine qua non* of the viability of the kibbutz system.

Intertwined with this is the integration of manual and white-collar work. Keenly aware that work has so often become "a curse of fate," the pioneers set out with a recognition of the necessity for a full and balanced life, and sought to ensure that their model of collective living guaranteed that the individual was free to undertake all different kinds of work.[197] The unique economic model they created falls somewhere between the Fair-Share labour system and the Anti-Quota model;[198] members occupy work positions for varying lengths of time, with routine daily jobs such as kitchen and dining hall duties performed on a rotation basis. In the early years, for example, members would work in the kitchen every few months, in the cowshed every half year, in the vegetable garden and with animals by seasons and in the fields, while also taking on whatever administrative jobs needed doing.

Ensuring that all members shared in every kind of work was felt to create fulfilling and rewarding work that, as the Betanya member says, "ceases being attached or inferior"—that is to say, all work has equal social value, with no distinction existing between "respectable" and "degrading" work roles. With a member working in the dairy one week, in the factory the next, in the fields the next, and so on, the system of rotation meant that work was arranged in such a way that no one was expected to spend all his time in drudgery, with specialised abilities giving no one exemption from unpleasant or dull tasks, nor conferring any right to greater share in the amenities of the community. As Maurice Pearlman observed in an article in *Community Overseas*—a pamphlet produced by the Community Service Committee in the 1950s—despite a degree of specialisation in health and education services,

> drudge work such as serving table [and] washing up…is done by all without class consciousness. Not only do women share all but the heaviest of the men's work, but men also share the kitchen tasks that traditionally are the lot of the woman. A doctor is on the same footing as a dustman, and a lecturer of high educational attainment may be found prefacing his lecture by clearing up the tables after a meal.[199]

The kibbutz pioneers set out with the belief that their communities should "unite all the workers, whether they employ muscle or brain, provided that they derive their livelihood from their own labour, and not from the exploitation of others."[200] The central tenet of the kibbutz's economic activity is the idea that a socio-economic model that holds particular kinds of work in higher esteem than others is less logical and fair than one that holds them all in equal regard.

By the same token, within the kibbutz system, human attributes were considered equal, intellectual acumen respected no more than manual dexterity, or physical ability no more than organisational or administrative skills.[201] With workers deciding their own specific tasks and the method by which they carry out these tasks, the kibbutz, to this day, exhibits "a unification of conception and execution in the labour process such that no differentiation exists between mental and manual labour."[202]

Kibbutz Industry: Management Without Authority

The system described above was, quite literally, created by the kibbutz founders. Although the settlements have been in a continual process of evolution since their inception, it is this system that has underpinned the organisation of their economic life throughout the movement's history. Even though the small kvutzot and kibbutzim of the Second and Third Aliyot evolved into large-scale agro-industrial enterprises during the 1930s and 1940s, the kibbutz managed to ensure that their values and practices were translated and adapted as the basis for the organisation of large-scale industrial activity.

Until the 1930s, agriculture had been the mainstay of the kibbutz's economic activities, with kibbutz industry amounting to little more than a "workshop economy." The kibbutz pioneers' early hostility to the idea of industrial enterprise stemmed from their aspirations of inverting the Jewish socio-economic structure of the Diaspora by rejecting bourgeois, industrial urbanism in favour of an organic, agricultural existence. Industry was seen as an anathema to those who subscribed to A.D. Gordon's ideas about taking root in the land and spiritual renewal through reconnection with nature. Nevertheless, the second half of the century saw the process of industrialisation becoming the focus of the movement's attention. Around the time the state of Israel was created, the movement began devoting its energies to both rationalising and adapting to this transition, with adoption of new technologies and the acquisition of necessary industrial skills becoming the key priorities for the kibbutzim's economic development.

Industrial expansion gave rise to new challenges for management and organisation, making it more difficult to maintain the high degree of direct democracy, self-labour and workers' decision-making that had been possible in the smaller settlements of the early years of the kibbutz movement. Participatory self-management and workplace democracy in the early kvutzot were facilitated not only by the small size and intimate nature of the communities, but by universal comprehension of the urgency of the tasks facing the early communards and the pioneering spirit, or *élan*, which one Degania member described as "our feeling of inner strength that urged us to pool our forces in order to create something of value in our communal work, something different from the existing patterns."[203]

As the settlements grew larger and as projects became more ambitious, members found themselves presented with the reality that such work requires some kind of management, and records from general meetings at Degania at that time record how members were "unable to divide ourselves into managers and the managed."[204] As a means of rectifying the situation without having to stratify the settlement into managers and underlings, the Degania members decided to divide their settlement into two separate kibbutzim in order to restore what they felt to be the constructive atmosphere achievable only in a small group.

Traditionally, the smaller kvutzot tended to adopt this approach, deliberately trying to keep the population of each of their settlements to a minimum, with the assumption that for direct face-to-face democracy to function properly, settlements had to be as small and intimate as possible. But ultimately, due to the necessity of building an economy capable of supporting mass immigration, the demands of demographic increases and, later, the prospect of imminent statehood, all the kibbutzim had to expand. Although industrialisation and demographic expansion made it harder to maintain as high a level of direct democracy as in the intimate agricultural settlements of the early years, new mechanisms developed within the communities that allowed the kibbutz to ensure that it imposed its own economic culture on the industrial enterprises it created. An "ideological conformity" to the original values and practices was maintained, thus enabling the kibbutz to sustain "a form of industrialism that is free, working and classless."[205]

Such an ideological environment was achieved through the development of a "horizontal" management structure composed of a network of managerial committees, democratically elected by the general assembly of members and operating via a system of regular rotation. To each branch was assigned a branch manager, with each branch consisting of several autonomous units operating independently—the factory, fields, avocado and apple groves in the production branch, for example, and the laundry and kitchen in the consumption branch. Each of these had separate work groups with their own supervisor and a coordinator who set overall objectives for the various teams. Aside from the planning and administrative functions he or she carried out, the coordinator worked with the team just the same as any other member. According to Rosner,

> Work teams develop camaraderie and high esprit de corps. Six to twelve members work together side by side in the fields..., workshops or factories. They eat breakfast and lunch together and have regular meetings... In an atmosphere of mutual trust and responsibility close relationships are forged and often carry over to social life.[206]

Decision-making within these groups was carried out on a directly democratic basis, with each team free to choose a supervisor responsible for the day-to-day operations of the team. The supervisor divided tasks among team members who then decided for themselves how to perform the work, and kept an overview of the work process.

Continued adherence to the principle of systematic rotation ensured that employment in the kibbutz's industrial sector was never a permanent occupation, with members dividing their working life between the factory and other work branches.[207] Who worked where on any given day was usually decided the previous night by an elected committee, but the allocation of jobs would often be decided more openly and informally, with a dozen or more members assisting the committee every night to ensure that individuals' work preferences were taken into account. The allocation of jobs had, to the greatest extent possible, always taken individual members' preferences into consideration, ensuring that everyone was free to follow their own particular strengths and interests. Economic diversification obviously meant that a great deal of logic also came into play, in terms of matching labour assignments with personal aptitude, but it was still the personalities, wishes and desires of the people involved that more often than not remained the dominant determinants of work allocation.[208]

Before settling into a job, members would work in various branches to find the one that suited them best, and were free to request a change of work unit at any time. Although, for a short period, every member might find himself sent to work in an area where he was most needed, after a while everybody would be doing what he chose to do.[209]

This system survived virtually intact well into the 1980s, and it is essentially the system that the kibbutzim use to this day, although recent developments have led to an increased complexity in the network of committees and administrative bodies. Having said that, widespread bureaucratisation across the movement and the increasing use of full-time managers (a very recent phenomenon and one not yet common to all kibbutzim) has attracted accusations of the movement abandoning its original values. If Christopher Warhurst's study of Kibbutz Geffen in 1999 is anything to go by, although the management structure he encountered there reflects the increased complexity of economic organisational structures, kibbutz industry, even then, retained the principles of workplace democracy and self-management visible in the early settlements, just extended to a larger economic scale.

Each work branch, according to Warhurst, organises a committee to take responsibility for each production branch, all of which are ultimately subordinate to the economic affairs committee. Participation in the economic affairs committee is carried out on a voluntary basis and is supplementary to normal day-to-day work. The factory committee represents a joint kibbutz-factory management group acting as a form of supervisory board discussing policy related to the factory.

The board consists of senior managers, departmental managers, the kibbutz secretariat, two or three workers from the factory and one kibbutz member not from the factory ("to give a non-official view from the kibbutz membership").[210]

Even with this complex web of committees and managers, the kibbutz managed to prevent the emergence of a managerial hierarchy of "managers and managed," as the members of kibbutz Degania had once feared. Even today, the function of managers on most kibbutzim remains far removed from those in a capitalist business, their role entailing "the co-ordination and not the control of workers or work in progress."[211] Neither the work coordinator, supervisor, nor anyone else in a managerial position has the power to dismiss a worker. Decision-making still takes place on a participatory basis, and any conflict that arises in the workplace must be brought before the work group who talk it over collectively.

Warhurst recounts that one kibbutz worker said of his line-manager: "He is the manager but he can only ask me to do things, he cannot tell me."[212] The manager in question confirms that,

> It's not my job to impose discipline on the line. If I'm working with other members there's no difference between us. It's not my job to teach them discipline or responsibility. Discipline should come from the members themselves—self-discipline. It's not something that I'm supposed to do.[213]

So, by virtue of his position, a manager is afforded no greater degree of power or status than any other worker, and the regular rotation of those in managerial office ensures that managers take part in menial jobs just like any other kibbutz member. Managers and workers alike enjoy considerable autonomy as to how they carry out their own work roles, and it is left up to the individual to do his job as he sees fit. According to one supervisor: "[I am] completely free in how I do the job. Nobody tells me how to produce, not even the production manager." He continues, "I'm not fussing to know all the small details. I believe that you have to give people room to manoeuvre... Everyone has their own way of working. I know this and let them get on with it. I get involved only if there are problems."[214]

Despite the difficulties that arose in terms of reconciling demographic expansion and technological advancement with original ideological goals, the kibbutz movement has strived to ensure that a maximum degree of freedom and egalitarianism in decision-making remain central pillars of the *modus operandi* of kibbutz industry. As the role of managers is nominal, rather than one that enables them to wield any kind of coercive power or affords them greater levels of reward or status, any hierarchies that *are* found within the kibbutz are de-emphasised. Direct democratic election and the regular rotation of office holders prevents the development of a separate managerial class.[215]

Efficiency Without Coercion

It is important to note that there remains no official minimum labour contribution requirement on the kibbutz. Its "management" has never kept a formal check on who works, when and for how long. The only regulator being the self-motivation of each and every worker. With the worker in charge of his own life, rather than simply being a tool in a production process directed from above, he is free to make his own decisions regarding the work he does, how he does it—and even *when* he does it. "That members were under no compunction to even remain at their place of work," writes Warhurst, "is attested by the constant stream of bicycles leaving and returning to the factory throughout the working day. Every member...would at some time, leave the factory to conduct personal business."[216]

But, with such personal freedom a near-immutable principle in the economic life of the kibbutz, coupled with the absence of managerial authority, the threat of sanctions, or the promise of monetary reward, how does the kibbutz ensure that production goals are met? What would happen, for example, to a kibbutz member who is slacking off work? During the 1920s, when presented with this question, one member of Degania simply answered: "We would not love him."[217] Simplistic though it may seem, over the course of the past century this attitude has played a key role in defining the ethos of the kibbutz labour model. Conformity to productivity norms has traditionally been secured by "a socially defined framework of sanctioning and behaviour prescription based on public opinion and peer pressure"[218]—a by-product of the intense intimacy of interpersonal relations between kibbutzniks, characteristic of relationships in a *gemeinschaft*-type society like the kibbutz.

Thus, an individual's work reputation remains vitally important for social cohesion and for ensuring that the participatory economic model can successfully function, with attitudes towards a kibbutznik's productivity and/or labour contribution based on the "knowledge...and opinions held by the community about individuals and their perceived effort and commitment." The medium of transmission is basically gossip or hearsay, or as one kibbutz sociologist put it, "informal interpersonal communications."[219] Through the pressures of public opinion then, rather than through a typically market-driven system of meritocracy, the kibbutz is able to ensure conformity to its social norms and labour expectations.

Communal Consumption

Collective possession and control of the means of production implies common enjoyment of the fruits of that production. Accordingly, the kibbutz's system ensures that the product of the community's labour remains at the disposal of all its members. The kibbutz has always sought to ensure that its members' needs are catered to in a full and egalitarian way, basing its approach to consumption on the elimination of any connection between one's input and what one receives in return.

The draft kvutza constitution of 1924 stipulates certain basic items such as food, housing and clothing that were to be "defrayed out of the common account." In practice, this translated into a system wherein community members' economic needs were comprehensively satisfied by the kibbutz. Everything from food and clothing right down to cigarettes (a packet a day for those who wanted them) was provided for by the kibbutz. With private property nonexistent, the individual's accommodation was owned by the kibbutz and he therefore paid no rent. He had no food bills since he ate in the kibbutz dining room, and his clothes were borrowed on a weekly basis from the communal clothing store, rather than being personal to him. Smaller personal items, like combs and toothbrushes, were obtained from the communal store. Children were educated at the expense of the community. Should a kibbutznik fall ill, the kibbutz would foot his medical and hospital bills.[220] Although each kibbutznik received a small allowance for trips outside the kibbutz (every member was entitled to an annual holiday at the kibbutz's expense), within the community itself, no money was used. And nor did it need to be, since members' day-to-day economic needs were wholly provided for out of the common account.

The kibbutz retained this status as a moneyless society until well after Israel's independence, with solidarity, public opinion, and "the social identification of the individual with the system and its administration"[221] remaining the sole guardians against the potential for waste and over-consumption that inevitably accompanies free distribution. In a paper entitled "The Use and Division of Income in the Kibbutz" presented at an international conference on communal living in 1981, Amir Helman identified a system of distribution and consumption that reflected the enduring influence of the "to each according to his needs" approach on the kibbutz of that era, with every member continuing to receive an equal quantity of free goods determined by the kibbutz.[222]

However, the 1980s would subsequently witness the erosion of this system. For a variety of reasons (discussed in Chapter 5) the ideological consciousness on which the kibbutz had previously relied as the primary stabiliser of its economy began to atrophy.[223] Increasing over-consumption of free utilities led to the kibbutz initially beginning to meter energy usage, meaning that since members now had to pay for the electricity they used, they had to have their own money. Private accounts were thus introduced into kibbutz life for the first time. Such changes rapidly filtered into other areas of consumption such as eating arrangements, with the communal dining halls—previously the focal point of kibbutz's communal life—replaced, in the majority of kibbutzim today, with pay-as-you-go cafeterias.

Kibbutz Polity: The No-Government System

The economic model of the pre-1948 kibbutzim was built on the principles of communal ownership of property, with production in the hands of the community and consumption according to Marx's maxim "from each according to his ability to each according to his need." With economic activity and workplace decision-making taking place on an egalitarian and participatory basis, neither the reproduction nor the transformation of labour power depended on the relations of production through which goods and services are produced and distributed.[224] In other words, relations of production in the kibbutz's economic model were not those of employer and employee. Coupled with the absence of wage labour, this meant that kibbutz members were not subject to exploitation or subordination, and therefore that the social and economic antagonisms inherent in free market economies were absent.

Let's return for a moment to Kropotkin. Adapting the critique of political economy first put forward by Marx, the Russian anarchist argued that the political system of a given society should be a reflection of its economic structure.[225] To each new economic phase of life he saw a corresponding new political phase (absolute monarchy corresponded to serfdom, representative government to capital-rule and so on). In a society where the distinction between capitalist and labourer has disappeared, government of any kind would be superfluous: "Free workers," Kropotkin wrote, "would require a free organisation, and this cannot have any other basis than free agreement and free cooperation... The no-capitalist system implies the no-government system."[226] Accordingly, given the structure of the kibbutz's economic relations, this "no-government system" is one to which the settlements have tried to adhere since the very earliest days of their existence.

Relying on direct membership participation in all areas of its day-to-day running, the ultimate authority of collective governance is the general assembly or *asefa*, as it is called in Hebrew. The general assembly, of which every kibbutz member was a part, met on a weekly basis, traditionally in the communal dining room, and was the forum in which the community's decision-making took place. In it, kibbutzniks could confront social, political and economic issues or consider new candidates for membership. Every member had one vote and decisions were made by majority vote. Direct participation and involvement of all in the general assembly was expected (though while this expectation may have been adhered to in the communities' younger days, today only about 35 percent to 40 percent of the members attend the general assembly's sessions).

The direct democracy that the pioneers sought to achieve involved every member of the kibbutz engaging in the decision-making process, and the views of every member given equal consideration. During the earliest years of the movement, when the populations of many of the kvutzot hardly made it into double figures, the decision-making process was, by nature, informal and sporadic, characterised by spontaneous direct democracy and loosely formed organisational institutions.[227] Decisions were made strictly by consensus, with informal group discussions, debates and arguments—again, usually taking place in the communal dining room, without a chairman or fixed agenda—being the main forum in which political activity took place.

It was assumed by the earliest kibbutz communards that the work would get accomplished without having to endow any individual or group with power over their associates—and during this early period it did. But with demographic expansion and economic diversification came a recognition that the face-to-face democracy and consensus-based decision-making achievable in the small, intimate communities of the early years had to evolve. Although the diversification, expansion and the increased economic complexity of the kibbutz meant that some kind of formal organisation was necessary, this recognition was still coupled with an ideological commitment to prevent any one individual or group from acquiring personal power, and to subvert the formation of an "entrenched bureaucracy"— i.e. a separate political class or ruling elite—within the kibbutz. [228]

It was with this in mind that the kibbutz's decision-making structures evolved. According to the 1924 draft kvutza constitution, the general assembly remained the "supreme organ of the kvutza," as it had traditionally been, but it now took upon itself the responsibility of appointing "executive organs that are to run current affairs for a certain term."[229] So, while the general assembly remained the ultimate forum in which major policy decisions were decided, certain responsibilities beyond that were delegated to various committees.

An executive committee elected by the general assembly, in turn, elected a secretary for a one or two year term, and sub-committees were appointed to deal with various aspects of community life. Areas such as work allocation, culture, services, economic planning, cultivation, personal relations, health, education, sports, entertainment and so on would all have their own committees. In addition to these, a secretariat, usually consisting of secretary, treasurer and economic coordinator, was nominated from and elected by the general assembly. These various administrative offices were held on a temporary basis and rotated after a predetermined period of time, usually ranging from between one and five years.

With the implementation of this system of administrative offices it was still held as axiomatic that members elected to these positions must not be afforded any material advantage over their peers. Their opinion was not to outweigh that of any other kibbutznik, and they would not enjoy any more prestige or status than anyone else. With those elected to these offices enjoying no special privileges or material rewards (the rewards derived solely from the "satisfaction of serving and from the appreciation of everyone for the person who fills the post,") and frequent rotation of leadership positions and the participation of up to 50 percent of kibbutzniks on various committees at any given time, the kibbutz system of democracy remained geared towards preventing the formation of any kind of powerful and entrenched bureaucratic elite.[230]

All kibbutz members serving on committees were to carry out their special duties at night, with no excuse other than ill health accepted for not working on the land during the day—secretary, treasurer, economic coordinator and everyone else.[231] The role of these office-holders was seen as purely organisational, and did not bring with it the ability to back their recommendations with any kind of sanctions or coercive or quasi-governmental power. Committees, for example, even in the administrative functions they fulfilled, remained under the scrutiny of the community in general. Any policy decisions were still thrashed out by the general assembly in open meetings. According to kibbutz sociologist Josef Blasi, writing in the mid-1980s,

> The close community structure, economic equality, direct-democracy and the absence of wage differentials work together to discourage the formation of elite groups. Of the several central mechanisms that reduce stratification, foremost is the collective system of reward. Members are nominated to public offices, not elected; thus, "influence campaigns" seldom occur. Power in such offices and committee posts is coordinating and executive, not definitive. People persuade, relate and direct. The general assembly, however, defines, decides, and sets the limits and policy for officials. Officials receive power from the community, not from the people who held power previously.[232]

So the "power" of the officers is further restricted by the fact that major decisions are still made, not by them, but by the general assembly of kibbutz members with whom the ultimate authority regarding matters of governance remains. The general assembly, in effect, held on to its function as "the supreme organ" of the kibbutz, retaining the prerogative to remove an officer at any time should he fail to live up to the expectations of the community.

Over the years, the increased complexity of kibbutz social organisation and demographic expansion have resulted in this system's evolution into an enormously complicated and comprehensive network of committees, each charged with responsibility for the organisation and management of the many diverse areas of the kibbutz's social and economic life. Although expansion meant that social relations became less intimate and less visible, this diffuse decision-making system of interrelated committees, branches and groups continues to underpin the life of today's kibbutzim. There may be more committees than there were, and their functions may be more specialised, with kibbutz politics spread across the variety of consulting and executive groups that have become the new decision-making centres, but sovereignty still ultimately rests with the general assembly of members in which all the functions of the kibbutz's political process are still integrated.

Order Without Law

Just as the kibbutz's participatory labour model is held together by public opinion, gossip and social consciousness, it is these same informal mechanisms that are the primary stabilisers of the community's social and political life. The kibbutz employs no formal enforcement mechanisms to safeguard social cohesion, and relies instead on the social pressures of group life and the intense intimacy of interpersonal relations within the community to ensure voluntary adherence to its self-imposed, collectively-decided behavioural norms. The fact that social relations are so intimate on the kibbutz means that the direct exchange, airing and resolution of views on an informal basis is an everyday feature of kibbutz life. This face-to-face interaction is seen as essential for direct democracy to flourish, irrespective of the presence (or otherwise) of official legislative and supervisory institutions.[233]

In a paper entitled "Laws and Legalism in Kibbutz," presented at an international conference on communes and kibbutzim in 1985, Avraham Yassour suggests that, by their very nature as organic societies based on voluntary association, communal responsibility, mutual trust and collectively-decided agreements, the kibbutzim simply have no need for formalised rules and sanctions enforced by a specialised body of coercive legal institutions.[234] Apparently attesting to the veracity of Yassour's claim, Josef Blasi's study of Kibbutz Vatik, published in 1986, notes that the community had never experienced any serious crime in its entire lifetime. In a letter to London's *Freedom* newspaper in 1940, a British airman stationed in Palestine recorded a similar observation. Within the kibbutzim, he wrote, "The problem of violence has simply not arisen," and he suggests that across the kibbutz movement as a whole this trend is not exceptional.[235] Yassour's own study similarly finds that the very phenomenon of crime "factually disappeared" within the settlements.[236]

These remarks on the non-existence of crime were all made at a time when many of the communities were of equivalent size to small towns, or at least large villages, many of them housing well over a thousand people each. Although neither Blasi nor Yassour reflect on the other pressures conducive to solidarity within the communities that could have bolstered the ability to maintain a crime-free existence, for an organisation the size of the kibbutz movement to have survived for the best part of a century without having experienced any serious crime is clearly still no mean achievement.

Inextricably linked to this absence of crime is the fact that the kibbutz has achieved a level of social wellbeing almost unheard of in the modern industrialised world. Blasi records how suicide, mental illness, juvenile delinquency and drug abuse have been almost totally eliminated among their membership, an accomplishment due in large part, according to sociologist Menechem Rosner, to a sense of belonging and a common identity promoted by the cooperation, mutual help and solidarity of the peer group.[237] "The emotional attachment of the individual kibbutz member to his peer group," writes Rosner, "and to the kibbutz as a whole almost eliminated the feelings of isolation, of loneliness in the crowd, of anomie, so familiar to modern mass society." The very nature of kibbutz membership, he says, "creates a feeling of belonging, of sharing the fate of others, which are the conditions for real synergy and cooperation between human beings."[238]

"The feeling of living a meaningful part of something larger than oneself receives constant social reinforcement," agrees Daniel Katz. "Total rather than partial inclusion is the rule."[239] The role played by this synergy in the apparently glowing success story that is the kibbutz's social life is echoed throughout much of the literature written on the kibbutz movement by members and outside researchers alike. While the lessons to be drawn from this must be accompanied by an acknowledgement that the kibbutz is obviously not without its problems (particularly in the very recent years, when trends towards individualism have threatened to undermine the tight-knit community structure), in comparison to the rest of Israeli society, the kibbutz is still a veritable laboratory for students of social psychology and criminology.

In their book *Reform through Community* (1991), social scientist Michael Fischer and education philosopher Brenda Geiger describe an experimental project in which a number of young offenders were invited to live and work as members on kibbutzim in lieu of the final third of their prison sentences. Focusing on the offenders' perceptions of their own experience on the kibbutzim, Fischer and Geiger explain how the protective environment, daily routines, egalitarianism, peer group support, acceptance and trust provided by the kibbutz way of life yielded involvement, commitment and higher self-esteem. Relating the kibbutz ways of ensuring a harmonious social order to theories of social psychology and criminology, Fischer and Geiger argue that the kibbutz's way of life provides insight into how a combination of group dynamics and social learning in a context of meaningful work and acceptance are conducive to solving the problems of anomie in modern society.

Education on the Kibbutz

For the founding generation of kibbutzniks, the "solidarity of the peer group" identified by Rosner as a key determinant of the kibbutz's peaceful and cohesive social relations was born from the hardships of their situation. It was born from *élan*, from pioneering spirit, and also from the simple fact that many of the earliest settlements sprang from the nucleus of a group of friends who had grown up together, made Aliya together, and lived communally prior to founding their kvutzot.

For subsequent generations however—those born *into* the kibbutz—the duty of fostering peer group solidarity fell on the kibbutz's education system. Needless to say, the question of family and child-rearing was the subject of intense disagreement within the movement from day one, and still constitutes one of the most enduring, complex, emotive (and also myth-ridden) disputes surrounding the kibbutz movement.

Apart from practical considerations, the birth of the first children into the kvutzot gave rise to a major ideological crisis. Should the parents bring up their child, or should it be in someone else's care? Should children live with their family or in separate accommodation? Were children "private property" or did they belong to the group? The answer to the latter was, in many respects, fairly clear. Since the communal life of the early settlements saw all expenses defrayed collectively, it was taken as self-evident that the expenses of childrearing and education should be borne by all. Nobody was to be exempt from this just because he or she had no children.[240] Moreover, it was felt that an individual approach to parenting would be detrimental to collective work, and it was taken as read that the arrival of a child into the kibbutz should not interfere with the egalitarianism and participation of communal life.

But the arrival of the first babies in Degania presented another, much more far-reaching problem for the communards. When the first children were born on the settlement, their parents were dismayed by their selfish tendencies, and in constructing the kibbutz education system, made it a priority to ensure that these traits were replaced by cooperation, mutual sympathy and mutual concern. Within the kibbutz, the education and socialisation of youth came to be considered a joint enterprise of the parents, *metaplot* (house mothers), *madrichim* (guides) and teachers, who between them took joint responsibility for planning and implementing various educational programs.

The education system the kibbutz created was based on the idea that children should also live in their own community environment, a "community of youth" that would make the peer group the major socialising force rather than the traditional nuclear family structure. From infancy onward, children on most kibbutzim lived together in the children's house, where their parents visited for a few hours every day and for most of the day on Shabbat and holidays.[241] Children were raised and educated in groups, usually of around sixteen, who remained together from nursery school through to high school. Life within these groups was guided by the same democratic principles that governed the kibbutz's adult society.

The youth society (composed of adolescents aged thirteen to eighteen) existed as a self-governing body in its own right, with its own general assembly, work and social committees. The *madrich* guided the group and interceded only if the children's behaviours deviated drastically from kibbutz norms. Agricultural or other vocational training was valued just as much as academic learning, and, from the earliest possible age, children were encouraged to do useful work and take up their natural role in the productive life of the community.[242]

With an emphasis on solidarity and cooperation, competition between groups was encouraged only to the extent that it increased group solidarity and teamwork. As the community took on many of the duties traditionally assumed by the parents, even after the rapid abandonment of the more "extreme" communist practices (in many kibbutzim, prolonged separation between parents and children quickly proved too much for both parties), the education system continued to ensure that the authority structure of the traditional nuclear family did not exist.

Whether or not this education system was either successful or healthy is a question that has caused a great deal of debate (but not so much in the way of consensus) among psychologists and sociologists all over the world. But perhaps more interesting is the quite remarkable degree to which the kibbutz education system polarises opinion even among those who actually went through it. Of her upbringing at Kibbutz Nachshon, Dorit Friedman recalled how "it was inhuman, really inhuman."[243] Other kibbutzniks blame their schooling for strained parent and sibling relationships that were never overcome. Childcare experts have described how "unnatural feelings" about extended parent-child separations persist even among second- and third-generation kibbutzniks who never experienced a traditional family upbringing.[244]

On the other hand, one of the first children to be born at Degania recalled, in later life, a happier childhood, during which the "mutual concern for one another," nurtured from the earliest age to the point where it became intuitive, an impulse that the individual obeyed instinctively, meant that "it never occurred to me that I could have an orange and not share it with all the children."[245] Although the education system of the kibbutz evolved largely through trial and error (mainly error, some would say—by the late 1970s most kibbutzim had abandoned many of the practices outlined above and returned to traditional family life), it was this feeling of non-reflexive mutual aid and solidarity that the early kibbutzniks were attempting to encourage in their offspring. It was this that formed the basis of the education system they created. For the same reason, educational ideas were also central to the *modus operandi* of many of the European youth groups that contributed to building the kibbutzim of the 1920s and 1930s. Hashomer Hatzair is a particular case in point. As an educational youth movement, Hashomer Hatzair believed that educational training, and the particular kind of discipline fostered through participation in a youth group, was the key to collective settlement and the most essential and effective means of building a viable and sustainable community. A good insight into the kind of educational framework they were trying to create is obtained by looking at the organisation's activities in Europe in the 1930s.

The movement divided itself into age groups (*shichvot*): Bnei Midbar (nine to twelve years old); Zofim, subdivided into Zofim Zeirim (twelve to thirteen) and Zofim (fourteen to fifteen); and Bogrim, again subdivided into Zofim Bogrim (sixteen to seventeen) and Zofim (eighteen and over). According to kibbutz researcher Michael Tyldesley, the Bnei Midbar worked "using an emotional approach based on customs, symbols and commandments of the movement," whereas the Zofim program was based on "character-building and establishing the basis for a Marxist-Zionist worldview." The Bogrim worked on broadening their understanding of the politico-ideological roots of Hashomer Hatzair in light of the organisation's situation and role in Jewish community-building in Palestine, while the Zofim worked with texts like the *Communist Manifesto* and writings by Kropotkin and Landauer.[246]

This educational system was to be the bedrock on which Kibbutz Artzi would be built; its "organic" kibbutzim maintaining social cohesion and ideological conformity—and thus coherence and sustainability as socio-economic units—because its members had all gone through this educational process. Hashomer Hatzair's emphasis on the development of this "ideological collectivism" as an educational youth movement came to be institutionalised in their kibbutzim.

The Kibbutz Federations

From an early stage, high levels of inter-community reciprocity and the beginnings of relatively complex trade and communication networks began to develop among the settlements. The idea of federation has been central to the kibbutz movement since its inception, with Landauer, Arlosoroff, Buber and Yaari, to name but four of the most influential ideologues in the early movement, all envisioning a Jewish nation in Palestine built on an association of communal settlements (arguably in some ways appositional to the other "macro" vision of the kibbutz talked about during the early development of the Gedud and Kibbutz Hameuhad). Federations—loose, sporadic, and spontaneous at first—assumed many of the responsibilities usually taken on by the state.

The idea of formalising the trend towards federation remained just an idea until 1925. The minutes of a meeting of kvutza representatives held at Degania the previous year show that, although the question of a federation of kvutzot had not yet been investigated, it was considered "important insofar as it may improve relations among the kvutzot,"[247] and mutual aid seen "as a way of spreading the communal idea."[248] According to Martin Buber's famous retrospective analysis though,

> Even in its first undifferentiated form a tendency towards federation was innate in the kvutza, to merge the Kvutzoth [sic] in some higher social unit; and a very important tendency it was, since it showed that the Kvutza implicitly understood that it was the cell of a newly structured society. With the splitting off and proliferation of the various forms, from the semi-individualistic form which jealously guarded personal independence in its domestic economy, way of life, children's education etc., to the pure communistic form, the single unit was supplanted by a series of units in each of which a definite form of colony and a more or less definite human type constituted itself on a federal basis.

The fundamental assumption was that the local groups would combine on the same principle of solidarity and mutual help as reigned within the individual group.[249]

In his chapter on Kropotkin in *Paths in Utopia*, Buber acknowledges the Russian anarchist's belief that "a socialistic community could only be built on the basis of a double intercommunal bond, namely the federation of regional communes and trade communes variously intercrossing and supporting one another."[250] It was more or less along these lines that the kibbutzim would evolve.

The communities established by the various pioneering organisations of the Second and Third Aliyot gradually gravitated towards one another, laying the groundwork for the subsequent development of the federations. Gedud HaAvoda evolved into Kibbutz Hameuhad (United Kibbutz), the Hashomer Hatzair kibbutzim coalesced into Kibbutz Artzi Hashomer Hatzair (the National Kibbutz Movement of the Young Guard). Hever Hakvutzot (the Association of Kvutzot), the first federation formed in 1925, became part of the Ihud Hakvutzot Vehakibbutzim (The Union of Collective Settlements) in 1951.

Throughout the twentieth century, the movement operated on this federal basis with principles of mutual aid between kibbutzim, as they underwent a complex and extensive process of splits and mergers. Today, The Kibbutz Movement—an amalgam of the two largest federations, TAKAM and Kibbutz Artzi—houses some 94 percent of the country's total kibbutz population, the Kibbutz Dati, the Religious Kibbutz Movement, making up the remaining 6 percent.[251]

With representatives from every kibbutz, each federation organises a central authority with annual and extra-ordinary assemblies. At any given time, a kibbutz has around 6 percent of its members working full time on federation business, assignments that are rotated approximately every two years. As well as planning, research, evaluation, consultant work and occupational and educational training programs, the federations provide comprehensive healthcare, social insurance and various other federation-wide services, including economic and technical advisory services such as the Kibbutz Industries Association (KIA), a voluntary organisation, established in 1962, that represents and advises all the industrial projects throughout the movement.[252] While each kibbutz is an autonomous entity, the bonds of mutual aid and cooperation evident from the very inception of the movement remain concrete in these national federations. The progressive tax system, organised by the federations, which enables the more established kibbutzim to help younger or weaker settlements, is a contemporary example of the kind of aid that existed between the early kibbutzim.

Although the federations' primary role involves co-ordinating activities within and between kibbutzim, they have also traditionally played a big part in the life of wider society. A noteworthy example of this is the Branch for Involvement in Israeli Society, a unit established to create programs to help Israel's underprivileged.

While the federations co-ordinate national political programmes and develop the expected norms of conduct for the member kibbutzim in terms of consumption, educational programs and regulations in various other spheres of life, the kibbutz secretariat in Tel Aviv has no real power, as such, over the individual kibbutzim. Unless a decision of the secretariat is accepted and ratified by the general assembly of each kibbutz, the central authority has little power of coercion, allowing the individual kibbutzim to retain their basic autonomy.[253]

The Histadrut

The kibbutzim are self-contained social models in themselves, bound together in this federative structure, but they have always been connected to the country's trade union movement, the Histadrut. Quite apart from its enormous influence in defining the ideological self-understanding of the kibbutz movement, in the context of this discussion the Histadrut is an interesting organisation in its own right. Founded in Haifa in December 1920, the Histadrut was created to provide a federation for all Jewish workers, to promote land settlement, and to stand up for workers' rights, as well as to provide services such as an employment exchange, sick pay and consumer benefits for its members. More than simply being a trade-union movement in the conventional sense however, the Histadrut became something of an "alternative society" during the pre-state years.

From 1920 onwards, the Histadrut would own and control a wide variety of different enterprises throughout Palestine, and it was, for a time, the largest employer in the country. As well as owning numerous businesses and factories, it had its own network of schools and ran teachers' seminars, libraries and cultural clubs across the country. Workers' councils in the cities and the kibbutzim ran various cultural programs, sponsored sports clubs, and established flourishing publishing houses.[254] In pre-1948 Palestine, as Laqueur notes,

> A trade union member had no need to move far outside the compass of the Histadrut sector, even if he did not work in one of its enterprises. He could do his shopping in a cooperative store, deposit his money in a workers' bank, send his children to Histadrut-sponsored kindergartens and schools, and consult a doctor at the Kupat Holim (Histadrut Sick Fund), which was ultimately to provide medical services for 65 percent of the total population, a semi-official national health service in fact. But for the fact that the Histadrut did not own cemeteries, it would have been true to say that the Histadrut provided the great majority with all amenities from the cradle to the grave.[255]

Within two years of its inception, the Histadrut had over 8,000 members, representing just over half of the Jewish working class in Palestine. By 1927, now with 25,000 members, it incorporated 75 percent of the country's entire Jewish workforce. Although the creation of the state meant that some of the functions it had previously fulfilled were no longer needed, the organisation would remain an important mainstay of the labour movement and continued to provide key welfare functions until the 1990s.

Anarchism in the Kibbutz?

To characterise the kibbutz's unique model of organisation described in this chapter as a microcosm of state socialism or Marxism, as many have done, would be a mistake. Although, by the early 1930s, the wider discourse of settlement was framed almost entirely within a Marxist-Leninist ideological context, and the official line of the kibbutzim had, as a reflection of a larger Israeli political discourse (and particularly that of the Histadrut), become avowedly pro-communist, the model of politico-economic organisation created within the kibbutz itself differs so enormously from that of most theoretical blueprints for, or historical examples of, state socialism that the two systems are simply not analogous. While the essential preconditions of *state* socialism as defined by Marx or his followers are not present in the kibbutz system, the key characteristics of anarchist socialism are clearly visible.

This is the line taken by Israeli journalist and kibbutz member Giora Manor, whose 1993 article "The Kibbutz: Caught Between 'Isms'" attempts to dispel the idea that the kibbutz is the practical example of Marxism or a microcosm of state-based forms of socialism that it is commonly thought to be. Manor argues that the shift towards Marxist ideas that began during the 1920s actually had no real bearing on the reality of kibbutz life but merely created "an ever-widening chasm between ideology as expressed in slogans and manifestos, and reality."[256]

Anarchism, Manor claims, "was still implemented in kibbutz life but never mentioned.[257] He believes this discrepancy between ideology and praxis was felt most acutely by the kibbutz's educators, whose task it was to explain to the youngsters the theory of the community into which they had been born. During the 1930s, this task was made particularly problematic by the staunch anti-Zionist stance of communists all over the world (some kibbutz leaders spoke of the "unrequited love affair" between the USSR and the kibbutz movement). But even after the kibbutzim's official pro-communist stance was made easier to rationalise by the USSR's fighting against Hitler during the Second World War and its subsequent influence in the United Nations' decision to vote for the creation of the state of Israel, "the educators went on to pay lip service to Marxism, but did not try to connect it to kibbutz theory."[258]

Manor suggests it became unfashionable within the kibbutzim to formulate any theory regarding the basic principles of the kibbutz in a wider ideological framework, noting that, "until the 1950s hardly anybody noticed the absurdity of preaching Marxism while living according to the principles of anarchism."[259] While this argument must be set in a framework in which the importance of

Marxism—specifically Leninism—to Palestinian Jewish and early Israeli society could not be overstated, Manor's claim that the adoption of a Marxist-socialist worldview resulted in a "complete divorce between kibbutz theory and kibbutz practice," rather than in the abandonment of anarchism as a way of life, is one that has some basis.

While the rhetoric may have become Marxist, in terms of the communities' internal structure and praxis, the kibbutzim actually moved closer towards social anarchism during this period than conventional analyses might suggest. Although the amalgamation of agriculture and industry meant a divorce from the cosmic Tolstoyanism of the early, agriculturally-orientated kvutzot and resulted in the kibbutzim having to re-think their organisational structures, economic diversification brought the communities closer to Kropotkin and Landauer's ideal of the local-level integration of industry and agriculture than they had previously been. The introduction initially of small, light-industrial workshops and their subsequent integration with larger scale industry and intensive, technologically advanced horticulture and agriculture, as eco-anarchist Graham Purchase argues, resulted in the kibbutz model becoming "exactly the sort of modern communal village/small town life which Kropotkin had envisaged."[260]

Chapter 5

A New Kibbutz Movement?

The Kibbutz in the Twenty-First Century

"For anarchists and old fashioned socialists, the kibbutz movement in Palestine…was an example of how people could live and work together without the state, the boss and the incentives of capitalism. Alas, it would appear that the kibbutzim now exist only in name, in that they have abandoned all the values and objectives that made them unique."
—*The Raven: Anarchist Quarterly, Summer 1995*

Interviewed in 1999, Noam Chomsky remarked that the early kibbutz communities "came closer to the anarchist ideal than any other attempt that lasted for more than a very brief moment before destruction."[261] Internally, the communes certainly proved themselves capable of creating and sustaining a functioning social system based on the principles of classical anarchist theory, but in addition to providing a comfortable and egalitarian existence for their own membership, during the pre-state period, they also succeeded where other utopian experiments failed. They managed to extend this to a national level, effectively building an entire national infrastructure on the success of cooperative labour organised through a federated alliance of horizontally run communal societies.

The organisational and economic structure of the Yishuv in the early years of Jewish settlement consisted of a panarchistic pattern of various co-existing collective, quasi-collective and not so collective institutions, from the kibbutzim and the virtually all-encompassing Histadrut federation at one end of the spectrum, through to capitalist enterprises like the Rothschild colonies at the other.[262/263] Alongside the Jewish cooperative bodies that formed the backbone of the Yishuv's economy, the Palestinian economy kept going the whole time. The Arab villages, themselves run in a broadly collective fashion, continued to grow crops and take their produce to market in Hebron, Be'er Sheva and Jaffa. Until the Arab revolt of 1936, the two economies were largely integrated, with certain commodities (vegetables for instance) produced mainly by the Arab sector and others, including various sorts of fruit, imported from neighbouring Arab countries.[264]

Although they were ultimately under the jurisdiction of foreign powers at all times, this decentralised network of communes, cooperatives and other collective and quasi-collective enterprises proved itself capable of carrying out most of the major functions usually undertaken by the centralised institutions of capitalism and the state. On the back of collective endeavour, industry, agriculture, all manner of cultural and social programs and even a rudimentary national health service were successfully coordinated. Individuals were free to adhere voluntarily to the system of their choice and join and leave the jurisdiction of the communities at their own discretion.

The Betrayal of a Dream

As we have seen, this situation was something that many of the kibbutz founders initially hoped would become a permanent arrangement. In terms of capability, it might well have been able to. The fact that this vision would ultimately not come to fruition is attributable to a series of larger-scale betrayals that occurred during the British Mandate period, as the dream pursued by the early communards was systematically manipulated and hijacked by the emerging Zionist institutions of the state-to-be.

A clear portent of what was to come, and arguably one of the earliest and most distinct points of betrayal, can be seen in events surrounding Kibbutz Tel Yosef in the Jezreel Valley in the early 1920s. Established in 1922 by members of the Gedud HaAvoda, Tel Yosef was an offshoot kibbutz of Ein Harod. In the summer of 1923 it was to become the focal point for the culmination of escalating tensions between the Ahdut HaAvoda and the Gedud HaAvoda. Since its inception in 1919, Ahdut HaAvoda aimed to bring the Gedud under its control, and under the leadership of the man who would become Israel's first Prime Minister, David Ben-Gurion, it made attempts to move towards a merger. In the run-up to the second Histadrut convention in 1922, at which point the Ahdut HaAvoda's control of the Histadrut was still not yet secured, Ben-Gurion approached the Gedud and the rest of the Jezreel Valley kibbutzim in an attempt to broaden and strengthen the Ahdut HaAvoda's support-base.

On December 3, Ben-Gurion addressed a meeting of kibbutz representatives convened at Tel Yosef, where he spoke of his concerns about the viability of the Histadrut as it existed at that time and stressed the need for a "strong organised body that will lead the way for the masses of workers."[265] He complained of the Histadrut's weakness and its inability to effectively control the different elements existing within it, arguing that the priority from that point forward was to strengthen the organisation, which, he said, "can and should be everything in this country," but was "not yet created."[266] Ben-Gurion declared his intention to make the kibbutzim his power base, and asked for their support of his attempts to control the sources of funding in the hands of the World Zionist Organisation. He argued that, without an independent financial basis, there would be no hope for achieving autonomy.

Ben-Gurion was a man with a considerable talent for manipulation. While he knew perfectly well that all this would be more than acceptable to the kibbutzim, at no point did he mention anything about ideological partnership.[267] Many representatives of the kibbutzim at that time envisaged the Histadrut taking the form of a nationwide "cooperative of organised bodies," but Ben-Gurion felt that the labour federation would be much easier to control if it was composed not of groups, but of individuals.[268] He knew that if the kibbutzim had their way, and the Histadrut became a body that gave priority to socialist, ideologically-driven communes that demanded economic egalitarianism and complete autonomy, it could quite easily become a serious competitor to Ahdut HaAvoda. This was a risk Ben-Gurion was not prepared to take. After the second Histadrut convention, when it became clear that the Gedud had no intention of merging with Ahdut HaAvoda, he decided to eradicate this threat once and for all.

Given the make-up of the two organisations' respective leaderships, this was never going to prove particularly problematic for a man of Ben-Gurion's political abilities. The leadership of the Gedud did not have his talent for manipulation, preferring instead to make a habit of actually practising what they preached. "Unlike Ahdut HaAvoda," writes Ze'ev Sternhell, "not only did the Gedud adhere uncompromisingly to the principles of equality and mutual aid administered through the common treasury, but its leaders set a personal example."[269]

"They laboured strenuously, first in laying roads and afterwards in the fields of the Jezreel Valley," Sternhell explains. "They laid the foundations of Ein Harod and Tel Yosef with their own hands and suffered with the rest from weakness and malnutrition. That was their great mistake. Instead of embarking on a political career, taking over the administrative jobs in the Bureau of Public Works while that was still possible and seizing key positions in the Histadrut, they continued to work hard and realise the principles of equality, autonomous labour and personal example. While [the leaders of the Gedud] were setting up... kibbutzim, spreading Gedud companies from the Upper Galilee to Jerusalem, and building and stonecutting, the heads of Ahdut HaAvoda were making politics into a profession, setting up an apparatus and binding thousands of isolated, unorganised workers to the Histadrut without regarding themselves as being for a single moment obligated to set a personal example."[270]

As a way of weakening his political opponents, and in light of the escalation of tensions between the Gedud and Ahdut HaAvoda, Ben-Gurion decided to look again at Shlomo Lavi's demand that kibbutz Ein Harod be taken away from the Gedud. Lavi sought the dissolution of the Gedud through the elimination of its common treasury, and he wanted to prevent any possibility of the finances allocated to Ein Harod being transferred to other settlements. To this end, he essentially accused the Gedud of embezzlement. Armed with a variety of allegations concerning the misuse of resources, he approached the Histadrut authorities asking that the supply of money to the Gedud's treasury be cut off.[271]

On December 2, 1922, Lavi made an official declaration about the Gedud's alleged actions. Ben-Gurion made no reference to Lavi's allegations—though he was well aware of them—when he addressed the meeting of kibbutz representatives at Tel Yosef the following day (asking for their support at the Histadrut convention), nor did he in the following weeks. He saved it up for what he felt was the right moment. When this moment came, he "applied the full force of the Histadrut steamroller on behalf of the Ahdut HaAvoda."[272] Although the Gedud's adherents at Tel Yosef vastly outnumbered Lavi's supporters in Ein Harod, the Histadrut demanded that the joint economy be divided equally between the two settlements.

Tel Yosef refused point blank to divide up the property. After delivering an ultimatum, which was ignored, Ben-Gurion retaliated against the kibbutz. "Ben-Gurion acted swiftly and with cruelty," writes Sternhell of the event, "and he did not shrink from using any means, including withholding medical aid, food supplies, and other necessities. A blockade was imposed on Tel Yosef...nothing could be expected of Gedud members except complete surrender."[273]

Pawns

The Tel Yosef affair, which took place in May and June 1923, marks the first point at which the dream of an organic commonwealth of autonomous, egalitarian communities was betrayed. The emergent state apparatus, led by up-and-coming career politician David Ben-Gurion, usurped the utopian possibilities of the kibbutzim, while preserving the myth of that utopia for his own political purposes. With Ben-Gurion's seizing control of the means of distribution and using it against an individual kibbutz in retaliation for its refusal to obey the order of a central authority, the creation of a new kind of society effectively stopped being a realistic proposition. After that, it was only a matter of time before the kibbutz movement turned from a nationwide socialist experiment, within a non-state mandatory entity, into a collectivist component of a state-driven, command economy.

If the first betrayal was of the utopian moment, the second was of the *revolutionary* moment. In a sense, this was also a betrayal by a state, but not the proto-Zionist state apparatus that was taking shape in Palestine. This was a betrayal by the underlying reality that Zionism was, from the outset, in the service of colonialism. Given the larger web of power politics in which the kibbutz project had been entangled from the very beginning, this was a betrayal waiting to happen.

For the European Jewish youngsters of the late nineteenth and early twentieth century who had been educated in socialist ideologies, Zionism wasn't just about seeing the end of exile and the re-creation of Eretz Yisrael. It was about creating a fresh society, in a new place. It was a project to which this generation could readily subscribe, a competing trend to Marxist currents, and one able to compete due to its ability to attract those people who did not see their calling and self-realisation lying in conventional European revolutionary activities. This was the *real* cause: a revolution without an opponent, in which radicals would be afforded the opportunity to build something totally new, from scratch.

While these idealistic youngsters were building their kvutzot, however, the institutions of political Zionism were in the background, buying up land and forging diplomatic relationships with the British government. This was particularly so after the First World War with the establishment of the Mandate, when political power in Palestine was assumed by the British, and by Zionist organisations. The subsequent emergence of interests based on the division of the world into two antagonistic blocs during the mid-1940s meant that the future of the Jewish community in Palestine became a question of economic and strategic concerns, of setting up a permanent stronghold in a region rich in natural resources though the installation of an agent of the West. Executive influence over the question of statehood lay not with the workers in the kibbutzim, but with the global superpowers.

Thus, it was Zionism's colonialist dimension that would ultimately be the final nail in the coffin of the early kibbutz pioneers' original vision. Independence would not, as was desired, come from "collective will," but, quite literally, from the United Nations. The fact that this had been the case right from the very beginning was a reality to which the early communards were tragically oblivious. Whatever ambitions the radicalised youngsters of the Second and Third Aliyot may have arrived with, the scope of the Zionist movement and the utopian projects it sheltered had always been restricted by the external influence of the Western states, and by their enmeshment in the multiple webs of power that the involvement of these foreign actors entailed.

Regardless of how successful the kibbutzniks were in creating and sustaining a radical new way of life within their settlements, these communities' long-term potential as a national political force had always been structurally inhibited by their being pawns in Western states' foreign policies. This reality, unaccounted for in the anarchist and socialist ideologues' explanations of the functioning and destiny of agricultural communities on which the communards drew, made it almost inevitable that the kibbutzim would end up being absorbed by a state themselves.

Though Diaspora Jewish interests on the right were certainly a catalyst on the road to statehood and played a part in shaping the national character of the young Israel—as emphasised by Italian anarchist Alfredo Bonanno, who blames the Jewish-American and international lobbies for cajoling the US into "push[ing] the small but fierce Israel into the role of policeman of the Middle East"—the role of Western imperialism in reversing the utopian ethos of the Jewish community in pre-state Palestine was, in fact, more symbiotic in character.[274] During the 1950s, Ben-Gurion and the early state leadership proceeded to lead Israel from one foreign sponsor to the next, in an attempt to make the country "useful" on the international stage. Thus, an impoverished, vulnerable and solicitous Israel, looking for friends, offered itself up as the worst kind of tool to the West, in exchange for protection and money.

This is the conclusion reached by Ralph Miliband and Marcel Liebman in an exchange of letters, beginning on the eve of the 1967 war and published later under the title *The Israeli Dilemma*. Liebman and Miliband's discussion of the relationship between Zionism and Western imperialism focuses specifically on the British and French in light of the Sinai War, and on France's subsequent adoption of Israel during the beginning of the disturbances in Algeria. The authors—two left-wing Jews with very different positions on Israel—in varying degrees excoriate Israel for its readiness to prostitute itself for whatever European power Ben-Gurion happened to be courting at the time.

Yet, it is important to note the distinction in Liebman and Miliband's argument between their identification of Israel's utility as a metaphorical Middle Eastern aircraft carrier for the Western powers (*à la* Bonanno), and the more pertinent issue of how the country's role as such impacted Israel's internal ethos and ideology, regardless of how the state's foreign and domestic policies might differ: given Israel's poverty and desperation for support during its early years, its leaders' abandonment of even a pretence of socialism and liberalism was hardly surprising. By making itself so readily available, cosying up to the West, Israel's leadership inevitably ended up accelerating the transformation of their state in many ways, including a rapid shift in national ideology that would see the gradual redundancy of the kibbutz idea.

The End of the Kibbutz Movement?

The kibbutzim's role in Palestinian-Jewish society and the Zionist project/s is one thing, but what of the way of life *within* the communities? Since 1948, the settlements have, to some extent, existed as islets of social anarchism within the shell of the state, but, since the Declaration of Independence, the movement has been steadily diluting its radical way of life. While the settlements used to be widely written about and held up as an exemplary socialistic society—famously hailed by Buber as "the experiment that did not fail"—the majority of contemporary kibbutz-related literature is today more concerned with chronicling "the end of the kibbutz movement."

State absorption had a profound impact on the way that the kibbutz worked, not least because the influx of new members brought into the movement by the state were no longer coming from a radical position, but instead a much more conventional, Social-Democratic background. Throughout the second half of the century, enthusiasm for the idea of belonging to a radical pioneering organisation similarly declined, accelerated as many of the children born into the kibbutzim began to marry people outside the movement, thus undermining the settlements' ideological bedrock.[275] During the latter half of the century, as the settlements became progressively more introverted and less involved in national politics, the status of the kibbutz gradually eroded both within its own eyes and within Israeli society as a whole.

In spite of this, the kibbutzim still managed to retain their anarchic communalist way of life for many years after state absorption. In some respects, Buber's view of the kibbutzim as the "experiment that did not fail" would remain true for several decades, as the communities continued to bear a considerable resemblance to Kropotkin's vision of anarchist communes for many years yet, though now within the shell of the state. Within forty years of *Paths in Utopia*'s publication, however, Buber's sanguinity would be called into question once and for all, as the movement entered a period of drastic transformation auguring a rapid and radical divorce from the socialist ideals that it had been struggling to uphold throughout the second half of the century.

The Crises of the 1980s

The kibbutz's problems began in earnest with the victory of Menachem Begin's Likud government in 1977, an unprecedented event in Israeli history that heralded a seismic shift in the make-up of Israel's political landscape. From there on in, Israel underwent a process of major economic change, with ownership of the economy moving from the state and the Histadrut into private hands for the first time in the country's history. Along with Mapai, the Histadrut had effectively exercised complete control over the country's economy until that point, and was now drastically scaled back, organised labour stripped of its influence.

Concomitant with this change was the broader process of globalisation occurring throughout the industrialised world. International currents set in motion by the policies of Margaret Thatcher and Ronald Reagan quickly engulfed Israel. The first and most significant transformation was the country's merger with the global market and sudden exposure to the forces of the world economy, resulting in widespread privatisation and cutbacks in the public sector.[276] These changes were accelerated by Likud's subsequent elimination of all restraints on financial trading in 1985, which eased conditions for foreign investment and paved the way for Israelis to invest abroad, as well as helping to develop Israel's financial market.[277] Import duties, which had averaged 13 percent in the 1970s, dropped to 1 percent by the end of the 1980s, and import penetration (as a share of GDP) rose from 37 percent to more than 50 percent over the same period.[278]

These economic changes hit Israel hard, crippling the productive sector and causing small businesses nationwide to collapse into bankruptcy. Most of Israel's traditional industries sustained severe damage, and although the kibbutzim managed to survive this period, they did so at grave cost. In 1982, the movement was showing profits of 345 million NIS (New Israeli Shekel), but spiralling inflation (which peaked, in 1985, at 400 percent), combined with the price of produce controlled by government policy, and the banks joining forces to exploit mutual guarantees among the kibbutzim (giving them unlimited, expensive credit for high-risk investments) changed this. Between 1984 and 1988 the kibbutzim lost around 470 million NIS per year to the country's banking system.[279] Believing that inflation would keep their debts at a manageable level, the kibbutzim had borrowed excessively during the early part of the decade, but when the government brought in austerity measures, bringing inflation down to 20 percent per year, the settlements were left with a mountain of debt that they were unable to repay. By 1988, they collectively owed something in the region of 12 billion NIS, a figure that brought with it astronomical interest payments.[280]

Although socialist in comparison to its more recent conservative and neo-liberal incarnations, as the first government in the country's history not led by the Labour Movement, Likud was not exactly sympathetic to the kibbutzim's situation. Despite remaining a major contributor to the country's economy, the movement found that it no longer enjoyed the prestige, influence or degree of representation that it had previously in Israeli society, and for a long time, suggestions for a wholesale recycling of the movement's debts fell on deaf ears. In January 1989, the election of a national unity government of Labour and Likud, headed by Yitzhak Shamir and Shimon Peres, provided something of a reprieve, and that year the kibbutzim, the government and Israel's state-owned banks managed to sign an agreement to restructure the movement's debt.

Unfortunately, this came too late to reverse the damage sustained during the crisis period, not least because the most serious injuries suffered were not purely economic. Government policy during the 1980s deprived the federations of their ability to channel resources to individual kibbutzim, thus undermining relations between the movements and leading to the federations losing much of their influence. As the individual settlements became increasingly introverted and preoccupied with their own internal problems, mutual aid between kibbutzim began to atrophy, the implications of which were spelled out most graphically to kibbutz members by the Beit Oren Affair of 1987.[281] In common with most kibbutzim, Beit Oren had found itself caught up in severe economic and social crisis during the early part of the decade, the result of government economic policy, exacerbated by demographic changes within its own membership that saw an increasing number of elderly people and fewer young people able to shoulder the economic burden. In an unprecedented move that sent shockwaves throughout the kibbutzim, the movement responded to Beit Oren's plight by cutting off its financial support to the settlement and suggesting that veteran members leave.

The Beit Oren Affair was one of a series of events that battered kibbutz members' confidence and economic security during the 1980s. Moreover, the disconnection that took place between the kibbutz movement and the Israeli state under Begin was a major shock. With Likud claiming to represent an entirely new direction for Israeli society to follow, this had a devastating impact on the kibbutzim's self-image.

A painful process of introspection was compounded by changes in the ideological direction of Israeli society during that decade. Neo-liberalism was on the rise, and its emphasis on individualism meant that the struggle to create a collectivist national ethos was relegated to the periphery of the country's social consciousness. Following similar trends in the West since the late 1960s, Israel's historically secular consensus was superseded by a return to religion and a revival of both ultra-Orthodoxy and nationalist spirituality. The kibbutzim, with their typically liberal political outlook and secular political culture, came to seem outmoded and unworthy of respect.[282]

These varied and dramatic ideological shifts fuelled an ever-growing crisis of faith in the pioneering ideal of Zionism, which in turn severely dented confidence in the kibbutz way of life and contributed to the weakening of social cohesion within the communities. In short, although the movement managed to survive the crises of the 1980s, it emerged not only with a vast quantity of debt that it had to find a way of repaying, but with its entire *raison d'être* severely damaged in every possible respect. Lacking both institutional and cultural legitimacy, and equally conspired against by Zionism's imbrication with Western imperialism, it appeared that the end of the road had arrived, and with it, the death of any possible emancipatory, Jewish-led social projects in historic Palestine. Indeed, Israel had proved itself to be the dead end that its critics had always said it was—the death of the kibbutz movement just one of many examples of the Jewish community's failure to do anything positive with its achievements in the region.

The Contemporary Movement

This breakdown of confidence in the classic kibbutz lifestyle led to far-reaching organisational changes within the kibbutzim. Across the movement, radical transformation became the defining feature of the kibbutz of the 1980s and 1990s as the settlements struggled to adapt to deal with changing conditions. In practice, this entailed many of the settlements taking on a complexion far removed from the anti-market intentions of their founders. The last two decades of the twentieth century witnessed a rapid and sustained move toward less communal living, as the kibbutz, little by little, jettisoned the vestiges of its collectivist heritage in an attempt to deal with the mounting external pressures.

The current legal status of the movement defines two distinct kinds of kibbutzim: Communal Kibbutzim (*Kibbutzim shitufi'im*), in which only minimal changes have been made from the original principles, and New-style/Changing Kibbutzim (*Kibbutzim mitchadshim*), in which considerable changes have been and are being made. The movement today is in a process of transition, with each kibbutz having to decide to which category it belongs. Around thirty kibbutzim are currently organised in the *Zerem Shitufi* (Communal Stream), opposed to radical changes in kibbutz lifestyle, and around a hundred similarly organised in

Ma'agal Shitufi (Communal Circle), which includes those kibbutzim which, while changing, remain committed to adhering to the basic principles of kibbutz life.

Although the majority of the kibbutzim have attempted to maintain their original ethos in the face of adversity, an ever-increasing minority are officially turning their backs on socialist ideology altogether, explicitly turning to capitalism. Among the first of these was Kibbutz Kfar Ruppin, which, in 1999, converted its industrial and agricultural branches into limited companies, established a holding company for them and distributed shares to its members on the basis of seniority.[283] While the privatisation of kibbutz assets has so far only been realised in a minority of kibbutzim, many within the movement see it as simply a matter of time until this trend becomes more far-reaching.

The threat this poses to egalitarian and communal ownership of the means of production remains a serious concern in relation to the precariousness of their economic future. Although only a minority of kibbutzim have explicitly chosen to take this market-based path, with most of the settlements today built around hybrid economies, the number of settlements following in Kfar Ruppin's footsteps—twenty-two at the outset of the new millennium—is rising every year.

While most settlements are currently in the process of making difficult decisions as to whether or not to go down the path of privatisation, the movement as a whole has nevertheless taken on a palpably capitalist complexion. During the 1980s, when traditional management systems came to be seen as anachronistic and a factor in the economic failures of that decade, many kibbutz members proposed that horizontal management should be replaced by modern management practice, even if this meant that participatory democracy suffered as a result.[284]

The managerial structure of most of the kibbutzim's industrial enterprises today resembles a complex, centralist hierarchical organisation more akin to that of any large, capitalist business than to the functioning anarcho-communist economic unit it once was. Boards of directors run the economic branches, and the industries in particular, with business management now separated from the socio-political system. Economic decisions are therefore no longer subject to social considerations.

Increasing separation of economic management from the kibbutz milieu—directorates with external managers now replacing the traditional committees drawn from the general assembly—drastically undermined the kibbutz's character as a gemeinschaft society in which the collective was responsible for and involved with every aspect of the running of the community. The 1990s also saw methods of differential reward according to seniority, function, and effort creeping into the kibbutz system.[285] Kibbutz Ein Zivan was the first to introduce differential salaries in 1993, and by the outset of the new century, more than a third of the kibbutz movement had followed suit. Now that a manager of a factory, for example, receives a much larger personal allowance than a factory worker or agricultural worker, an important cornerstone of the kibbutz's egalitarianism has been lost.

In the political sphere, demographic changes and stratified differentiation led to the nature of the communities' democratic political decision-making system changing almost beyond recognition, and direct participatory democracy, in many cases, coming under threat from an increase in the use of representative bodies and ballot voting. Direct democracy, in the form of the general assembly, has been widely replaced by elected councils, and the general assembly itself now "resembles an annual shareholders' meeting more than it does the traditional assembly of all kibbutz members."[286]

By the same token, since the late 1970s, the kibbutz has seen radical changes to the way it ensures the maintenance of social order. Individual freedom—already under threat from the ever-expanding web of bureaucracy and increasingly authoritarian committees well before the crises of the 1980s—has been radically undermined by the widespread formalisation and institutionalisation of the general assembly's decisions, a phenomenon that Yassour warned, as far back as 1985, was "subvert[ing] the continual development and readjustment which are vital to the existence of the kibbutz as a voluntary communal society."[287]

Reinventing Utopia

If one generalisation can be made as to the current state of the movement—and generalisations are not easy given the rapidity with which changes are currently taking place—it's that the contemporary kibbutz bears little resemblance to the fiercely ideological settlements of the movement's younger days. Yet, to dismiss the kibbutz idea as simply another failed experiment in the history of anarchism on this basis would be premature.

There are two reasons for this: First of all, while the structure and day-to-day functioning of the contemporary kibbutz is certainly not nearly as close to classical anarchism as it once was, generally speaking, the movement still functions in a manner clearly distinct from the capitalist or state socialist models. The enduring influence of the movement's early anarchistic character means that there are still lessons to be absorbed from its way of life. The International Communal Studies Association insists that, while the kibbutz of today only remotely resembles the early twentieth century movement, in the vast majority of cases it has so far managed to preserve its uniqueness as a community of solidarity, with common ownership of means of production, despite the physical and organisational changes that have taken place since the 1980s.[288]

Warhurst's longitudinal ethnographic study of Kibbutz Geffen, carried out during the 1990s, indicates that, irrespective of the movement's assimilation into a market economy, integration of labour, direct democracy (albeit in a highly evolved and rapidly atrophying form), non-hierarchical management systems, absence of authoritarian structures in the political or economic spheres and communal production/consumption are still very much in evidence within the community itself. This is, of course, in comparison to capitalist society rather than to the kibbutz's own previous incarnations, yet even so, as Warhurst observes in his study, the essential preconditions of capitalism (or state socialism as defined by Marx), were still absent in the kibbutz, even as the movement prepared to enter the twenty-first century.[289]

But perhaps of greater long-term significance, given the rapid and apparently irreversible downhill slide the kibbutzim appear to be on, is that the historical development of the movement has always been characterised by a distinct dialectical pattern. Since their inception, the communities have been in a continual process of change, responding to the many challenges presented to them, not only by the changing forces of the outside world, but also by the varying political, social, ideological and demographic developments within their membership. The current phase of the movement is no exception.

Samar

Towards the end of the twentieth century, in response to the movement's shifting further and further from its original ideological goals, new projects began to emerge throughout the country. As children of the traditional kibbutz began to set up new communities as a reaction to what they saw as the failure of the traditional ones, a new epoch in the dialectic of the kibbutz's development began.

One of the most audacious of these projects—in many ways the flagship of a new generation of anarchist-orientated communal experimentation—is Kibbutz Samar. A small settlement of well under a hundred permanent members, situated about thirty kilometres inland from Eilat, Samar was founded in 1976 by kibbutz children who were trying to remedy what they felt were the shortcomings of the kibbutz their parents had created. "Basically we felt that our parents had got it wrong," explains one of the community's founders. "We were all from kibbutzim about forty years old, and we were acutely aware of the alienation between the kibbutz member and the kibbutz establishment. We knew all about the tyranny of the work roster and the humiliating dependence on committees. We forged our principles in revolt against the established kibbutz and have held onto them ever since."[290]

Most kibbutz children of that generation saw exactly the same erosion of personal freedom and dignity on their parents' kibbutzim as Samar's founders did, but the majority naturally believed that this authoritarian and humiliating kind of communalism was a given. Many simply left the kibbutzim as a result, adopting the attitude that "if this is communalism, then we don't want it any more." The youngsters who founded Samar, on the other hand, were adamant that another kind of communal life was possible—one that could reconcile individual freedom with communal responsibility—and set out to prove as much.

Samar's members have never called themselves anarchists. They did not set out basing their way of life on anarchism (even today, most of the members are not familiar with anarchist ideologies), and the settlement they created has never explicitly called itself an anarchist kibbutz. Yet that is precisely what it has become known as. Understanding from the experience of their parents' kibbutzim that authority is the root cause of the humiliation and degradation of the human being, the founders set out purely and simply to eliminate every element of mainstream kibbutz society that involved the domination of one person by another. As a result, Samar came to function according to the principles of pure, communal anarchy, without any kind of hierarchical or authoritarian structures or any of the organisational functions that have undermined communal life in the original kibbutzim.[291]

The community's founders made it a priority to ensure that there would be none of the institutions, committees, formalised regulations, binding decisions or personal budgets that they felt subverted individual liberty on their parents' kibbutzim. In place of authority, there would remain only personal relationships between individual equal human beings, and the settlement would be regulated solely by the sense of personal responsibility of each member towards their fellows.

Samar, in other words, functions more or less exactly as the early kvutzot did. Its modest size and intimate nature allow it to employ a system based on total trust, face-to-face democracy and mutual responsibility. Direct democracy and active participation by members in the decision-making process is the norm. There, the informal general meetings by which the kibbutz regulates its affairs are a far cry from the complex network of bureaucracy and committees that have come to characterise communal life on the original kibbutzim. Perhaps more important than the general meetings, which themselves are sporadic, to say the least, is the constant informal dialogue that is central to Samar's life. A willingness to talk and to discuss everything openly means that a culture of constant, organic conversation is a fundamental part of the kibbutz's existence.

Samar's income is derived mainly from agriculture. A date plantation, a dairy and plant nurseries provide the economic base, but Samar is a fluid and dynamic society not averse to economic diversification. According to one of its inhabitants, "the kibbutz develops according to the wishes and the needs of the members," and as such, it is distinct from the complex web of committees that have recently become the bugbear of the traditional kibbutz. "At Samar, if someone wants to do something, he or she assembles an ad hoc committee and does it."[292] This approach has allowed continuous experimentation with a range of new cooperative enterprises, with varying degrees of success.

Whereas, in many of the older kibbutzim, the autonomy of the individual has come under threat from increasing bureaucratisation and the institutionalisation of regulations, at Samar it is manifested in every sphere of kibbutz life. While the allocation of labour, for example, in the larger, established kibbutzim is the responsibility of a nominated committee, in Samar, there is no work roster. It is up to the individual members to decide when, if, in what branch and for how long they work. While collective consumption on the traditional kibbutzim has for many years taken the form of a collectively-dictated budget for each member, Samar's members have revived the system used on the very earliest kvutzot—a communal purse from which members are free to take as much as they think they need.

"At first there was a fixed monthly allowance," one member recalls, "but we opted for the open box system pretty quickly and have kept it open ever since. Everyone takes what he wants and nothing is written down."[293] Today this system takes the form of a communal creditcard account. It works fine.

The settlement's social and political life is based on voluntary acceptance of decisions by each individual member, with no coercion or any kind of statutory sanctions. The recognised behavioural limits ensuring social cohesion are arrived at collectively, and harmonious social life is maintained solely by people voluntarily abiding by the socially defined norms out of a sense of responsibility towards the community.[294] While the kibbutz does have administrative officers, these have been reduced in number "to an absolute minimum," with the few committees that exist at Samar doing so only on an informal, ad hoc basis.[295]

Samar's system is not without its problems. For instance, as one member says, "we can never be sure how many people are going to report for work on a given morning. Maybe ten will show up on a day when only two are needed. Alternatively only three may be available when there is a load of work to be done. Then I have to go and recruit people from other branches. If they agree to come, that's fine; but if they don't, there is nothing I can do about it."[296]

The reality, however, is that Samar does seem to work. Writing in *The Jerusalem Report*, Michael Liskin tells us that "while the kibbutz movement as a whole is in the throes of economic and social decay, Samar is blossoming."[297] Unlike its Second and Third Aliya forebears Samar has had to contend with fierce competition from a highly-developed capitalist economy, not to mention a political climate generally hostile to the interests of the kibbutz. That Samar survived the crises of the 1980s entirely unscathed, and has continued to go from strength to strength while the rest of the movement is falling apart, is no mean achievement.

The Urban Kibbutzim

Samar is, has always been, and will probably remain a unique exception in the kibbutz movement, believed even by its own membership to be a one-generation phenomenon. Nevertheless, it exists as part of a new generation of projects heralding a fresh phase in the history of the kibbutz. This a phase that has, at its core, a visible and deliberate reconnection with the anarchistic ethos of the early years of the movement, a response to the decay that has set into the mainstream kibbutzim with their dealignment from their original principles.

Rising up alongside the kibbutz movement there currently exist a growing number of new settlements and quasi-anarchic, kibbutz-style organisations across Israel, created in response to the crises and privatisation that have challenged the kibbutzim since the 1970s. This alternative communal movement consists largely of urban, non-agricultural, small commune-type groups whose members live communally and pool their salaries, but do not necessarily work together.

Attempts to integrate the kibbutz idea into an urban environment were being made as early as the mid-1940s. With widespread expansion and industrialisation taking place in kibbutzim nationwide, and with the institutions of the newly-created Israeli state assuming responsibility for many of the tasks previously undertaken by the kibbutz federations, certain groups within the mainstream movement began to question the role of pioneering—and even the purpose of the kibbutz itself—in this rapidly changing environment. Many came to the conclusion that for the kibbutz movement to maintain its influence in Israel it must be directly involved in the country's urban areas. Accordingly, attempts to integrate the kibbutz into an urban environment were being made as far back as 1947, when a group of 200 people set up a kibbutz in Efal, near Tel Aviv, with the goal of living on a kibbutz while working in the city.

The Efal settlement was to be short-lived, however, falling apart just four years after its inception. Most subsequent attempts to integrate the kibbutz idea into towns and cities across Israel have met with similarly unqualified failure. Communities established in suburbs of Jerusalem, Haifa and Herzliya soon found themselves unable to integrate into the surrounding society and, although still in existence, simply became "kibbutzim near towns." In 1968, a group from the Habonim Dror youth movement established a settlement near Haifa, which they named Kvutsat Shaal. Shaal fared little better than its predecessors, however, and disintegrated in 1972.

There are currently four "urban kibbutzim," however, that can justifiably be viewed as success stories. The largest of these, Reshit, was established in a Jerusalem suburb in 1979 and currently has around a hundred members. Alongside Reshit are Migvan in the western Negev city of Sderot, one kilometre from the Gaza strip (best known internationally as the target of relentless attacks by Qassam rockets since the Disengagement in September 2005), Bet Yisrael in Jerusalem, and Tamuz, situated in the small development town of Beit Shemesh eighteen miles west of Jerusalem.

Tamuz

Tamuz was established in the summer of 1987 by nine individuals who, in common with many of their generation, found themselves increasingly disenchanted with the mainstream kibbutz movement where they were born and raised. With privatisation creeping into the kibbutz seen as both the cause and effect of the breaking down of community, Tamuz's founders realised that the kibbutz was becoming unwilling, and more importantly *unable*, to fulfil the role it had previously played in addressing the needs of the country. Like the kibbutz pioneers more than half a century before them, they aimed to create a "just society" based on equality, mutual aid and cooperation, ideals that they felt were increasingly being abandoned by the main body of the kibbutz movement.

In the highly developed country that Israel had become—with agriculture no longer so central to the economy, the country's borders now protected by the army and the Left no longer enjoying hegemony of the political landscape—Tamuz's founders came to the conclusion that addressing the needs of contemporary Israel could best be achieved by locating their settlement within an urban environment. The settlement they founded became, in its own words,

> An urban kibbutz, a small Jewish community, and like the traditional kibbutz, Tamuz is a collective. Its 33 members function as a single economic unit, expressing the socialist ideals of equality and cooperation, ideas and praxis. However, unlike the traditional kibbutz, we are located in an urban environment, keeping us in tune with what is happening in society around us.[298]

Unlike the traditional kibbutz, Tamuz owns no cooperative agricultural or industrial enterprises. Members work regular jobs and their individual incomes go into a common fund. Aside from the obvious differences however, the economic arrangements by which Tamuz functions are otherwise more or less congruent with those of the traditional kibbutz. The collective owns several cars, assumes responsibility for the financing of education, health, and transportation and so on. Members live in family units in collectively-owned housing, maintaining separate households, and allowances are distributed on the basis of family size— thus loosely "according to need."

In common with many urban communards of their generation, Tamuz's members reject the increasingly indirect kind of democracy and often debilitating degree of bureaucracy that have crept into the larger, traditional kibbutzim. Instead, they opt for direct, face-to-face democracy attainable in small, intimate groups. Believing that, for a society to be truly democratic, it must involve an individual's active engagement in the political process and direct participation in the running of the community, Tamuz's decision-making takes place in various different collective forums centring around the general meetings, held on a weekly basis.

These meetings are frequently divided into smaller discussion groups, with seminars taking place every two months for longer, more detailed debate on more general subjects. The settlement's small size means that it seldom resorts to the kind of ballot voting adopted in recent years by most of the older kibbutzim. In contrast to the traditional kibbutz, there are no committees making decisions for the individual member.[299]

That individuals are free to make their own decisions about their personal lives is emblematic of the heavy emphasis placed on individual autonomy at Tamuz. This emphasis sets the group ethic of the urban kibbutzim apart from the asceticism of the traditional, tightly-knit kvutza; members of Tamuz are fundamentally and vehemently opposed to the subordination of the individual to the group. In place of that notion, the community adopts the maxim that "the freedom of man must be expressed in every moment of communal life."

This attempt to reconcile individual freedom and socialist communalism is central to almost all the groups within the new wave of communal experimentation that sprang up in the latter half of the twentieth century. Israeli journalist Daniel Gavron observes that the ideas of "sacrifice for the common cause, the subservience of the individual to the group, the personal deprivation for the sake of the superior communal goal" simply do not feature in the lives of today's urban communards as they once did in the mainstream kibbutzim. Tamuz members, he says, like those of the other urban kibbutzim, are "almost obsessed with their individual autonomy [and] their personal freedom."[300]

Members of the urban kibbutzim, Gavron writes, view the communal life as, "more than anything else, a means to greater personal freedom and fulfilment. It is not that they are unaware of the society around them—quite the reverse: they are making supreme efforts to reach out to the populations of the towns where they live. Their involvement and interaction with Israeli society at large for the most part preceded similar attempts by the conventional kibbutzim, but where the traditional kibbutz aimed to lead the Zionist enterprise, the modern urban kibbutz aspires to create a superior quality of life for its members while making a contribution to the quality of the surrounding society."[301]

The Tamuz system is based solely on mutual trust and mutual responsibility: "It is axiomatic that every member wants what is best for the community," says one of its inhabitants. "But it is also assumed that the community aims to benefit the individual member. The members believe that the two things are interdependent."[302] Accordingly, there exist no mechanisms of coercive authority at Tamuz, whose members believe that "control mechanisms…are based on the assumption that people try to take advantage of each other and must be prevented from doing so." According to one member, "the Tamuz assumption is that, given the opportunity, people prefer a life based on trust and partnership, [rather] than one based on exploitation and deceit. In the absence of control mechanisms, continuous dialogue between the members is maintained."[303]

From its inception, Tamuz has engaged in various educational and social projects in the surrounding area. In 1996, in cooperation with Beit Shemesh residents, its members established a non-profit association, Kehilla, which seeks to develop projects in the field of social involvement and works to promote dialogue between the area's diverse population groups. Kehilla attempts to assist weaker social groups through community organising and self-help, it runs various kinds of study groups for both children and adults, and attempts to cultivate community frameworks in Beit Shemesh and its environs that contribute to the empowerment of the town's residents, at the same time trying to counter the alienation and disintegration of Israeli society's social frameworks.[304] A separate organisation by the name of Yesod (an acronym for "A Social Democratic Israel"), through its publication *Society*, works to promote public debate on issues such as economics, politics, and culture.

The Tnuat Bogrim Groups

Tamuz and the urban kibbutzim represent only one part of a variegated mosaic of new, urban social models that exist within Israel at the outset of the twenty-first century. As the mainstream kibbutz drifted further from its roots, an increasing number of young people across the country began to subscribe to the sentiments of Tamuz's founders, and the 1990s saw an exponential upsurge in the number of groups leaving the kibbutz movement to set up their own communal projects based on the original kibbutz idea. At the time of writing, there are upwards of 1,500 people living communally across Israel, entirely unconnected to the kibbutz movement. This number is increasing steadily each year.

Approximately three-quarters of these are members of the Tnuat Bogrim or "graduate movement" groups of the youth movement Noar Oved ve'Lomed (Working & Student Youth Movement), otherwise known by its acronym NOAL. As kibbutz life was supposedly the ultimate fulfilment of their ideology, the kibbutz's abandonment of its original values left graduates of the youth movement without a means of achieving either *hagshama* (self-realisation) or any structure for bringing about change in Israeli society. Many NOAL graduates began to look for alternatives. In the creation of new, more intimate settlements, they saw a way of achieving hagshama by practising the youth movement's ideology and values in their everyday lives.

Historically involved with the building of traditional kibbutzim, NOAL graduates responded to the crises of the 1980s by abandoning their usual role within the kibbutz movement proper, and instead, evolved into a distinct new stream of (what Habonim Dror's James Grant-Rosenhead describes as) "small, intimate, consensus-driven, anarcho-socialist groups."[305] The new NOAL graduates of the 1990s "decided to cut out the kibbutz intermediary from their traditional symbiosis. They retained their small, intimate group life as separate new adult communities after they graduated from the youth movement and the army. Instead of integrating into a traditional kibbutz, they took on responsibilities within the youth movement which were formerly undertaken by the kibbutz emissaries."[306]

These graduate groups formed communes, kibbutzim, single groups, or groups of groups all over the country, and since the 1990s, such organisations have been taking root in every major town and city. Other socialist Zionist youth movements, who had been having the same discussions as NOAL about their future direction, began to form their own graduate groups along similar lines. Examples of these are Hashomer Hatzair's Pelech and Machanot HaOlim's Na'aran, among many others. The graduate groups that form the bulk of this new wave of urban communal experimentation generally consist of between ten and forty individuals. According to Grant-Rosenhead, each is "trying to work towards social justice and equality in Israeli society, through a wide variety of educational and social initiatives on both local and national levels. The number and variety of these groups is growing each year, and the rate of growth is increasing too."[307]

During the 1990s, these groups gained in strength and number, and tentatively formed a rudimentary network. In 2000, what had begun as a disparate miscellany of experimental communal projects, came together under the banner of Ma'agal Hakvutzot (the Circle of Groups), an umbrella organisation set up to "support the expansion of the communal idea in Israel, to nurture solidarity between groups, to promote important educational projects and to work towards an Israeli society, both on an economic and political level, based on social democratic values."[308]/[309]

Kvutsat Yovel

Nearly all of those involved in these communities are Israeli-born, but the Diaspora youth movement Habonim Dror has four groups (and counting)—established by immigrants from Great Britain, the United States, Mexico and Australia—located in three different urban centres across the country. One of these, situated in the northern town of Migdal Ha'Emeq some thirty miles south east of Haifa, is Kvutsat Yovel. Initially consisting of six Habonim graduates (four from England, two from North America), Yovel began in Jerusalem in 1999 before moving to its present location. I visited Yovel for the first time in June 2006, and spoke to one of the group's founding members, Anton Marks.

Originally from Manchester, Anton made Aliya to Israel in early 1999 and has since been at the forefront of Habonim Dror's communal endeavours in the country. He describes the ideological inspiration behind the establishment of these new "anarcho-socialist" communities—which he and many others see as "the seeds of a new kibbutz movement"—as the intellectual progeny of much the same combination of Judaism and socialism that motivated the early kibbutz pioneers.

"From the socialist camp," Anton says, "you're talking about people like Marx and Engels. From the socialist-*Zionist* camp you're talking about people like Moses Hess, [Ber] Borochov, [Nachman] Syrkin, and so on, and also of course the anarchist writers such as Kropotkin, Landauer and Bakunin." The influence of Martin Buber's "I-Thou" philosophy is also central to the groups ideology, with interpersonal relationships seen as a fundamental determinant of the nature of communal life. The fact that these new groups choose to describe themselves as "kvutzot" rather than kibbutzim is itself a deliberate and conscious alignment with the intimacy of the small anarchistic settlements of the early years.

"One of the things that's very clear to us" says Anton, "is that we're trying to build on something that's come before us, to try and learn those lessons and not make those same mistakes again, but also to take the beautiful things that are there. So yes, there are things that are conscious, and there are things that are semantic. Kvutza has a different meaning to kibbutz; it denotes something much more intimate; we do use the term kibbutz as well, but in the context of "kibbutz of kvutzot.'"

This phrase, "kibbutz of kvutzot," refers to the urban groups that have fused to form larger communities, a process that, at the time this book goes to press, is the defining trend within Israel's new communal scene. Within these conglomerates, a great importance is placed on the individual kvutza within the larger structure, so enabling the intimate relationship building between individual people that members see as the absolute *sine qua non* of community. Although the "kibbutzim of kvutzot" are expanding rapidly, with more and more kvutzot being set up each year, the individual kvutzot themselves are limited in terms of their ambition towards expansion. "The emphasis on smaller units," Anton explains, "is a lesson learned from the original kibbutz movement. Communities of hundreds of people cannot possibly reach the levels of trust, openness and understanding that a group of ten people can."

As with the early settlements, it is this trust, openness, and mutual understanding that enable the communities to function in the way that they do. Indeed, like Samar, these groups share many characteristics with their early twentieth century forerunners, and consciously so. *Kehillatenu* occupies a central place in the Yovel communards' long list of inspirations, and the communal ethic embodied in the settlements of the Second and early Third Aliyot provides the ideological template for the new groups' activities.

Each group has a communal purse, directly democratic internal decision-making structures and shared responsibility for domestic duties, all of which are geared towards ensuring the maximum degree of political and material equality for its membership. Within each group, the maxim "from each according to his ability to each according to his need" has been actualised, and coercive authority is nonexistent, community life based instead on free-flowing discussions, mutual aid, mutual trust and total freedom. "As an example," Anton elaborates, "my group has one bank account where all our earnings are deposited. We each have an ATM card to that one account and can withdraw money at our own discretion. It works purely on trust and a shared sense of responsibility." According to Yovel's members, this setup has worked very well for nearly eight years.

The absence of factory, farm, date plantation, olive groves, or any other collectively-run enterprise providing the groups' economic base means the kvutzot are by no means comparable, economically, to the full-cooperatives that the kibbutzim were. Anton emphasises, however, that these new communities do, in fact, see themselves as having a means of production, even though it is not as immediately obvious as the factory or rolling farmland of a traditional kibbutz. "All of the different movements have officially established non-profit organisations," he tells me. "In terms of what we do day-to-day, we work in teams with other people...involved in various educational and social projects. We raise money based on those projects; we carry out outside fundraising in all sorts of places to help us to *run* those projects. The money that's 'fundraised' comes into the movement, so again in terms of our financial arrangements, we're all getting according to our needs, as opposed to what the outside market tells us that we're worth."

Located mainly in the development towns, which house a large proportion of the country's most underprivileged and marginalised groups, the kvutzot attempt to integrate into mainstream society in an effort to tackle what they feel are the salient issues of the day—issues their members claim the traditional kibbutz, as well as the Israeli government, are comprehensively failing to address.

All but one of Yovel's members work in education in one way or another—mainly in projects run by the Kibbutz of Kvutzot in Migdal Ha'Emeq and Nazareth Illit, of which the kvutza is a part. As far as they are concerned, education is the primary determinant of meaningful long-term change in Israel. According to Anton, however, "the secondary education system in Israel has deteriorated in many areas, including a significant reduction in teaching hours and an increase in class sizes. In addition, the system leaves many students behind—more often than not students that come from an impoverished background. (Forty percent of all children in Israel are living under the poverty line.) Western capitalism has bludgeoned its way into what was once one of the most progressive societies in the world."

The new generation of urban communards undertake projects designed to help remedy this situation. These projects are geared towards encouraging empowerment and coexistence, nurturing relationships of mutual aid, solidarity and tolerance in a society they view as a profoundly unequal and discriminatory. Within each movement, teams composed of members from different groups work together on a whole host of different projects, including running a boarding school for disadvantaged youth, teaching English to Arab children, organising after-school clubs, museum-guiding, establishing and running democratic schools, legally representing the rights of working youth and establishing seminar centres.

All this may seem a far cry from the agrarian philosophy of the early pioneers, but necessarily so, for the context in which the new groups are operating is vastly different from the conditions that the early immigrants found on their arrival in Palestine. Twenty-first century Israel is one of the most advanced industrialised nations on the planet, and with this comes a whole new set of problems very different from those faced by the kibbutz pioneers. "In the old days of the movement," Anton explains, "the bottom line was about creating a country, and creating a new human being, building an economy based on agriculture, settling the land, defending the borders. Those needs are not the same—the needs today are more the social needs of the country, narrowing those gaps, and recognising that these are the needs of the country in the twenty-first century... We see the ways of dealing with those needs as being based on the same values—it's just the methods that are slightly different."

At the time of this writing, the various communal projects are at the stage in their development when they are having much the same discussions about the future direction of their movement as the kibbutz representatives were in their early 1920s meeting. The strengthening of inter-community ties and moves towards federation are at the top of the agenda. The coalescing of groups under the umbrella of Ma'agal Hakvutzot can, in itself, be seen as an indication of this trend, as can increasing local-level cooperation between groups and the growing-together of kvutzot within "kibbutzim of kvutzot." While each kvutza retains its own autonomy, the organisation already involves a great deal of inter-group activity. Dialogue between communes is a regular feature of the new movement's activities, emblematic of an attempt to nurture the kind of mutual aid between groups as exists between individuals within each group.

Building the Future?

The traditional kibbutz has not "failed," but it has encountered serious problems that have led not only to an increasingly marked disconnect with the classical anarchist ideas on which the movement was initially based, but also to a corresponding weakening of the kibbutz movement's relevance to mainstream Israelis. The new urban communal groups thus constitute an important new phase in the development of the kibbutz. This reconnection with the small-group ethos of the kibbutzim's early years highlights the urban communes as an entirely modern organisation whose concerns and priorities betray an increasing unease with the present direction of Israeli society. Given the degeneration of the original movement and the generally ideologically bereft state of Israeli society as a whole, it is fascinating to see how this new generation is consciously reinvoking the movement's anarchist progenitors as inspiration for its future direction.

While the new urban communal groups are not nearly as close to the ideas of Kropotkin as the original kibbutzim were, both graduate-movement kvutzot and urban kibbutzim still embody many anarchistic traits in their social and political organisation. Although it might well be too early to speculate as to these projects' future, as their evolution into a nationwide network of extended neighbourhood communities gathers pace, they still potentially represent inspiration or a template for those who are attempting to combat capitalist hierarchies by building the future society in the here and now.

Unlike the traditional kibbutz model of self-contained, federally-connected settlements, that these new groups are embedded within towns is a crucial and definitive characteristic. Many projects their members undertake serve to help integrate the settlements into local communities. This idea invites immediate comparisons to Landauer's vision of the preliminary stages of the transition to a future anarchist order (see Chapter 6). Anticipating contemporary notions of prefigurative politics, Landauer envisaged the gradual transition to a stateless society taking place as communal, anarcho-socialist groups grew up within, and alongside, the existing state—eventually succeeding it. He maintained that "the pioneers in spirit would be those who begin with the independent realisation of collective life within community groups which will join the federated alliance and which will maintain the new socialist way of life *within the old world*."[310] This federation, he said, would gradually replace the centralised capitalist state, as the consolidation and expansion of the new communities gradually eroded its complex mechanisms of control and suppression.[311] It is interesting to see elements of this being reinvoked contemporarily, particularly so, given that Yovel's James Grant-Rosenhead specifically chooses to attach Landauer's term "anarcho-socialist" to the new communal groups.

A key feature that distinguishes the graduate movement groups from the urban kibbutzim (Tamuz, et al.) is that the former have a youth movement attached. While the urban kibbutzim represent more of a "lifestyle choice" for their members and see themselves very much as "one-generational communities," the graduate groups, like Anton's, are part of a continuing movement. With new members joining all the time and the organisation both increasing in number and spreading to more neighbourhoods in Israel's urban areas, we can see the beginnings of an anti-authoritarian, consensus-driven structure rising up within the Israeli state—*alongside* it—in the form of a federated alliance of communal groups not far removed in their particular communal ethic from those described by Landauer as the pioneer nuclei of a new society.

Where this nascent society will go next remains to be seen. "It's a long process," Anton says. "I definitely see it becoming more and more meaningful in terms of dealing with the needs of this country. I'd like to think that we're not just trying to paper over the symptoms of a pretty rotten society [but] that we're building an alternative society at the same time as being involved in the existing one. I'd like to think that yes, at some point in the future, we'll reach that critical mass, the point where the alternative society is no longer the alternative society, that the *existing* society is the alternative society. That's the vision."

Chapter 6

The Kibbutz Movement and Israeli Anarchism

Contemporary Perspectives

"You don't know what order with freedom means! You only know what revolt against oppression is! You don't know that the rod, discipline, violence, the state and government can only be sustained because of you and because of your lack of socially creative powers that develop order within liberty!"
—*Gustav Landauer, 1913*

Given the sheer magnitude of issues resulting from the Jewish settlement of Palestine during the early twentieth century, it is to be expected that the aspirations and achievements of the pre-1948 kibbutz communities are rarely recognised by modern anarchist movements. Drowned out by the din of anti-Zionism and the condemnation of Israeli oppression on which most leftist critiques of the region's politics are focused, the social lessons of experiments such as the kibbutz movement are lost to the outside world, not to mention most Israelis. At the same time, it is also true that many self-identified anarchists have abandoned the core battle between labour and capital in favour of any anti-Zionist cause, frequently indulging in forms of anti-Semitism typical of many contemporary anarchist movements.[312]

In short, a good proportion of today's militant anarchist left knows nothing of the ideologies that informed the early period of communal experimentation in Palestine, much less the internal workings of the early kibbutzim. The fact that the early kibbutz movement came "closer to the anarchist ideal than any other attempt" and was, as this book has demonstrated, a crucial chapter in the history of anarchism, remains of little interest. Though one may ascribe this oversight to any number of factors, including racism towards Jews or anger at Israel for its government's policies towards the Palestinians, whatever the reason for ignoring the aspects of the historical anarchist project implemented in Palestine and Israel, it reflects a tendency to concentrate anarchism's ideological achievements in First World contexts such as Europe. This should not be taken lightly, as many ideological and social innovations by the left are frequently made in Third World and otherwise global southern contexts.

To this end, this chapter considers how activists on the ground in Israel are at the forefront of today's movement towards a stateless commonwealth in historic Palestine, an idea foreshadowed in many of the ideologies prevalent during the early years of the kibbutz movement. Is it recognised among their ranks that this precedent exists? Is it known that this was the original aim of the Hashomer Hatzair olim, for example? And is it acknowledged that, for a while at least, this system actually worked? The kibbutz movement may well have internally come closer to the anarchist ideal than any other such experiment. However, in the absence of permanent state structures prior to Israeli independence, these federated islands of communalism also together proved themselves able to take on many of the functions usually assumed by the centralised institutions of capitalism and the state, as part of a decentralised pattern of settlement not too far removed from the "organic commonwealth" envisaged by figures like Buber, Landauer and Kropotkin himself.

Anarchism in Israel

Despite the early kibbutzim's ties to anarchist ideologies and the actualisation of social anarchist ideas within these communities, they have never been officially affiliated to any formal anarchist movement in the country. Although a minority from among the founding generation had connections to the Yiddish-speaking anarchist movements in their countries of exile, there were no such organisations in Palestine until well into the 1940s.

The influx of western European survivors of Nazism who arrived in the region in the wake of the Second World War included many influenced by libertarian ideas, and it was this wave of immigration that began to sow the seeds of Israel's mainstream anarchist movement.[313] The first formal organisation was established in the late 1940s by a group of Polish immigrants in Tel Aviv, and from the mid 1950s, the nascent anarchist scene centred on the Yiddish-speaking group Agudath Schochrei Chofesh (ASHUACH), the "Freedom Seekers Association," founded in Tel Aviv by Russian-born writer and philosopher Aba Gordin.

Problemen/Problemot, the monthly review Gordin established, ran until the late 1980s. Following its initiator's death in 1964, the review was directed by Shmuel Abarbanel, and then by Yosef Luden. Although the organisation itself numbered only about 150 members, the conferences ASHUACH organised in the late 1950s and early 1960s, on the philosophy of anarchism, drew hundreds of people.[314]

As in many other countries, the end of the 1960s sparked a renewed interest in anarchism in Israel. During the latter part of that decade, and the early years of the next, the country's anarchist movement began to take shape with more and more groups coming together, gaining impetus and inspiration from the student movement in Europe and the various revolutions taking place outside

Israel. In 1974, an anarchist group in Tel Aviv was named in honour of Gustav Landauer, in recognition of his ideas' impact on the formative years of the Jewish communitarian movement in the country.[315]

The emergence of new protest movements in the 1980s in opposition to the continuing occupation of the West Bank and Gaza, and to the Lebanon conflict, together with Israel's then-nascent punk scene, the animal rights movement, the rise in conscientious objection, and the first Intifada, saw Israeli anarchism steadily gaining more and more momentum throughout the decade, with numerous anarchist student cells starting during this period. Many of the country's radical left-wing groups around at that time—whether self identified as anarchist or not—saw some involvement by anarchists. The anti-capitalist, anti-Zionist Trotskyite group Matzpen (Compass), founded by former members of the Israeli Communist party in 1962 and active until the late 1980s, is one such organisation.[316]

Contemporary Israeli Anarchism

The contemporary anarchist movement in Israel came together during the wave of anti-globalisation activism that took place across the world in the late 1990s. In addition to the 300 or so Israeli anarchists, and a few hundred Palestinian sympathisers and allies (anarchism is historically not a well known intellectual current in Arabic culture and there is no formal Palestinian anarchist movement as such), there is a significant international presence on the ground in Israel and Palestine. This consists primarily of European and North American volunteers connected to the International Solidarity Movement (ISM), a Palestinian-led organisation, established in 2001, that encourages volunteers from around the world to take part in nonviolent protest against the Israeli military in the West Bank and, until disengagement in 2005, the Gaza Strip.

Although Israel's anarchist movement is small in comparison to its European and North American counterparts, sections of it are highly active. A sizable proportion of those involved participate in the peace, environmentalist and animal rights movements, but since the beginning of the second Intifada in 2000, the activities of anarchist groups—like those of any other radical leftist organisation in Israel—have been focused almost entirely on opposition to the Occupation in Palestine, and in particular against the construction of the Separation Wall. Numerous organisations of joint resistance to the Occupation exist throughout the country.

Ta'ayush (Arab–Jewish Partnership)[i], for example, created in the autumn of 2001 by Jews and Palestinian Arabs of Israeli citizenship, engages in many different solidarity actions in the occupied territories. The Anarchists Against the Wall (AATW)[ii] initiative, a direct action group established in 2003 in response to the construction of the Separation Wall, similarly works alongside Palestinians

i http://www.taayush.org/
ii http://www.awalls.org/

in nonviolent resistance to the Occupation, taking part in demonstrations and direct actions against the wall in particular, and the Occupation in general, across the West Bank.

While destructive/preventative action against the Occupation is the movement's main focus, the construction of practical alternatives is considered an important thread of anarchist activity in the region. Grassroots peacemaking comes in a variety of different forms, with many of the country's anarchists actively involved with the numerous kernels of cooperation and solidarity that exist throughout Israel. In addition to Jewish-Arab initiatives like the Negev Coexistence Forum,[iii] the women's solidarity group Bat Shalom,[iv] the Arab-Jewish Center for Equality, Empowerment and Cooperation[v] in the Negev and the children's and youth centre Netivei Ahava (Paths of Brotherhood) in Jaffa, the more prominent examples often referred to in anarchist literature include cooperative communities like Neve Shalom/Wahat al-Salam (NSWAS),[vi] an experimental village situated half way between Tel Aviv and Jerusalem, where Jews and Arabs have lived and worked together for over three decades.

Established in 1976 as a joint venture by Jewish and Arab Israelis, Neve Shalom carries out educational work to promote peace, equality, mutual understanding and cooperation between the two peoples. The village is one of the few in the country with bilingual, multicultural schools in which Jewish and Arab children are educated together in both languages and taught the culture and traditions of each people. It is also home to the School for Peace, which runs workshops for young people and adults in conflict-resolution training, and a Pluralistic Spiritual Center. In addition to its educational institutions, NSWAS operates a program that provides humanitarian assistance for Palestinian villagers affected by the conflict.

New Profile,[vii] a volunteer organisation run by feminist women and men opposed to the militarised and bellicose consciousness of Israeli society, also has some anarchists involved. Supporting the right to conscientious objection, not presently recognised in Israeli law, the organisation provides help and advice to those wishing to abjure Israeli militarism and opt out of military service. It calls for the recognition of the individual's right to act according to his or her conscience, and for the option to express one's social commitment by means of alternative civic service, and advocates a fundamental overhaul of the education system to give young Israelis an upbringing that promotes the practice of peace and conflict resolution, rather than one that perpetuates a society that sees military prowess as a supreme and overriding value.

---

iii http://dukium.org/
iv http://www.batshalom.org/
v http://www.nisped.org.il/
vi http://www.nswas.org/
vii http://www.newprofile.org/

Israeli Anarchism and the Kibbutzim

Israelis who come to think of themselves as anarchists today tend to arrive at that stance first and foremost through their immediate objection to the military and their belief that citizens of Israel have an obligation to resist the immoral policies and actions carried out in their name, rather than from a theoretical background or in-depth historical understanding.[viii] In light of their focus on what they see as more immediate concerns, the role of ideology in informing their outlooks and actions is largely de-emphasised.

Viewing their most pressing goal as ending the Occupation and restoring Palestinians' rights, many Israeli anarchists believe that only when this has been achieved can substantive discussions begin about the kind of society they would like to see in the future. This "one step at a time" approach means that theoretical anarchist frameworks are largely alien to some people working within the groups that see themselves as "anarchist."

It would be fair to say that the role of libertarian socialist ideologies in informing the ideas of those involved in the early kibbutz communities doesn't exactly play a prominent part in defining the ideological or historical self-understanding of most of today's activists. That contemporary radicals consign today's kibbutzim to the dustbin of radical experiments goes without saying, but there are also many within Israel's anarchist camp who are wholly unaware of the historical presence of anarchist ideas in even the earliest years of Zionist settlement. "Most of today's radicals would laugh if you suggested that the kibbutzim had anarchist roots," one activist suggested to me recently. "When Israel's anarchists look back on the early years of the movement, they see it in a very negative light—not just as part of a racist state-building project, but a project that, even within its own communities, tried to stifle individuality and make everyone the same."

According to anti-war activist and New Profile member Tali Lerner, "Even twenty years ago, the same technical idea as Kropotkin wrote about existed in the kibbutz. But what people saw was this idea being run so *badly* that that's what they remember. How oppressive the kibbutz became in its later years towards its own members is anarchists' main impression of what the kibbutz was about, and that's the impression that stays with them. They won't think "Well, in the 1930s, it really worked."'

The Kibbutzim and the Military

The experience of the early communards is one with which many of today's Israeli anarchists would have difficulty relating. "Reading people's letters from the Second and Third Aliya kvutzot," Lerner said to me, "you realise that these people were so deeply emotionally invested in things on a level that most of today's

viii   The following section is based on a series of interviews with Israeli activists in Tel Aviv in 2006 and 2007 radicals would see as utter naivety. This is *so* distant from the experience of today's radicals. We're much more cynical today, much more individualistic."

Perhaps the main reason, however, for contemporary activists' disdain for the kibbutzim, is that they have become so inextricably intertwined with the Israeli state, and, in particular, its militaristic policies towards the Palestinians. Indeed, in the first three decades following independence, the country's fiercest fighters were drawn from the kibbutzim, including the Israel Defence Force's core military leadership.

The first baby born at Degania, for example, was Moshe Dayan, the famous warrior and politician who achieved worldwide fame during the 1967 Israeli-Arab War as the architect of Israel's military victory. The ideological shift that occurred within the communities from the 1930s onwards—from socialism to a nationalist-militarist ethos, as the movement became a bastion for Zionist colonisation against the interests of the Palestinian population—is a major barrier to anything approaching objective consideration of the kibbutzim for many of today's anarchists. According to Israeli activist and author Uri Gordon,

> In terms of their internal structure as communes, the early kibbutzim of course had a great deal of correspondence with anarchist principles, and yes, this was a system that proved itself capable of providing for a large number of people. The kind of system the communities employed is well known in Israel. But when these communal islands are transformed into the food-basket of a country and the source of its elite soldiers, as far as today's anarchists are concerned any achievements that the kibbutzim might have had before 1948 are hardly relevant to today's struggles.[317]

The Yishuv (through its defence force auxiliary, the Haganah) had essentially been organised as a military entity since the establishment of the Jewish self-defence organisation Hashomer in 1909. During the 1930s, the sections of the movement's membership that initially had favoured organising and solidarity with their Arab co-workers began to dwindle, and many people were thrown out of the kibbutzim for speaking out against the racism inherent in the "conquest of labour." According to one Israeli activist I spoke to, the point at which those radicals who weren't ready to convert their Zionism into a right-wing, nationalist movement were kicked out of the settlements was the point at which the kibbutz forfeited its relevance to radical thought.

This was also a period—and to some extent this is known among today's anarchists—during which many of the original radicals were also leaving the kibbutzim of their own accord, disillusioned with the new ideological direction their settlements were taking. Fourth International socialist Rudolf (Rudi) Segall, who arrived in Palestine from Germany in 1934, inspired by the ideas of Gustav Landauer, lived on a Hashomer Hatzair kibbutz from 1935 to 1939. In an interview in 2001, he spoke of his and many of his comrades' disenchantment with their new reality: "It is no miracle that a high percentage of the Israeli military elite came from the Kibbutz," he said. "For some of us the contradiction between the socialist ideal and the behaviour in relation to the resident population became ever bigger, so…a large group left the Kibbutz in order to carry out political work."[318]

Changing Perspectives

In short, the kibbutz is viewed by contemporary Israeli anarchists not for what it once was, but for what it has become. In *light* of what it has become—both in terms of its oppressiveness towards its own members and of its external face as an establishment Zionist institution—the way in which the kibbutz was actually run, and the lessons to be learned from its early economic and political structure, fade into insignificance. This is exacerbated by the inevitable tendency, prevalent among today's younger radicals, to apply modern anarchist ideas to discussion of the early kibbutzim, and therefore to lose sight of the historical context in which the communities were operating. ("Even the very earliest kibbutzim couldn't possibly have been anarchist," one member of the New Profile initiative said to me, utterly bewildered by the very suggestion, "because they used work animals.")

Given that most of Israel's anarchists arrive at their beliefs in reaction to the limits of Israeli liberal/left politics, their tendency to ignore or overlook the lessons to be learned from the early kibbutz movement is not surprising. To the young generation, the kibbutz is the establishment. For many, the fact that it served for so long as the source of elite units in the IDF and the country's political leadership is, itself, enough to limit interest. But why is it that so few within the contemporary anarchist movement remain conscious of the prevalence of anarchist ideologies in the early years of the kibbutz movement?

Among those activists whose knowledge of Zionist history extends beyond the partial story peddled by the Israeli education system, media and *hasbara* (Zionist education aimed at foreigners), there is some acknowledgement that the creation of the state, and the kibbutzim's subsequent link to it, meant the historical perspective of many within the kibbutz movement—and the Zionist movement as a whole—changed dramatically. "When you think about it, it's hardly surprising that today's radicals know so little of their forebears' politics," Lerner said to me. "When the state was set up, everything that happened before 1948 was twisted to fit what was acceptable to the *new* Zionism, the sole focus of which was the state. Ben-Gurion and other figures from that generation deliberately tried to erase everything that happened before 1948."

"The entire movement in Israel was to delete everything that happened before the state was everything," Lerner adds. "You can't say whether or not it was designed to bury the anarchist ideas specifically, but that was certainly one effect. Anarchism was no longer spoken about. The idea that the kibbutzim were going to create a new society had stopped being a realistic proposition by the mid 1930s—by that point there was a state-in-waiting and the kibbutzim were coopted—but around the time of the creation of the state, the entire notion that the kibbutzim had ever been aiming to build a new society in Palestine as a *socialist* project rather than an exclusively Zionist one was systematically erased. The entire anarchist or radical socialist notion in Jewish history was altered, as everything was changed into this new one perspective of Zionism: 'Zionism *is* the state of Israel.' Everything was focused on making this happen."

It goes without saying that the role of anarchist ideology among the early settlers is absent from the Israeli educational curriculum. While figures like A.D. Gordon and Chaim Arlosoroff and groups like Hashomer Hatzair are well known, the influence Kropotkin, Landauer and Tolstoy had in informing their ideologies is rarely taught—but it is also seldom talked about among the elder generation of kibbutzniks who were actually there. The young generation of anarchists— many of whom were raised in kibbutzim—have first hand experience of this, and many agree that even kibbutzniks from the founding generation today look back at the early years very differently from the historical accounts that appear in documentation from the time.

Outside researchers and kibbutz authors note this same tendency, some concluding that the fact that some of the individuals who had previously been promoting radical leftist ideologies would later dismiss the role of such ideas is a product of an "anti-ideological ideology" that emerged within the kibbutzim, compounding the proletarianisation of intellectuals.[319]

The No-State Solution

While the achievements and aspirations of the early kibbutzim may remain largely alien to many grassroots activists, they have been noted in much of the scholarship emerging in recent years from the Israeli anarchist movement. In his book *Anarchy Alive!*, Uri Gordon notes the anarchist principles of the pre-state settlements and the presence of anarchist literature among the early communards, observing how, while their methods may not have been the same as those of today's anarchist movements, and while they remained largely oblivious to their reality as pawns in a larger imperialist project, the early kibbutzniks' form of constructive activism has continued significance to contemporary anarchist struggles in the region.[320]

In drawing up his grand strategy for moving towards a "no-state" solution to the Israel-Palestine impasse laid out in a 2003 article entitled "From Mutual Struggle to Mutual Aid," Chicago-born Israeli Bill Templer elaborates on this relevance in more detail. Acknowledging the impact of anarchist ideals on the founding generation of kibbutzniks, Templer suggests that their example might be borrowed for a renewed move towards the kind of stateless commonwealth originally envisaged by many of the movement's founders.[321]

Putting forward a proposal for a "staged transformation"—moving from an interim stage of two states to a unitary, bi-national state, and on to what he tentatively terms a "Jerusalem Cooperative Commonwealth"—Templer argues that the first steps towards meaningful peace lie in laying the groundwork for "a kind of Jewish-Palestinian Zapatismo, a grassroots movement to 'reclaim the commons.'" This would mean making constructive moves towards direct democracy, participatory economics and autonomy for the people of both national entities in the region—in other words, as he puts it, effectively moving once again "towards Martin Buber's vision of 'an organic commonwealth...that is a community of communities.'"

Building the Future, Now

As well as stressing the importance of re-examining ideas from Buber's pre-1948 Brit Shalom (Peace Alliance) and post-independence party Ihud (Union), Templer notes the role played by Gustav Landauer in shaping Buber's anarcho-utopianism, and singles out the German theorist as a potential source for the renewal of utopian thought within Israeli society. Using Landauer's idea of hollowing out hierarchical capitalist structures and top-down bureaucracies through the creation of practical libertarian alternatives, Templer argues that the first crucial steps towards a stateless solution lie in a process that he calls "autonomous prefiguring."

In other words, social transformation must be focused on building from the bottom up, through the construction of progressive, anti-authoritarian spaces within the shell of the existing order, beginning at the level of the household and neighbourhood. Templer regards the creation of autonomous, directly democratic neighbourhoods, "Household" and "Home Assemblies," neighbourhood associations, employees' associations, cooperative housing associations, "people's assemblies," alternative schools and innovative forms of home schooling as potential beginnings for self-emancipation.

Templer suggests that important models for this kind of constructive action can be found in the new wave of communitarian experimentation that has taken place across Israel during the last few decades, such as the renewal of the libertarian tradition in many of the various new anarchist-oriented forms of communal living.

As well as highlighting the example of Kibbutz Samar (which he acknowledges is "in significant ways internally an anarcho-communalist mini-model, whatever its external entrepreneurialism in the Israeli economy"), Templer views the urban kibbutz model and the work of today's urban communards as a form of prefigurative politics of precisely the kind he has in mind. He cites Hashomer Hatzair's graduate movement group, Pelech, in particular, as an example. Templer contends that the urban commune idea could, in conjunction with existing seeds of rapprochement and solidarity like Neve Shalom/Wahat al-Salam and organisations of joint resistance to the Occupation such as Ta'ayush, Stop the Wall and the various other Jewish-Arab initiatives, be adapted and used as part of a move towards this potential stateless future

It is not only in the new wave of urban communal groups in which Templer sees the seeds of anarchist communalism. Irrespective of the capitalist structure they have developed during recent years, even some of the existing agricultural settlements—including the kibbutzim and moshavim—could, he believes, be transformed into incubators for positive change. "By dint of size," he argues, "the kibbutzim...can be targeted as potential foci for new forms of direct democracy and experimentation with Home Assemblies, as ever more Israelis seek to re-establish control of their civil society at a scale of local community... In transposing pareconic ideas,[322] new mini-kibbutzim in Israel could begin experimentation with the principles and structures of parecon. Indeed, a few could become a microlab for such change."

Between Theory and Praxis

When it comes down to it, the construction of practical, permanent anti-authoritarian alternatives is not high on the agendas of contemporary anarchists—even though many might insist otherwise. With the activities of today's radicals on the ground focusing on the Occupation and Palestinian solidarity actions in the West Bank, questions of community-building and the construction of grassroots alternatives, in reality, receive less attention.

Moreover, the creative resistance that *is* in evidence often tends to be seen as useful only to the extent that its constructive endeavours are accompanied by destructive/preventative actions. According to Templer's vision, however, it is *precisely* through these creative enterprises, through the creation of new forms of participatory economy and autonomy designed to promote equality, diversity and mutual aid, that the conflicting national narratives contributing to the conflict can be defused and the present situation ultimately overcome.

Although it might be among the most elaborate programmatic plans for moving towards a no-state solution, Templer is not the only self-identified Israeli anarchist to name-check the kibbutz movement and its quasi-anarchic offspring as potential sources of inspiration for those hoping for an anarchistic future for the region. Among those who have similarly cited the communes as templates for social transformation are Landauer aficionado and self-styled "mystical anarchist" Doreen Bell-Dotan, who remarks how the urban commune idea, in particular, could be seen as a method for positive social change both in the region and abroad.

Bell-Dotan also notes that the model of the classical kibbutz—"as anarchic as ever a society was"[323]—might itself be borrowed by those seeking to create an anarchist society overseas. Dan Sieradski (AKA Mobius), the New York-based journalist and founding publisher of *Jewschool.com*, records how some anarchist activists in Israel have talked about reinvigorating the small-group ethos of the early years by establishing spiritual anarchist kibbutzim in the country.[324] Similarly, kibbutz thinkers like Giora Manor, Muki Tsur and Haim Seeligman have recently underlined the importance of re-examining anarchist theory within the mainstream kibbutzim as a way of reinvigorating the utopian ethos of the early communities.

The difference between these writers and the bulk of the movement on the ground is that all of them are approaching the kibbutz, as this book itself does, in terms of its internal structure as a model of social anarchism. In the face of the daily horrors of the Occupation, many contemporary anarchists couldn't care less about models of social anarchism—much less learning from the kibbutz idea— and most would treat such ideas with a high degree of cynicism. The question is, does this point to a failing on the part of the theorists, or a blinkeredness that the anarchists who form the landscape of anarchist resistance in Israel should be attempting to overcome? In response to the perpetual disparagement of the kibbutz idea from her country's contemporary left, one exasperated Israeli anarchist, writing on a web forum recently, had this to say:

> Jesus fucking Christ! Isn't there *anyone* on any of these Anarchy lists that has the fortitude of character and generosity of spirit to be an Anarchist? Isn't there *one* who isn't full of shit? Isn't there *one* who has what it takes to recognise something that's *potentially* great? If you had one Anarchic cell in your bodies you'd be *celebrating* the Kibbutz and wanting to give them any support you can. Instead you criticise. I guess that's all you're good for.

Epilogue

March 2008

Yuvi Tashome arrived in Israel as a young girl in the autumn of 1984. She and her family were among the 33,000 members of Beta Israel airlifted to the country from refugee camps in the Sudan during Operation Moses, one of a series of dramatic rescue operations orchestrated by the Israeli government and Israel's intelligence service, the Mossad, when famine and civil war threatened Ethiopian populations during the 1980s and 1990s.

Under the provisions of Israel's Law of Return, more than 120,000 Ethiopian Jews have settled in the country during the last three decades. Like many of the minority ethnic groups who've immigrated to Israel, the Ethiopian Jews have experienced serious difficulties integrating into Israeli society. While many of their central- and eastern European brethren arrived with educational qualifications and job skills, the olim of Beta Israel came from a subsistence economy, and in many cases found themselves ill-equipped to work in an industrialised, first-world environment. Not only did they have to start virtually from scratch in education and employment skills, but, like the Mizrachi immigration two decades before them, the Ethiopian Jews found themselves facing prejudice, discrimination and racism from both Israeli society and the official establishment.

Vast amounts of government money have been poured into the absorption of Beta Israel, but progress has been slow. Figures released in 2007 indicate that the socio-economic disparities between Israel's Ethiopian community and the rest of the country's population are not going away. The gaps remain plain to see in impoverished neighbourhoods, skyrocketing unemployment and the highest high-school dropout rate of any Jewish group in Israel.

Average per capita income among Israel's Ethiopian community is around half that of all other Israeli Jews, and significantly lower even than that of the country's Arab population.[325] Inequalities and discrimination in the education system mean that Ethiopian youth often fall behind in basic skills early in their schooling. Around 40 percent of Ethiopian adults don't have an education beyond elementary school level. In deprived neighbourhoods in the country's development towns— the modern equivalent of the tent cities of the 1950s—drug use and criminal activity, practically unheard of among Ethiopian Jewish communities before they came to Israel, is increasing dramatically.

Now in her early thirties, Yuvi has had firsthand experience of the problems that Israel's Ethiopian community has to confront. Her status as a second-class citizen, she says, was hammered home to her during her childhood, when she went from living among other Ethiopian families to attending a religious boarding school in Hadera, then a high school at a religious kibbutz near Ashkelon, and later when she found herself rejected for jobs because of her ethnicity. After completing her army service, Yuvi worked for many years in programs run by the Society for the Protection of Nature in Israel (SPNI) designed to help integrate Ethiopian youth into Israeli society. "When I was working with Ethiopian kids there" she tells me, "I began to realise quite how serious the gaps were that exist between Israeli society and Ethiopian society here in Israel."

"As an Ethiopian immigrant in Israel you have to erase everything Ethiopian in order to be Israeli," Yuvi said. "When you first get here, they erase your name and give you a new one. When we arrived they asked me my name and I replied 'Yuvnot.' The girl didn't understand what I said, so she said 'OK, from now on you're going to be Rahel.' So I was Rahel until after my army service. All through my childhood I wanted to be Israeli so much, so I was Rahel, my accent was Israeli; I didn't like Ethiopian food, only Israeli food; I dressed Israeli and so on. The Ethiopian part of me was completely pushed aside. I didn't want to deal with it."

Drawn up by the majority Ashkenazim, official absorption processes have often failed to account for the particular social and cultural needs of minority ethnic groups. Yuvi sees this identity crisis experienced by so many of the Ethiopian olim as a significant contributor to the alienation felt among the Ethiopian communities. "When two Ethiopian kids are speaking Amharic in class," she explains, "the teacher will intervene and force them to speak Hebrew. When parents come to the school, the teacher will often have to translate what he says to the parents to their child, or vice versa. If you ask an Ethiopian youngster about Ethiopia or about his Ethiopian name, he'll say 'I don't have any Ethiopian name—only Israeli.' I think it's a big problem. I think that this is a big part of the underlying cause of a lot of the things that are happening to Ethiopian youth— the crime, the drugs and so on."

It was only when she started working with Ethiopian youngsters in the SPNI that Yuvi found herself able to reconnect with her own Ethiopian identity. "SPNI is about hiking," she says. "It's about knowing the country. When I was hiking with the kids and we talked about the history or the geography of Israel we'd always need to speak about Ethiopia. Let's say we talked about the mountains around Nazareth, we'd find a similar area in Ethiopia and draw comparisons with that. This way, once you've helped them draw out their Ethiopian identity, the Ethiopian kids who didn't want to hear about Nazareth would listen because you begin with Ethiopia, and Ethiopia interests them."

"So of course to work with the kids I needed to go home and ask my parents all about Ethiopia, about the hiking there, about the plants, the animals—everything I wanted to use when I was teaching the kids. This was the first time I'd really asked my parents anything about where we'd come from."

Gedera

In 2005, Yuvi was among the co-founders of a community in Gedera established to operate initiatives aimed at helping the town's underprivileged Ethiopian population. The decision to move to Gedera, which is home to around 1,700 Ethiopian families, was born of Yuvi's desire to work with the youth population of one neighbourhood in particular, Shapira. "I used to work with a lot of the kids in Shapira when I was in SPNI," she told me, "and it seemed that something very strange was happening there. Every year the situation with the neighbourhood's youth was getting worse and worse. If, in the first year, they smoked cigarettes, in the second it'd be alcohol. If the second year it was alcohol, the next it would be drugs. I began to feel that I was investing a lot of time and energy here and something was not moving, so I wanted to figure out what it was."

"There are a lot of programs aimed at helping Ethiopian society in Israel," Yuvi explains, "but basically they're not working. After five, six, twenty years, things here are not getting better. I began to realise that the main problem is that the motivation for everything was coming from outside—from the government, from foundations and so on. Within the Ethiopian community itself, there's no real motivation to do anything. It's just a cycle of poverty and disempowerment."

"When I talked to my parents about their life back in Ethiopia I was amazed, because they were so activist, they were so motivated. But here it's the opposite. People are just sitting and waiting—waiting for what, I don't know. In Ethiopia, if you don't work, you don't eat. It's as simple as that, so the motivation's there already. It's built in. Basically my friends and I decided that we needed to come up with ways of getting the motivation for change in the Ethiopian community here to come from the families and the kids themselves."

The community Yuvi and her friends established calls itself Garin Kehillati "seed of community." Although comparisons have been made with the urban kibbutz model, the community actually has little to do with the new generation of contemporary derivatives of the kibbutz idea.[326] Its basic premise is to bring people to live together in an extended neighbourhood community, bound together not by kibbutz-style economic communalism, but by a common social mission. Today, two and a half years since the garin first took root in the town, its initial nucleus of three families has evolved into two separate neighbourhood communities. Yuvi's alone now consists of eleven families, six of whom are Ethiopian immigrants, the rest *sabra* Israelis and Russian olim.

The communities operate a wide range of local-level initiatives in the surrounding area, including educational and social projects, a community garden and a non-profit organisation, Haverim Bateva, all of which aim to restore a sense of belonging to the town's alienated youth by strengthening their Jewish-Ethiopian identity. Every two weeks, the families meet for *Bet Midrash* (communal study), during which they learn about Ethiopian religion and culture, study other cultures and belief systems, discuss social problems, and share ideas about the future direction of the community and its role in helping the surrounding society.

"Everyone who wants to come and be a part of our community basically can. I don't think that there needs to be a separation between the Ethiopian community and the other families living here. We're all the same; all of us are immigrants. It doesn't matter if you're black or white, religious or not religious— as long as you accept and respect the other, you're welcome." The community, she tells me, is in a permanent process of evolution and still developing all the time. "We're constantly asking ourselves how we can improve what we're doing. For example, with eight children in the community, we're now talking about opening a kindergarten and bringing in Ethiopian kids from the neighbourhood to be with our own children."

In addition to the eleven families, the community counts among its number thirteen young people from the neighbourhood aged between twenty and twenty-five, all of whom are volunteering in the locality, half of them as permanent members of the garin. "We started to work with this group three years ago," Yuvi tells me. "This year, six of them go to university, so we we're very happy about that. That's a real success story for us."

Rather than leaving Gedera, this group goes to college in the town and comes back home in the evenings, and as Yuvi explains, this was an important part of the idea behind beginning the garin in the first place. "The Ethiopian families living in this neighbourhood have been trapped in a kind of cycle," she says. "The stronger kids from the neighbourhood always end up leaving to go on to university, so the ones who stay behind are the ones drinking, the ones who dropped out, or who didn't go through the army or whatever. So when you're a young child growing up here, these are your role models. The idea of having this young community staying in the neighbourhood was to provide alternative role models for the younger kids, and already it's working. It's really working."

Taking the power back

Yuvi doesn't consider herself "political." She doesn't vote, and, although she identifies more with leftist elements within Israeli society than any other, she has little faith or interest in party-politics as an agent of social change. While the community's evolution wasn't exactly what you'd call an "ideologically-motivated" process, the various initiatives established by its members came into being as part of a quiet but calculated attempt to take local organising away from local government and back to the grassroots.

"In the neighbourhood that we're talking about," Yuvi tells me, "people just don't feel like it's their own. As an example, about a year ago a group of soldiers from a nearby army base wanted to do community work in Gedera, so they come to Shapira. Without bothering to ask anybody from the neighbourhood what they needed, they decided to paint the buildings. So they come to the neighbourhood at 10am, and when their two hours was up, they just stop painting, drop everything and go. The neighbourhood looked like trash."

About a week later, a huge picture of those soldiers, brushes in hand, appeared in an Israeli newspaper with a laudatory caption paying tribute to fine work these young people were doing for the community. "I was so angry!" says Yuvi. "Apart from anything else, how could someone have the nerve to come and paint my house without asking me?!"

"So I asked the people living there why they would do something like that, and they say, 'Oh, it's like that all the time here. If the mayor says it's OK, then there's nothing we can do. We don't have any power to resist that. A few people just have to go and clean everything up.' So we started thinking about ways of dealing with this. The first thing we did was to create a parents' group who wanted change, as a way of fighting against this tendency to just accept everything that anybody in authority said. If, for example, a teacher in the local school said 'your child's not allowed to do this, this and this,' and because of that he ends up quitting school and dropping out, all too often the parents would just say, 'Oh OK,' roll over and accept it. NO! You don't need to say, 'Oh OK' if you don't agree with it! There are a lot of other solutions!"

One of the other projects to emerge from this process was the community garden, brought into being as a way, not just of regenerating a neglected neighbourhood, but of strengthening the self-image and Ethiopian-Jewish identity of its inhabitants. "In Ethiopia," Yuvi explains, "people are very connected with the earth. Every family that has a house has a patch of land where they grow vegetables. So we thought OK, even though this community's living in an urban environment we still have a lot of places we can cultivate. So we asked one of the people from the parents' group, Asnaka, if he wants to help us to create a garden to see what would happen."

Asnaka, an Ethiopian immigrant in his early fifties, had recently been made redundant from his job with the municipality and was working various menial jobs in the town. "To start off with, he was really hesitant!" Yuvi says. "He said that he wouldn't know how to do that here, that he was unfamiliar with the soil—he was so afraid. So we said OK, let's ignore that, let's just start and see what happens. Asnaka went off with one of our members of staff to choose the vegetables he wanted to grow, and after a while, when he saw that there was actually something growing and there was something to eat, he was so excited. Once, we found him bringing his friends from his neighbourhood to see. 'Look!' he was saying, 'It's like Ethiopia!'"

Asnaka's now in charge of the garden and he takes all of the produce home with him. Following the success of the project, plans are now being put in place to cultivate other patches of land throughout the neighbourhood. "At the moment we're talking to Asnaka about developing a garden for every building in the neighbourhood," Yuvi says. "We don't know how it's going to be run exactly, but that's something that the families in each building need to sit down together and decide among themselves."

Reinventing the Revolution

Anarchism has long claimed to have understood the importance of going beyond theory and actually beginning to build the elements of a new society in the present. The kibbutz movement and the various other forms of autonomous and quasi-autonomous communal organisation that existed throughout pre-1948 Palestine represent probably the single most exemplary historical instance of such constructive activism in action. What Yuvi and her friends are constructing in Gedera can be seen as a comparable form of counter-hegemony, a "social counter-power" uniquely suited to the forces and dilemmas that have shaped, and continue to shape, modern Israel.

In spite of the inequitable treatment the Ethiopian-Jewish community has received from Israelis of both European and Arab descent, within this counter-power its progenitors are working through the greater historical stream of anarchist-utopian thought to pioneer a very particular form of autonomy, a form that highlights the efficacy of their particular brand of resistance in a political context moulded by issues of racial inequality and institutionalised ethnic discrimination.

The way that Gedera's Ethiopian community is dealing with these issues is in terms of universals. Though they clearly hanker for aspects of their Ethiopian existence and remain mindful of their heritage and identity, there is no "back to Africa" feeling here. Their dream of overcoming disempowerment, inequality and racism and finally being accepted as full and equal citizens of this land, while at the same time retaining their own unique character, identity and values, is a dream that resonates profoundly within today's wider conflict/s. It is this, ultimately, that makes modern Israel such an ideal setting for radical ideological experimentation. It is precisely because of the rich diversity of competing political and cultural narratives, each laying claim at once to their homeland and to the belief that they are all their own unique forms of natural reason, that they all naturally inhere in the fabric of Israeli life.

This also means, of course, that no one belief system can ever emerge as fully hegemonic, even though, in their right wing incarnations, they can also be hideously destructive. Yet, the Middle East is a region in a constant process of evolution and self-creation; its future, to borrow a modern cliché, is still very much unwritten. Although the aspirations of the early kibbutz communards have long since been consumed in Zionist state-making, the country they created remains a veritable microlab for radical social experimentation. Its communes are among the most advanced in the world, and the vast and diverse patchwork of alternative ways of living that exists within its borders offers unique opportunities for testing radical new forms of organisation.

As the kibbutzim themselves are forced to come up with solutions to a seemingly endless string of potentially mortal problems, some of their members have recently begun to ask whether such solutions could potentially be found in a renewal of the anarchist tradition within the movement's history. "Is it possible to cure some of today's maladies by using anarchism's tools?" asked kibbutz veterans Haim Seeligman and Muki Tsur in discussions at Yad Tabenkin in 1998. "Can we use them to create some kind of renewal process for the kibbutz?"

> There are, in the vast treasury of philosophers such as Gustav Landauer, Bernard Lazare, Kropotkin, and Paul Goodman, philosophical elements that can assist us in advancing our thinking. When the movement is in a process of change… we must enable the vacuum to be filled with new, constructive contents. In anarchism, as in Utopian thought, we can find such constructive contents.[327]

Many modern proponents of anarchism are today, however, advancing the need to break free from the stifling confines of abstract ideological systems altogether and establish exactly the kinds of community-based institutions seen at Gedera, as the seeds of an antiauthoritarian future. Tenants committees, allotments, local-level voluntary organisations, extended neighbourhood communities, alternative-education institutions and community gardens are all viewed as means by which people might be empowered to forge their own non-alienated futures within and alongside the existing order.

The beauty of the community established by Yuvi and her friends lies not just in the clear parallels with these kinds of ideas, but in the mentality behind its organic process of self-creation. In a land that knows the effects of political sectarianism and dogmatic conformity to rigid agendas and abstract ideologies better than any other, the kind of work being done in Gedera highlights the importance of the emotional life of the family and local community involvement in ensuring that politics remains rooted in immediate experience of everyday life, rather than bound within the stifling and often destructive constraints of ideology. Utopia, by this account, is not some abstract "no-place," somewhere in the far-off future or distant past. Utopia lives and breathes in those existential pockets of autonomy, those moments of freedom whose seeds lie lodged in the cracks and fissures of everyday society—not "outside of place," but here, now, constantly demanding realisation.

Appendix I

Jewish immigration to Palestine

Aliya	Year
First	1882–1903
Second	1904–1914
Third	1919–1923
Fourth	1924–1931
Fifth	1932–1940
Sixth	1941–1947

(*Source*: Viteles, H (1967) A history of the Cooperative movement in Israel, Vol. 2, London: Vallentine Mitchell.)

Appendix II

Exchange of letters: Goldman-Landauer

These translations of correspondence between Gustav Landauer and Nachum Goldman in 1919 were prepared by Professor Avraham Yassour for the International Conference, Utopia—Imagination and Reality, *held in Haifa in January 1990.*

* * *

Nachum Goldman
Berlin
14 March 1919

Mr Gustav Landauer
Munich
Wolf Hotel

The Very Honourable Mr. Landauer:

You have no doubt received my two telegrams with regard to the convention of the representatives from Eretz Israel and you realise that the convention will take place only at the end of April. We sincerely hope that you will have the chance to be in Berlin during that period and that you will be able to participate in the convention.

From Dr. Buber you already know that he plans to arrange a small preliminary convention in Munich in mid-April to study the question of building (national) settlements in Eretz Israel. You offered to cooperate with us in Munich and expressed willingness to assist us in drafting the proposals and the outline which we will want to present to the convention. I wish to propose to you today the most important points on which we need your advice; these are the result of counselling among friends here;

1. As a fundamental question in building the settlement, we see the problem of centralised vs. decentralised society. We here are all united in the desire that the settlement be based on a decentralised community system while the emphasis is on the community as a unit (by itself) in which the people have a direct relationship with one another. The difficulty in this question is only in determining which areas of social life demand a centralised structure, for instance, technical administration and economic life.

We request that you inform us of your opinion and, if possible, draft it in outline form.

2. With regard to the nationalisation of land, we are all united (in opinion) and with us as well, I believe, are most of the Zionists. With the nationalisation of land, we are also demanding the nationalisation of the resources (water, coal, etc.)

3. Very difficult and unclear to us is the question of industry. Only a few amongst us are Marxists in the sense that we demand socialisation of the means of production. Before our eyes is the image of a factory organised on the basis of association in which the workers participate as owners and have equal rights concerning all problems of distribution of profits, administration, etc. The Controversy is as follows:

a) will the entire united community be credited with profits, or only the collective association of the given factory, something we suspect as dangerous, since a new, petit-bourgeois, capitalistic working class will spring up; furthermore, [circumstances will be created in which] the situation of the workers in a profitable factory would be better than that of workers in less profitable factories?

b) Is it not possible to combine the two principles: on the one hand, a single factory unionised on a cooperative basis and on the other hand, collectivized industry; this unique society will make possible supervision and far-reaching rights of intervention on the part of the public, which seem necessary, and not on the part of workers in the successful factories, who don't know how to defend themselves against penetration of new elements?

4. Also very difficult and unclear are the questions of trade arrangements. Are they to be nationalised or are they to be turned over to the settlements, and who will deal with the international exchange of goods etc.?

These are the same points which we have debated until now in our own circles and on which we are now asking your advice. On all these questions we will want, perhaps, to present outlines or proposals to the convention of delegates and we ask you to formulate your position in such an outline form. We can discuss any of the questions at length at our meeting in Munich, but it is most desirable if you could inform us beforehand in writing so that we may come somewhat prepared.

On other important questions (the Arab question, the agricultural settlements, terms of land acquisition, etc.), it is preferable that we discuss them here before approaching you with a request for advice on these matters also.

I hope that among all the preoccupations in which you find yourself in these days and weeks in Munich, that you will find, nonetheless, time to reply to our questions. I thank you in the name of all of us.

My very best wishes and regards,

Yours,

Nachum Goldman

* * *

Krombach (Schwaben)
19 March 1919

Dear Mr Goldman:

Buber has not written me. In any event, I shall be glad to participate in the small convention in Munich. If possible, I would like only then to decide on the matter of my participation in the larger convention of delegates in Berlin. The uncertainties on which I am dependent are too numerous. With regard to the questions, we can try to answer them together at the convention and in any event, I have no desire to give answers, rather, to point out additional questions to the problems you have brought up.

Decentralisation, and with it, freedom and volunteering are to be introduced to a wide degree in any place where there is no need to insist upon profitability and competitive power, that is, wherever it's possible, in the matter, to permit non-thrifty management of the economy. And here as well belongs the question of whether the economy, which is also called the 'state economy" (*Staatswirtschaft*) will be based on the productivity of work only or whether profitability is needed as well. A further question is whether by disregarding the existing centralised establishments (the System), can the growth of centralisation which the communities demand (to introduce) be made possible? Are we to judge the possibility according to the instance? And closely related to the question of centralisation are the questions of taxation, State economy, police, judicial administration, officialdom, representation system (democratic government). And with all this, it seems to me, nonetheless, possible not to demand beforehand all which will be necessary on the part of the State, but rather to leave to leave this to the development of the communities and their desires. Only then, when not the benefits of the organism, but rather the welfare of the individual is considered—this is the most important principle.

2. Nationalisation of the land must be a *fundamental principle*. It must become an existing actuality in the specific case of rare land resources which are claimed for the allied community (ore, coal, clay deposits, large waterways which serve as passage for the goods of the community, etc.). But we can usually realise this fundamental principle in various ways: leasing of land parcels by means of the community, community ownership and collective working of the land etc. Here too, the direction of Question 1 is influential. I think that each community should have its own means of marketing, which will be under its control in an independent manner, but excluding the abundant land resources which are owned by the united community. In fact here is the golden opportunity for taxation on the part of the whole: in communal acquisition of chemical fertilizer, agricultural machinery, marketing unions, etc. Also, suppose, in spite of the danger of waste, it is better to allow volunteering to develop than to decide beforehand on compulsion.

3. To be truthful, one needn't be a Marxist in order to refute the economy which is based on profits. Your posing the question has no meaning in my eyes. Here belongs more appropriately the question of equal exchange in trade, of financial operations without interest and of mutual credit. Afterwards, when we are able to solve these questions as far as possible, comes the turn of the following question:

4. National trade and trade with the rest of the world, which is still capitalistic. Both of these questions are secondary. If we can only solve the problems in Question 3, then there is no difficulty, since each product has a market value of its own, and with regard to the method of trading, supply and demand in the market can be advertised for example in the newspapers. The question of trade with foreign nations is dependent on the following circumstances: a) is there a surplus of products? b) are these superior in quality and inexpensive so that there will be buyers for them in the world market?

If the reply to these questions is positive then the community will be able to import the specific products that it needs. This is undoubtedly the (present) situation. It is not important to what degree it is vital, above all else *to nationalise foreign trade* and the individual economies as these are separable from the community economy. The supply of goods from abroad and their distribution must be the interest of the community; the community will see to it that there will be appropriate products for export, otherwise the situation will lend itself to debt and dependence on foreign countries.

I suggest that you and your friends think over my hurried comments and afterwards we'll attempt, in a joint effort, to reach the phrasing of an outline. Looking forward to seeing you and with warm regards,

Yours,

Gustav Landauer

Notes

1   Michael Löwy, *Redemption and Utopia: Jewish Libertarian Thought in Central Europe* (London: The Athlone Press, 1992), 65.

2   Graham Purchase, *Anarchist Society, & its Practical Realisation* (San Francisco, See Sharp Press, 1990), 4.

3   Jon Bekken, "Peter Kropotkin's Anarchist Communism" (http://flag.blackened.net/liberty/spunk/Spunk065.txt, February 20th 2005).

4   Kropotkin in Bekken, "Peter Kropotkin's Anarchist Communism."

5   Peter Kropotkin, "The Conquest of Bread," in *The Conquest of Bread and Other Writings*, ed. Marshall S. Shatz (Cambridge: Cambridge University Press, 1995), 133.

6   Peter Kropotkin, "Anarchist Communism," in *Anarchism: A Collection of Revolutionary Writings*, Roger N. Baldwin, ed. (New York: Dover Publications, Inc., 2002), 52.

7   Kropotkin in Paul Eltzbacher, "Peter Kropotkin," in *Anarchism: Exponents of the Anarchist Philosophy*, Steven T. Byington, trans., James J. Martin, ed. (New York: Chip's Bookshop, Booksellers and Publishers, 1970), 106.

8   As opposed to the individualist stream of anarchist thought, which stresses individual sovereignty and opposes the compulsory subservience of the individual to any form of external authority, including social collectivities.

9   Avraham Yassour, "Prince Kropotkin and the Kibbutz Movement," in *In a Kibbutz Commune (A Collection of Papers)*, Avraham Yassour, ed. (Haifa: University of Haifa), 31.

10 Avraham Yassour, "Prince Kropotkin and the Kibbutz Movement," 31.

11 Yaacov Oved, "Anarchism in the Kibbutz Movement," in *The Anarchist Communitarian Network* (http://www.anarchistcommunitarian.net/articles/kibbutz/kibbtrend.shtml, January 16th, 2005).

12 Landauer in M. Buber, *Paths in Utopia* (New York: Syracuse University Press, 1996), 46.

13 Landauer, G. "The Settlement, People and Land: Thirty Socialist Theses," in *Der Sozialist* (Berlin: 1907) trans. Crump, R., 6.

14 Buber, M. *Paths in Utopia*, 48.

15 G. Landauer, "The Settlement," in *Der Sozialist*, (Berlin: 1909) trans. Crump, R.

16 Joseph Blasi, *The Communal Experience of the Kibbutz* (New Brunswick, New Jersey: Transaction Inc. 1986), 179.

17 Barzel in Christopher Warhurst, *Between Market, State and Kibbutz: The Management and Transformation of Socialist Industry* (London: Mansell, 1999), 7.

18 Amir Helman, "Use and Division of Income in the Kibbutz" in *Alternative Way of Life: The First International Conference on Communal Living (Communes and Kibbutzim)*,

Yehudit Agasi and Yoel Darom, eds. (Norwood: Norwood Editions, 1984), 46.

19   This book is restricted to discussion of the kibbutzim comprised within TKM (The Kibbutz Movement), an amalgam of the two largest federations, TAKAM (the United Kibbutz Movement) and Kibbutz Artzi, which together house some 94 percent of the country's total kibbutz population. The remaining 6 percent is accounted for by the orthodox Religious Kibbutz Movement (the Dati federation). As well as being different in structure and praxis to the main body of the movement, Dati is, for obvious reasons, more ideologically complex in terms of its relationship to anarchism. While kibbutzniks of all the federations are (with very few exceptions) Jewish, theirs is predominantly a cultural or national Judaism rather then a religious one. Within the seventeen Dati kibbutzim and the two kibbutzim of the Poalei Agudat Israel (Pagi) movement), the ultra-orthodox kibbutzim, this is of course different. The Dati federation grew out of the Mizrachi (and especially the Hapoel Hamizrachi workers' strand) tradition of religious Zionism. Following the declaration of Israeli independence it formed a dovish faction in the National Religious Party. However, elements within it, and especially within its youth movement, B'nei Akiva were influenced by the right-wing, ultranationalist movement Gush Emunim (Bloc of the Faithful). Although Dati is not covered in this book, it is nevertheless worth noting that its kibbutzim are not without their own ties to anarchist thought—even though they are even more complex than the other federations. The memoirs of the anarchist Augustin Souchy, who had been a member of Landauer's Sozialistische Bund pre-World War I, include a couple of pages about his visit to Kibbutz Yavneh in 1951, and record how he was delighted to find that members of this Dati Kibbutz had been influenced and inspired by Landauer's ideas. (see: Michael Tyldesley, *No Heavenly Delusion: A Comparative Study of Three Communal Movements*, 131.)

20   C. Ward, "Editor's Postscript," *Fields, Factories and Workshops Tomorrow* (London: Freedom Press, 1974), 202.

21   S.F., "Reflections on Utopia," in *Freedom*, March 24th, 1962.

22   Pobedonostsev in Levon Chorbajian, *Studies in Comparative Genocide*, (Palgrave MacMillan, 1999), 237.

23   S. "Bilu"—an acronym based on a verse from Isaiah (2:5), "*Beit Ya'akov Lekhu Ve-nelkha*"—"Let the house of Jacob go!"

24   Qtd in Mordecai Schreiber, Alvin I. Schiff, Leon Klenicki, eds., "Bilu," *The Shengold Jewish Encyclopaedia*, 50–51.

25   Walter Laqueur, *A History of Zionism* (New York: Schocken Books, 2003), 75–76.

26   Rothschild began to buy land in Palestine in 1882, and his donations financed many of the early ventures, including the first settlement at Rishon LeZion. During the 1880s he became involved in founding Israel's wine industry when he helped Russian Jews flee pogroms and plant vineyards in their Palestine settlements.

27   Laqueur, *A History of Zionism*, 279.

28   Joseph Baratz, *A Village by the Jordan* (London: The Harvill Press, 1954), 52.

29   Arthur Ruppin, "The Picture in 1907: Address to the Jewish Colonization Society

of Vienna," *Zionism and Israel Information Center* (http://www.zionism-israel.
com/Arthur_Ruppin_1907.htm July 1 2008).

30   Ibid.

31   Ibid.

32   Nachman Syrkin, "Cooperative Settlement and Ahva," in *The History of the Kibbutz a
Selection of Sources—1905–1929*, ed. Avraham Yassour (Merhavia: 1995), 99.

33   Daniel Gavron, *The Kibbutz: Awakening from Utopia* (Lanham: Rowman & Littlefield,
2000), 19.

34   Baratz, *A Village by the Jordan*, 52.

35   Henry Near, *The Kibbutz Movement, A History Volume 1, Origins and Growth, 1909–
1939* (Oxford: Oxford University Press, 1992), 29.

36   Baratz in Near, *The Kibbutz Movement, A History*, 28.

37   Baratz, *A Village by the Jordan*, 43.

38   In his 1929 article "Buying the Emek, "Ruppin recounts how the Jezreel Valley (Emek
Yisrael) was purchased for settlement. A sizable part of this land, including the plot at
Umm Juni, was bought from absentee landlords—in Degania's case the Sursuk family
of Beirut. Most of the land was not in fact privately owned, and publicly owned
lands were usually not for sale to the Jews. In addition to the asking price, the settlers
paid often outlandish sums in compensation to the tenant farmers who had been
working the land; while this often assumed lesser priority for the Zionist authorities,
the necessity of retaining good relations with the Arab workers was something on
which early kibbutz literature—A.D. Gordon's essays in particular—places a great
deal of emphasis.

39   Yassour, "Introduction: Chapters in the History of the Kvutza and Kibbutz," in *The
History of the Kibbutz, A Selection of Sources—1905–1929*, 12.

40   "Degania, the Mother of the Kibbutzim, is 90 Years Old," *Communa* (http://www.
communa.org.il/dgania.htm, August 20th 2006).

41   "Degania, the Mother of the Kibbutzim, is 90 Years Old"

42   "Way of Life," *Degania* (http://www.degania.org.il/eng/life3.htm, September 7th
2006)

43   Ibid.

44   Warhurst, *Between Market, State and Kibbutz*, 57.

45   Literally "settlement"—abbreviation of *Hayishuv Hayehudi b'Eretz Yisrael* ("The
Jewish settlement in the Land of Israel") commonly used to refer to the pre-1948
Jewish community in Palestine.

46   Laqueur records that there was, during this early period of experimentation, a tendency
to stick rather dogmatically to the example of Degania. The fact that Degania had
consisted of twelve people, for example, had been purely accidental, but, for the
groups who set up kvutzot in its wake, this pattern became an ideological imperative.
In fact, during this period, Degania itself was still in a process of evolution and still
very much finding its feet. Early suggestions that none of its members should marry
during the first five years were shelved after the birth of the first child, for example,

which gave rise to a major ideological crisis—should the mother bring up her child, or should it be in someone else's care? Should children live with their family or in separate accommodation? Should female members work in all branches of agriculture, or was their place in the kitchen and the laundry? Were children "private property" or did they belong to the group? In the event, the Degania members during this time opted for a string of compromises but nevertheless their settlement became the template for subsequent settlements.

47   Warhurst, *Between Market, State and Kibbutz*, 57.

48   Ibid.

49   Yassour, "Introduction: Chapters in the History of the Kvutza and Kibbutz," 13.

50   Avraham Yassour, "Socialist Communal Ideas as Inspiration for the Inception of the Kvutza," *In a Kibbutz Commune*, 8.

51   Yassour, "Introduction: Chapters in the History of the Kvutza and Kibbutz," 8.

52   Ibid.

53   Syrkin, "Cooperative Settlement and Ahva," 98.

54   Buber, *Paths in Utopia*, 142.

55   Bowes in Warhurst, *Between Market State and Kibbutz*, 65.

56   Buber, *Paths in Utopia*, 143.

57   J. Baratz in Yassour, "Socialist Communal Ideas as Inspiration for the Inception of the Kvutza," 6.

58   Baratz in Near, *The Kibbutz Movement, A History*, 28.

59   M. Baratz in Yassour, "Socialist Communal Ideas as Inspiration for the Inception of the Kvutza," 6.

60   Avraham Yassour, "Chapters in the History of the Kvutza and Kibbutz" in *The History of the Kibbutz, A Selection of Sources—1905–1929*, 10.

61   Near, *The Kibbutz Movement, A History*, 13.

62   Buber, *Paths in Utopia*, 143.

63   Warhurst, *Between Market, State and Kibbutz*, 66.

64   Ibid.

65   Baratz, *A Village by the Jordan*, 79.

66   Ibid.

67   A.D. Gordon, "Thoughts and Letters," in *The History of the Kibbutz, A Selection of Sources—1905–1929*, 143.

68   A.D. Gordon, "Man and Nature," *A.D. Gordon: Selected Essays*, trans. F. Burnce (New York: League for Labour Palestine, 1938), 205.

69   Warhurst, *Between Market, State and Kibbutz*, 132.

70   L. Tolstoy in George Woodcock, *Anarchism* (Aylesbury: Pelican Books, 1963), 215.

71   Laqueur, *A History of Zionism*, 285.

72   Baratz, *A Village by the Jordan*, 82.

73   Ze'ev Sternhell, *The Founding Myths of Israel: Nationalism, Socialism, and the Making of the Jewish State*, trans. David Maisel (Princeton: Princeton University Press, 1998), 3.

74   Sternhell, *The Founding Myths of Israel*, 60.

75   E. Schweid in Sternhell, *The Founding Myths of Israel*, 57.

76   Ibid.

77   Ibid.

78   In his 1973 biography of Gustav Landauer, *Prophet of Community*, Eugene Lunn puts forward a superb analysis of the development of the leftist branch of *volkisch* romanticism in an attempt to highlight the inadequacy of understanding *volkisch* themes exclusively in terms of their latter-day association with "Nazism." Lunn underlines the fallaciousness of the belief that the romantic, *volkisch* nationalism of Herder has no other ideological descendents than the proto-fascist and xenophobic views of thinkers associated with integral nationalism, and argues that this simplistic, teleological view of European romantic *volkisch* currents, which sees political romanticism simply in terms of a unilinear development to fascism, is responsible for historians" tendency to overlook the left-wing strain of *volkisch* romanticism exemplified by thinkers like Landauer.

79   Michael Tyldesley, *No Heavenly Delusion: A Comparative Study of Three Communal Movements* (Liverpool: Liverpool University Press, 2003), 48.

80   Hune E. Margulies, "Dialogue and Urbanism: On Buber, Naess, Spinoza and the Question of Diversity," *The Martin Buber Homepage* (http://buber.de/material/urban).

81   A.D. Gordon, "Thoughts and Letters," 143.

82   Ruth Link-Salinger, *Gustav Landauer: Philosopher of Utopia* (New York: Hackett, 1977), 44.

83   Avraham Yassour, "The Survival of Social Models," in *In a Kibbutz Commune (A Collection of Papers)*, ed. Avraham Yassour (Haifa: University of Haifa), 4–5.

84   Yassour, "The Survival of Social Models," 5.

85   F. Oppenheimer in Link-Salinger, *Gustav Landauer: Philosopher of Utopia*, 43.

86   Link-Salinger, *Gustav Landauer: Philosopher of Utopia*, 43.

87   Yassour, "The Survival of Social Models," 5.

88   F. Oppenheimer in Yassour, "Socialist Communal Ideas as Inspiration for the Inception of the Kvutza," 9.

89   Yassour, "Socialist Communal Ideas as Inspiration for the Inception of the Kvutza," 9.

90   Yassour, "The Survival of Social Models," 5.

91   J. Bussel in Yassour, "The Survival of Social Models," 5.

92   Yassour, "The Survival of Social Models," 5.

93   Josef Trumpeldor in Oved, "Anarchism in the Kibbutz Movement."

94   Avraham Yassour, editor's note to Josef Trumpeldor, "Letters and Program" in *The History of the Kibbutz, A Selection of Sources—1905–1929*, 47.

95   Trumpeldor, "Letters and Program," 62.

96   Ibid., 52.

97   Ibid.

98   Ibid.

99   Ibid., 53–54.

100 Yassour, editor's note to Trumpeldor, "Letters and Program," 48.

101 Trumpeldor, "Letters and Program," 59.

102 Ibid., 58.

103 Near, *The Kibbutz Movement, A History*, 57.

104 Gustavo Esteva in B. Templer, "From Mutual Struggle to Mutual Aid: Moving Beyond the Statist Impasse in Israel/Palestine," *Borderlands E-journal* (http://www.borderlandsejournal.adelaide.edu.au/vol2no3_2003/templer_impasse.htm,February 20th 2005).

105 Blasi, *The Communal Experience of the Kibbutz*, 22.

106 Avraham Yassour, "Maintaining Equality in a Kibbutz Commune," in *In a Kibbutz Commune*, ed. Avraham Yassour, 16.

107 See: "Discussions in the General Assembly at Kibbutz Degania/From the Meeting Minutes" in *The History of the Kibbutz, A Selection of Sources—1905–1929*, 108–112

108 Oved, "Anarchism in the Kibbutz Movement."

109 Tyldesley, *No Heavenly Delusion*, 51.

110 Not to be confused with Habonim Dror (See chapter 5), which formed when the Habonim and Dror youth movements merged in 1982.

111 Oved, "Anarchism in the Kibbutz Movement."

112 Yassour, "Introduction: Chapters in the History of the Kvutza and Kibbutz," 21.

113 Oved, "Anarchism in the Kibbutz Movement."

114 Löwy, *Redemption and Utopia*, 128.

115 Buber, *Paths in Utopia*, 39.

116 Landauer in Löwy, *Redemption and Utopia*, 134.

117 Ibid.

118 Eugene Lunn, *Prophet of Community: The Romantic Socialism of Gustav Landauer* (Berkeley: University of California Press), 271–272.

119 Ruth Link-Salinger in Yassour, Avraham. ed., *Gustav Landauer on Communal Settlement: Exchange of Letters* (Haifa: University of Haifa), 21.

120 Ibid.

121 Ibid., 21–22.

122 At the time of writing it is unclear exactly which groups were involved in the meeting, but, as one of the few international organisations in existence in 1919, it is likely that Poalei Zion was involved. If this is the case, this comment indicates that although Poalei Zion has been pigeonholed as a Marxist organisation, this may not have been entirely accurate.

123 Ruth Link-Salinger, *Gustav Landauer: Philosopher of Utopia*, 53.

124 Buber in Oved, "Anarchism in the Kibbutz Movement."

125 All of these groups arrived in Palestine with some knowledge of Landauer's ideas, but it was not as systematic as in Hashomer Hatzair. The one exception to this is Werkleute,

whose members would later establish kibbutz Hazorea in the Jezreel Valley. Formed in 1932, Werkleute were very close to Buber, and it is inconceivable that he would not have introduced them to Landauer's ideas. But in 1938 the group (which by then had two kibbutzim in Palestine) shocked Buber by officially becoming part of Hashomer Hatzair—by that stage the latter was an avowedly Marxist organisation and this went totally against Buber's religious socialist outlook.

126 In 1915, the remainder of Ze'irei Zion would form a separate group, Dror, which was influenced by the teachings of the Russian Narodniks.

127 Michael Tyldesley, in conversation with the author, June 2007.

128 Gershom Scholem in Oved, "Anarchism in the Kibbutz Movement."

129 Manes Sperber in Löwy, *Redemption and Utopia*, 165.

130 Yassour, "Chapters in the History of the Kvutza and Kibbutz," 21.

131 Meir Yaari in Oved, "Anarchism in the Kibbutz Movement."

132 Ibid.

133 Manes Sperber in Löwy, *Redemption and Utopia*, 165.

134 Yassour, "Chapters in the History of the Kvutza and Kibbutz," 22.

135 "The Betanya Commune: Selections from Diaries" in *The History of the Kibbutz: A Selection of Sources*, ed. Avraham Yassour, 119.

136 Yaari in Oved, "Anarchism in the Kibbutz Movement."

137 Yassour, "Introduction: Chapters in the History of the Kvutza and Kibbutz," 21.

138 Landauer in Erhard Doubrawa, "The Politics of the I-Thou, Martin Buber, the Anarchist," *Erhard Doubrawa: Gestalt Therapy — Martin Buber, the Anarchist* (http://ourworld.compuserve.com/homepages/gik_gestalt/doubrawa.html#text, March 16th 2005).

139 It is interesting, perhaps, to consider one passage from the diary of Moshe, who recounts his motivations for going to Palestine: "During the November revolution in Vienna," Moshe writes, "I was among the young anarchists, whom I had joined several years earlier. During that period we dreamed of real revolutionary action. When the communist movement of the Spartakists took action in Munich, I was among those who went there to take an active part in bringing the revolution about. The revolt was not successful, and I, along with the rest, fell into enemy hands. In prison I thought, pondered, and questioned many things. I sought a project which would command great spiritual strength and action and achievement. There was none. There was only a tragic tangle lacking any *raison d'être*. Humankind! Here you walk about with the masses under the flag of the revolution. You make claims, become infatuated, crave purity, beauty and holiness in life. These same masses, what are their desires? Who knows? Will they not readily betray the souls of the seekers? In general, this whole revolution was devised in the streets amidst the crowds in mass, sporadic uprising... The spiritual accounting began with a genesis. The longing for a creative, authentic, independent, tangible deed was renewed. Things became clear. Only what you yourself realise in your lifetime will succeed, stand firm, and never betray you. The memory of the land of Israel came to mind. The plan was simple and

consistent."

140 Zvi Schatz, "Letters, Diary, Notes and Essays," in *The History of the Kibbutz: A Selection of Sources*, 91.

141 "The Betanya Commune: Selections from Diaries" in *The History of the Kibbutz: A Selection of Sources*, 124.

142 Ibid., 121.

143 Ibid.

144 Meir Yaari, "Two Essays on Hashomer Hatzair," in *The History of the Kibbutz: A Selection of Sources*, 166.

145 Ibid.

146 "The Program of the National Kibbutz Movement of the Young Guard," in *The History of the Kibbutz, a Selection of Sources*, 192.

147 Near, *The Kibbutz Movement, A History*, 152.

148 Merron in Tyldesley, *No Heavenly Delusion*, 129.

149 "The Program of the National Kibbutz Movement of the Young Guard," 192.

150 Oved, "Anarchism in the Kibbutz Movement."

151 Ibid.

152 Menachem Rosner, in conversation with the author, June 2006. See also: Michael Tyldesley, *No Heavenly Delusion*.

153 Shlomo Avineri, *Arlosoroff* (London: Peter Halban Publishers Ltd, 1989), 9

154 Link-Salinger, *Gustav Landauer: Philosopher of Utopia*, 73

155 Arlosoroff in Avineri, *Arlosoroff*, 104.

156 Avineri, *Arlosoroff*, 104.

157 Ibid.

158 Ibid.

159 Chaim Arlosoroff in Avineri, *Arlosoroff*, 105.

160 Jason, Schulman, "The Life and Death of Socialist Zionism," *New Politics* (http://www.wpunj.edu/newpol/issue35/schulman35.htm, February 2005).

161 Arlosoroff in Schulman, "The Life and Death of Socialist Zionism."

162 Yosef Aharonovitch in Shulman "The Life and Death of Socialist Zionism."

163 Arlosoroff in Avineri, *Arlosoroff*, 108.

164 Avineri, *Arlosoroff*, 107.

165 Oved, "Anarchism in the Kibbutz Movement."

166 Avineri, *Arlosoroff*, 10.

167 Ibid.

168 Quoted in Yassour, "Socialist Communal Ideas as Inspiration for the Inception of the Kvutza," *In a Kibbutz Commune*, 7.

169 Oved, "Anarchism in the Kibbutz Movement."

170 Yitzhak Tabenkin in Oved, "Anarchism in the Kibbutz Movement."

171 Oved, "Anarchism in the Kibbutz Movement."

172 Ibid.

173 Daniel Gavron, *The Kibbutz: Awakening from Utopia* (Lanham: Rowman & Littlefield,

2000), 46.
174 Yassour, "Introduction: Chapters in the History of the Kvutza and Kibbutz," 15.
175 Ibid., 22.
176 "Way of Life," *Degania Homepage* (http://www.degania.org.il/eng/life.htm, September 5ᵗʰ 2006).
177 Yassour, "Prince Kropotkin and the Kibbutz Movement," 31.
178 Ibid.
179 Oved, "Anarchism in the Kibbutz Movement."
180 See "Jewish Criticism of Zionism" by Edward C. Corrigan (*Middle East Policy*, Winter 1990–91, pp. 94–116) for a good overview.
181 Quoted in Corrigan, "Jewish Criticism of Zionism."
182 Albert Einstein in Corrigan, "Jewish Criticism of Zionism."
183 See Tony Greenstein, "Zionism: An Antidote to Socialism," *Movements For Socialism* (http://www.movementsforsocialism.com/archive/Zionism_greenstein.htm   March 16th, 2005).
184 Oved, "Anarchism in the Kibbutz Movement."
185 Moshe Goncharok, "The Yiddish anarchist press in Israel," trans. Jesse Cohen, *R.A. Forum* (http://raforum.apinc.org/article.php3?id_article=2368, March 16th 2005).
186 Joseph Lanir, *The Kibbutz Movement Survey And Data* (Tel Aviv: Yad Tabenkin, 1985), 1.
187 Ibid.
188 "Degania, the Mother of the Kibbutzim, is 90 Years Old."
189 Quoted in Yassour, "Maintaining Equality in a Kibbutz Commune," *In a Kibbutz Commune*, 14.
190 Warhurst, *Between Market, State and Kibbutz*, 72–73.
191 *The Communal Scene in Israel* (http://www.communa.org.il/e-israel.htm, September 18ᵗʰ 2006).
192 "Kibbutzim: Some Facts and Figures," *The Communal Scene in Israel* (http://www.communa.org.il/kibbutz.htm, September 18ᵗʰ 2006).
193 "Kibbutzim: Some Facts and Figures."
194 Melford Spiro, "Moral Postulates of Kibbutz Culture," in *Economic Democracy: Essays and Research on Workers' Empowerment*, Warner P. Woodworth (Pittsburgh: Sledgehammer Press, 2002), 138.
195 Uri Leviatan, "Relevancy of Kibbutz Experience to Society at Large" in *Alternative Way of Life: The First International Conference on Communal Living (Communes and Kibbutzim)*, eds. Yehudit Agasi and Yoel Darom (Norwood: Norwood Editions, 1984), 63.
196 "The Betanya Commune: Selections from Diaries," 124.
197 Trumpeldor, "Letters and Program," 67–68.
198 As defined by A. Allen Butcher in *Communal Economics*, 2002.
199 Maurice Pearlman in George Woodcock, *The Basis of Communal Living* (London: Freedom Press, 1947), 23.

200   Josef Trumpeldor in Warhurst, *Between Market, State and Kibbutz*, 68.

201   "A Meeting of Representatives of Kibbutz Groups: From the Meeting Minutes" in *The History of the Kibbutz, A Selection of Sources—1905–1929*, 211.

202   Warhurst, *Between Market, State and Kibbutz*, 137.

203   "Discussion in the General Assembly at Degania: Excerpts from the meeting minutes," 109.

204   Ibid.

205   Warhurst, *Between Market, State and Kibbutz*, 86.

206   Menachem Rosner in Fischer, Michael, Brenda Geiger & Hans Toch, *Reform through Community: Resocializing Offenders in the Kibbutz* (New York: Greenwood Press, 1991), 11.

207   Fischer, Geiger & Toch, *Reform through Community*, 11.

208   Warhurst, *Between Market, State and Kibbutz*, 136.

209   Helman, "Use and Division of Income in the Kibbutz," 50.

210   Warhurst, *Between Market, State and Kibbutz*, 98.

211   Ibid., 134.

212   Ibid.

213   Ibid.

214   Ibid., 137.

215   Ethnographic studies of the kibbutz carried out as late as the early 1980s indicated that industrialisation neither changed the kibbutz's basic social structure nor affected members' commitment to its original ideals, with the kibbutz having proven themselves capable of absorbing industrial development without undermining the ideological principles with which they had been conceived. Cross-cultural studies of direct democracy in industry in Italy, Austria, the U.S., Yugoslavia and the kibbutz in the 1980s found that, in comparison to capitalist industry, kibbutz industries at that time applied the principles of "Quality of Work Life" better than any other industrial settings tested. The kibbutz was found the most participative with comparatively egalitarian distribution of power and authority and the highest levels of informal participation in decision-making. The relations between kibbutz supervisors and other workers were found to be the most harmonious, with supervisors more receptive to new ideas and suggestions, and more willing to help and support their team. (See: Tannenbaum, A.S., B. Kaucic, M. Rosner, M. Vianello & G. Wieser (1974). *Hierarchy in Organizations: An International Comparison*. San Francisco: Jossey Bass., and Tannenbaum A.S. (1980). "Foreword." In *Work and Organization in Kibbutz Industry*, edited by U. Leviatan & M. Rosner. Norwood PA: Norwood Editions, XIII–XIX.)

216   Warhurst, *Between Market, State and Kibbutz*, 134.

217   "Degania," *Communa* (http://communa.org.il/dgania.htm, August 26th 2006).

218   Warhurst, *Between Market, State and Kibbutz*, 137.

219   Ibid.

220   Spiro, "The Moral Postulates of Kibbutz Culture," 138.

221 Helman, "Use and Division of Income in the Kibbutz," 47.

222 Ibid.

223 Ibid.

224 Warhurst, *Between Market, State and Kibbutz*, 73.

225 The chief difference between Marx and Kropotkin is that while Marx saw every political and social system as being directly determined by the specific economic base, Kropotkin viewed base and superstructure as being mutually influential and enjoying a symbiotic, interdependent relationship.

226 Kropotkin, "Anarchist Communism," 52.

227 Avraham Pavin, "The Governmental System of the Kibbutz" in *Crisis in the Kibbutz, Meeting the Challenge of Changing Times*, eds. Uriel Leviatan, Hugh Oliver & Jack Quarter (London: Praeger, 1998), 100.

228 Spiro, "The Moral Postulates of Kibbutz Culture," 142.

229 "Draft for Kvutza Constitution" in *The History of the Kibbutz: A Selection of Sources—1905–1929*, 181.

230 "Way of Life"

231 J.F.H. in Woodcock, *The Basis of Communal Living*, 22–23.

232 Blasi, *The Communal Experience of the Kibbutz*, 105–106.

233 Ibid., 100.

234 Yassour, "Laws and Legalism in Kibbutz (Abstract)" in *International Conference: Kibbutz and Communes, Past and Future, Abstracts of the Lectures*, ed. Avraham Yassour, (Tel Aviv: Yad Tabenkin, 1985), 28.

235 J.F.H. in Woodcock, *The Basis of Communal Living*, 23.

236 Yassour, "Laws and Legalism in Kibbutz (Abstract)," 28.

237 Blasi, *The Communal Experience of the Kibbutz*, 143.

238 Menachem Rosner in Fischer, Geiger & Toch, *Reform through Community*, 12.

239 Daniel Katz in Fischer, Geiger and Toch, *Reform through Community*, 12.

240 "Discussions in the General Assembly at Degania: Excerpts from the Meeting Minutes" in *The History of the Kibbutz: A Selection of Sources*, 108.

241 This was not the case on all kibbutzim—at Degania, for example, children have always lived with their parents.

242 Woodcock, *The Basis of Communal Living*, 23–24.

243 Dorit Friedman in Peg Lopata, "Mothering: The Infant Daycare Experiment," *findarticles.com*, Winter 1993 (http://findarticles.com/p/articles/mi_m0838/is_n69/ai_14658169, June 30th 2007).

244 Lopata, "Mothering: The Infant Daycare Experiment."

245 "Deganya, the Mother of the Kibbutzim, is 90 Years Old."

246 See: Tyldesley, Michael. *No Heavenly Delusion: A Comparative Study of Three Communal Movements*. (Liverpool: Liverpool University Press, 2003).

247 "A meeting of Representatives of Kibbutz Groups: From the Meeting Minutes" in *The History of the Kibbutz, A Selection of Sources—1905–1929*, 207.

248 "Draft for Kvutza Constitution" in *The History of the Kibbutz, A Selection of Sources—*

1905–1929, 180.

249 Buber, *Paths in Utopia*, 146–147.

250 Ibid., 42.

251 "The Kibbutz Movement," *The International Communal Studies Association* (http://www.ic.org/icsa/kibbutz.html, February 20th 2005).

252 Warhurst, *Between Market, State and Kibbutz*, 70.

253 Giora Manor, "The Kibbutz: Caught Between Isms," *The Anarchist Communitarian Network* (http://anarchistcommunitarian.net/articles/kibbutz/kcbisms.shtml, January 16th, 2005).

254 Under the auspices of the Am Oved and Sifriat Poalim publishing houses, set up by the Histadrut and Hashomer Hatzair respectively, more than 2,000 books were published. In addition to the Histadrut newspaper, *Davar*, the main Socialist parties also published their own newspapers—*Al Hamishmar* was Hashomer Hatzair's, *Lamerhav* Ahdut Ha'Avoda's. As Laqueur comments, "These were no common achievements: bigger and more powerful Socialist parties, such as those in Britain and France, had failed to maintain their daily newspapers. It was another illustration of the determination and resourcefulness of the Jewish labour movement, which, moreover, provided a specific way of life for its members and sympathisers."

255 Laqueur, *A History of Zionism*, 331.

256 Manor, "The Kibbutz: Caught Between 'Isms.'"

257 Ibid.

258 Ibid.

259 Ibid.

260 Graham Purchase, "Peter Kropotkin: Ecologist, Philosopher and Revolutionary," *University of New South Wales* (www.library.unsw.edu.au/~thesis/adt-NUN/uploads/approved/adt-NUN20041011.094306/public/01front.pdf, September 10th 2006), 242.

261 "Eight Questions on Kibbutzim: Answers from Noam Chomsky," *Znet Commentary* (http://www.zmag.org/ZSustainers/ZDaily/1999-08   percent5C24chomsky.htm, March 16th 2005).

262 Baratz, *A Village by the Jordan*, 101.

263 See: Max Nettlau's *Panarchy: A Forgotten Idea of 1860*.

264 Near, *The Kibbutz Movement, A History*, 178.

265 David Ben-Gurion in Sternhell, *The Founding Myths of Israel*, 205.

266 Ibid.

267 Sternhell, *The Founding Myths of Israel*, 205.

268 Ibid.

269 Ibid., 206.

270 Ibid.

271 Ibid.

272 Ibid., 207.

273 Ibid.

274 A. Bonanno, *Palestine! Mon Amour* (London: Elephant Editions, 2007), 9–10.
275 Doreen Ellen Bell-Dotan, "Anarchy in Praxis—Getting off the Ground" (http://www.geocities.com/dordot2001/AnarchyPraxis.htm, December 20th 2007).
276 Assaf Adiv, "Post-Zionist Israel: The rules have changed" *Challenge Magazine* (http://www.challengemag.com/en/article__187/post_zionist_israel_the_rules_have_changed December 20th 2007).
277 Gershon Shafir and Yoav Peled, *Being Israeli: The Dynamics of Multiple Citizenship* (Cambridge University Press, 2002).
278 Bichler & Nitzan in Assaf Adiv, "Post-Zionist Israel: The rules have changed."
279 Eli Avrahami, "The Changing Kibbutz" (http://www.kibbutz.org.il/eng/welcome.htm. August 13th 2006).
280 Ibid.
281 Ibid.
282 Ibid.
283 Gavron, *The Kibbutz: Awakening from Utopia*, 209.
284 Avrahami, "The Changing Kibbutz."
285 "The Kibbutz Movement."
286 Avrahami, "The Changing kibbutz."
287 Yassour, "Laws and Legalism in Kibbutz (Abstract)," 29.
288 "The Kibbutz Movement."
289 Warhurst, *Between Market, State and Kibbutz*, 72.
290 Gavron, *The Kibbutz: Awakening from Utopia*, 260.
291 Michael Liskin, "Anarchy Rules," *Anarchist Communitarian Network* (http://www.anarchistcommunitarian.net/articles/kibbutz/index.shtml, February 2003). Originally appeared in *The Jerusalem Report*, Volume X, No.19 January 17 2000, p.18.
292 Gavron, *The Kibbutz: Awakening from Utopia*, 272.
293 Ibid., 262.
294 Liskin, "Anarchy Rules."
295 Gavron, *The Kibbutz: Awakening from Utopia*, 259.
296 Ibid., 267.
297 Liskin, "Anarchy Rules."
298 James Grant-Rosenhead, "A New Kibbutz Movement," *Communa* (http://www.communa.org.il/newkibbutzmvt.htm, August 20th 2006).
299 Gavron, *The Kibbutz: Awakening from Utopia*, 247.
300 Ibid., 246.
301 Ibid.
302 Ibid., 247.
303 Ibid.
304 "Kehilla," *Tamuz Homepage* (http://www.tamuz.org.il/kehilla/).
305 Grant-Rosenhead, "A New Kibbutz Movement."
306 Ibid.

307 Ibid.

308 "Ma'agal Hakvutzot," *Intentional Communities* (http://directory.ic.org/records/?actio n=view&page=view&record_id=20282, September 6th 2006).

309 Initially, Ma'agal Hakvutzot incorporated most of the various new forms of communal experimentation, including 'the Tnuat Bogrim groups and the urban kibbutzim. Recent changes have led to the organisation becoming more of a framework for those groups that are not coming from a youth movement background, namely the Urban Kibbutzim and the various other independent communal groups.

310 Avraham Yassour, *The Withering Away Politics in Buber and Landauer's Utopianism* (Israel: Haifa University, 1990), 10.

311 Ibid., 9

312 April Rosenblum, *The Past Didn't Go Anywhere: Making Resistance to Anti-Semitism Part of All our Movements.* (Self-published, 2007. Download at www.thepast.info.)

313 Goncharok, "The Yiddish Anarchist Press in Israel."

314 Ibid.

315 Paul Avrich, "Gustav Landauer," *The Match!* December 1974, 10.

316 Uri Gordon, *Anarchy Alive! Antiauthoritarian Politics from Practice to Theory* (London: Pluto Press, 2008), 140.

317 Uri Gordon in conversation with the author, December 2007.

318 Daniel Berger, "Anti-Zionist, Revolutionary and Internationalist: Interview with Rudolf (Rudi) Segall," *International Viewpoint: News and Analysis from the Fourth International* (http://www.internationalviewpoint.org/article.php3?id_article=676, December 20th 2007).

319 Warhurst, *Between Market, State and Kibbutz*, 66.

320 Gordon, *Anarchy Alive! Anti-Authoritarian Politics from Practice to Theory*, 140.

321 Bill Templer, "From Mutual Struggle to Mutual Aid."

322 Parecon—an abbreviation of "participatory economics"—is a an economic system developed by activist and political theorist Michael Albert and radical economist Robin Hahnel during the 1980s and 1990s that uses participatory decision making as an economic mechanism to guide the production, consumption and allocation of resources in a society. Proposed as an alternative both to capitalist market economies and to centrally planned socialism or coordinatorism, Parecon has become widely seen as an "anarchistic economic vision."

323 Doreen Ellen Bell-Dotan, "Anarchy in Praxis—Getting off the Ground" (http:// www.geocities.com/dordot2001/AnarchyPraxis.htm, December 20th 2007).

324 See: Dan Sieradski, "Rejewvenation: Checking In," *Orthodox Anarchist* (http:// orthodoxanarchist.com/2005/10/28/rejewvenation-checking-in/).

325 Moti Bassok, "Report: Ethiopian immigrants earned half of average salary last year," *Haaretz* (http://www.haaretz.com/hasen/spages/845435.html, February 20th 2008).

326 Tamar Rotem, "First Kibbutz for Ethiopian immigrants opens in Gedera," *Haaretz* (http://www.haaretz.com/hasen/spages/947484.html, January 23rd, 2008).

327 Oved, "Anarchism in the Kibbutz Movement."

Bibliography

Adams, Jason. *Rethinking the Global context: Non-Western Anarchisms*. (www. geocities.com/ringfingers/nonwesternweb.html).

Adiv, Assaf. "Post-Zionist Israel: The rules have changed." *Challenge Magazine* (http://www.challengemag.com/en/article__187/post_zionist_israel_the_rules_have_changed).

Albert, Michael and Robin Hahnel. *Looking Forward, Participatory Economics For the Twenty-First Century*. Boston: South End Press, 1991.

"Anarchists and Jews: The Story of an Encounter." *The Jewish Studies Newsletter* Issue 9.009 (March 2000): 2. (http://www.h-net.org/~judaic/newsletters/9-009p2.txt).

Avineri, Shlomo. *Arlosoroff.* London: Peter Halban Publishers Ltd, 1989.

Avrahami, Eli. "The Changing Kibbutz." (http://www.kibbutz.org.il/eng/welcome.htm).

Avrich, Paul. "Gustav Landauer." *The Match!* (December, 1974).

Baratz, Joseph. *A Village by the Jordan*. London: The Harvill Press, 1954.

Bassok, Moti. "Report: Ethiopian immigrants earned half of average salary last year." *Haaretz*, (http://www.haaretz.com/hasen/spages/845435.html).

Beinin, Joel. "Knowing Your Enemy, Knowing Your Ally: The Arabists of Hashomer Hatza'ir (MAPAM)." *Social Text*, No. 28 (1991): 100–121.

Bekken, Jon. "Peter Kropotkin's Anarchist Communism." (http://flag.blackened.net/liberty/spunk/Spunk065.txt).

Bell-Dotan, Doreen Ellen. "Anarchy in Praxis—Getting off the Ground." (http://www.geocities.com/dordot2001/AnarchyPraxis.htm).

Berger, Daniel. "Anti-Zionist, Revolutionary and Internationalist: Interview with Rudolf (Rudi) Segall." *International Viewpoint: News and Analysis from the Fourth International* (http://www.internationalviewpoint.org/article.php3?id_article=676).

Blasi, Josef. *The Communal Experience of the Kibbutz*. New Jersey: Transaction Inc., 1986.

Bonanno, A., *Palestine! Mon Amour*. London: Elephant Editions, 2007.

Buber, Martin. *Paths in Utopia*. Syracuse: Syracuse University Press, 1996.

Butcher, A. Allen. "Communal Economics." In *Encyclopedia of Community: From the Village to the Virtual World*, edited by Karen Christenson and David Levinson. Thousand Oaks, CA: Sage Publications 2003.

Breines, Paul. "Germans, Journals and Jews/Madison, Men, Marxism and Mosse:

A Tale of Jewish-Leftist Identity Confusion in America." *New German Critique*, No. 20, Special Issue 2: "Germans and Jews" (Spring, 1980): 81–103

Chomsky, Noam. *Government in the Future*. New York: Seven Stories Press, 2005.

Chorbajian, Levon. *Studies in Comparative Genocide*. Palgrave Macmillan, 1999.

Corrigan, Edward. "Jewish Criticism of Zionism." *Le Revue Gauche— Libertarian Communist Analysis and Comment* (http://plawiuk.blogspot. com/2005_07_29_plawiuk_archive.html, August 28th 2006).

Cohn, Jesse. "Anarchy in Yiddish: Famous Jewish Anarchists from Emma Goldman to Noam Chomsky." *Lecture on Jewish Anarchists in History*. (http://www. geocities.com/CapitolHill/7404/anarchy_in_yiddish.html).

"Degania." *The Jewish Agency for Israel, Department for Jewish Zionist Education*. (http://www.jafi.org.il/education/noar/sites/degania.htm, August 20th 2006)

"Deganya, the Mother of the Kibbutzim, is 90 Years Old." *Communa* (http:// www.communa.org.il/dgania.htm).

Doubrawa, Erhard. "The Politics of the I-Thou, Martin Buber, the Anarchist." *Erhard Doubrawa: Gestalt Therapy – Martin Buber, the Anarchist* (http:// ourworld.compuserve.com/homepages/gik_gestalt/doubrawa.html#text March 16th 2005).

Raptis, Nikos. "Eight Questions on Kibbutzim: Answers from Noam Chomsky." *Znet Commentary* (http://www.zmag.org/ZSustainers/ZDaily/1999-08 percent5C24chomsky.htm).

Eltzbacher, Paul. *Anarchism: Exponents of the Anarchist Philosophy*. Trans. Steven T. Byington, ed. James J. Martin. New York: Chip's Bookshop, Booksellers and Publishers, 1970.

"The End of the Kibbutz Movement?" *The Raven: Anarchist Quarterly* #30, Vol. 8, Number 2 (Summer 1995): 149.

Fischer, Michael, Brenda Geiger & Hans Toch. *Reform through Community: Resocializing Offenders in the Kibbutz*. New York: Greenwood Press, 1991.

Frankel, Jonathan. *Jews and Messianism in the Modern Era: Metaphor and Meaning*. Oxford: Oxford University Press, 1991.

Gavron, Daniel. *The Kibbutz: Awakening from Utopia*. Lanham: Rowman & Littlefield, 2000.

Goncharok, Moshe. "The Yiddish anarchist press in Israel." Trans. Jesse Cohen. *R.A. Forum* (http://raforum.apinc.org/article.php3?id_article=2368).

Gordon, Aaron David. *Selected Essays*. Trans. Francis Bunce. New York: League for Labour Palestine, 1938.

Gordon, Uri. "Anarchism and Political Theory: Contemporary Problems." (http:// ephemer.al.cl.cam.ac.uk/~gd216/uri/1.8_-_Nationalism.pdf).

———. *Anarchy Alive! Anti-Authoritarian Politics from Practice to Theory*. London: Pluto Press, 2008.

Grant-Rosenhead, James. "A New Kibbutz Movement." *Communa* (http://www.communa.org.il/newkibbutzmvt.htm. August 20th 2006)

Greenstein, Tony. "Zionism: An Antidote to Socialism." *Movements For Socialism* (http://www.movementsforsocialism.com/archive/Zionism_greenstein.htm March 16th, 2005).

Harris, Neil. "Going against the grain." *Kibbutz Trends* 46 (Winter 2002). (http://www.habonimdror.org.il/booklet/37.percent20kibbutz percent20trends percent20on percent20anton.doc)

Helman, Amir. "Use and Division of Income in the Kibbutz." In *Alternative Way of Life: The First International Conference on Communal Living (Communes and Kibbutzim)*, edited by Yehudit Agasi and Yoel Darom. Norwood: Norwood Editions, 1984.

"Kehilla." *Tamuz Homepage* (http://www.tamuz.org.il/kehilla/).

"The Kibbutz Movement." *The International Communal Studies Association* (http://www.ic.org/icsa/kibbutz.html).

Knowles, Rob. "Political Economy from Below: Communitarian Anarchism as a Neglected Discourse in Histories of Economic Thought." *Anarchy Archives* (http://dwardmac.pitzer.edu/Anarchist_Archives/Kropotkin/Knowles.html, August 28th 2006).

Kropotkin, Peter. *Anarchism: A Collection of Revolutionary Writings*. Ed. Roger N. Baldwin. New York: Dover Publications, Inc., 2002.

———. *Fields, Factories and Workshops Tomorrow*. Ed. Colin Ward. London: George Allen and Unwin Ltd, 1974.

———. *The Conquest of Bread and Other Writings*. Ed. Marshall S. Shatz. Cambridge: Cambridge University Press, 1995.

———. *Mutual Aid: A Factor of Evolution*. London: Freedom Press, 1998.

Landauer, Gustav. *Anarchism in Germany and Other Essays*. Barbary Coast Collective, 2004.

———. *For Socialism*. Trans. D.J. Parent, eds. R. Berman and T. Luke. St. Louis: Telos Press, 1978.

———. "The Settlement, People and Land: Thirty Socialist Theses." Trans. R. Crump. *Der Sozialist*. Berlin, 1907.

Lanir, Joseph. *The Kibbutz Movement: Survey and Data*. Tel Aviv: Yad Tabenkin, 1985.

Laqueur, Walter. *A History of Zionism*. New York: Schocken Books, 2003.

Leichman, David and Idit Paz. *Kibbutz: An Alternative Lifestyle*. Yad Tabenkin, 1994

Leviatan, Uriel, Hugh Oliver and Jack Quarter, eds. *Crisis in the Israeli Kibbutz*. London: Praeger, 1998.

Leviatan, Uri. "Relevancy of Kibbutz Experience to Society at Large." In *Alternative Way of Life: The First International Conference on Communal Living (Communes and Kibbutzim)*, edited by Yehudit Agasi and Yoel Darom.

Norwood: Norwood Editions, 1984.

Link-Salinger, Ruth. *Gustav Landauer in Historical Transmissions*. New York: American Academy for Jewish Research, 1975.

———. *Oeuvres Gustav Landauer*. New York: American Academy for Jewish Research, 1976.

———. *Gustav Landauer: Philosopher of Utopia*. New York: Hackett, 1977.

Liskin, Michael. "Anarchy Rules!" *The Anarchist Communitarian Network* (http://www.anarchistcommunitarian.net/articles/kibbutz/index.shtml).

Lockman, Zachary. *Comrades and Enemies: Arab And Jewish Workers In Palestine, 1906–1948*. California: University of California Press, 2004.

Lopata, Peg. "Mothering: The Infant Daycare Experiment." *findarticles.com*. Winter 1993 (http://findarticles.com/p/articles/mi_m0838/is_n69/ai_14658169).

Löwy, Michael. *Redemption and Utopia: Jewish Libertarian Thought in Central Europe*. London: The Athlone Press, 1992.

Löwy, Michael and Robert Sayre. *Romanticism Against the Tide of Modernity*. Trans. Catherine Porter. Durham: Duke University Press, 2001.

Lunn, Eugene. *Prophet of Community: The Romantic Socialism of Gustav Landauer*. Berkeley: University of California Press, 1973.

Maurer, Charles B. *Call to Revolution: The Mystical Anarchism of Gustav Landauer*. Detroit: Wayne State University Press, 1971.

Manor, Giora. "The Kibbutz: Caught Between Isms." *The Anarchist Communitarian Network* (http://anarchistcommunitarian.net/articles/kibbutz/kcbisms.shtml).

Margulies, Hune E. "Dialogue and Urbanism: On Buber, Naess, Spinoza and the Question of Diversity." *The Martin Buber Homepage* (http://buber.de/material/urban).

Marshall, Peter. *Demanding the Impossible: A History of Anarchism*. London: Harper Collins, 1992.

Melnyk, George. *The Search for Community: From Utopia to a Cooperative Society*. Montréal: Black Rose Books, 1985.

Meyers, Nechemia. "Urban Communes—Kibbutzim Strike Root in Israeli City." *Zionism and Israel Information Center* (http://zionism-israel.com/city_communes_kibbutz.htm).

Near, Henry. *The Kibbutz Movement: A History Volume 1, Origins and Growth, 1909–1939*. Oxford: Oxford University Press, 1992.

Oved, Yaacov. "Anarchism in the Kibbutz Movement." *The Anarchist Communitarian Network* (http://www.anarchistcommunitarian.net/articles/kibbutz/kibbtrends.html).

Pavin, Avraham. "The Governmental System of the Kibbutz." In *Crisis in the Kibbutz, Meeting the Challenge of Changing Times*, edited by Uriel Leviatan, Hugh Oliver and Jack Quarter. London: Praeger, 1998.

————. *The Kibbutz Movement, Facts and Figures 2006.* Tel Aviv: Yad Tabenkin. 2006.

Purchase, Graham. *Anarchist Society and its Practical Realisation.* San Francisco, See Sharp Press, 1990.

————. "Peter Kropotkin: Ecologist, Philosopher and Revolutionary." *University of New South Wales* (www.library.unsw.edu.au/~thesis/adt-NUN/uploads/approved/adt-NUN20041011.094306/public/01front.pdf).

Reinharz, Shulamit. "An Urban Kibbutz in Jerusalem." *The Jewish Advocate* (http://www.thejewishadvocate.com/this_weeks_issue/columnists/reinharz/?content_id=2834).

Rosenblum, April. *The Past Didn't Go Anywhere: Making Resistance to Anti-Semitism Part of All our Movements.* (http://pinteleyid.com/past-read.pdf).

Rotem, Tamar. "First Kibbutz for Ethiopian immigrants opens in Gedera." *Haaretz* (http://www.haaretz.com/hasen/spages/947484.html).

Ruppin, Arthur. "The Picture in 1907: Address to the Jewish Colonization Society of Vienna." *Zionism and Israel Information Center* (http://www.zionism-israel. com/Arthur_Ruppin_1907.htm).

Sayre, Robert and Michael Löwy. "Figures of Romantic Anti-Capitalism." *New German Critique* No. 32 (Spring, 1984): 42–92

Schulman, Jason. "The Life and Death of Socialist Zionism." *New Politics* (http:// www.wpunj.edu/newpol/issue35/schulman35.htm).

Shafir, Gershon and Yoav Peled. *Being Israeli: The Dynamics of Multiple Citizenship.* Cambridge University Press, 2002.

Sieradski, Dan. "Rejewvenation: Checking In." *Orthodox Anarchist* (http:// orthodoxanarchist.com/2005/10/28/rejewvenation-checking-in/).

Spiro, Melford. *Kibbutz: Venture in Utopia.* Harvard: Harvard University Press, 1972.

————. "Moral Postulates of Kibbutz Culture." In *Economic Democracy: Essays and Research on Workers' Empowerment,* edited by Warner P. Woodworth. Pittsburgh: Sledgehammer Press, 2002.

Sternhell, Ze'ev. *The Founding Myths of Israel: Nationalism, Socialism, and the Making of the Jewish State.* Trans. David Maisel. Princeton: Princeton University Press, 1998.

Templer, Bill, "From Mutual Struggle to Mutual Aid: Moving Beyond the Statist Impasse in Israel/Palestine," *Borderlands* E-journal (http://www. borderlandsejournal.adelaide.edu.au/vol2no3_2003/templer_impasse.htm)

Tyldesley, Michael. *No Heavenly Delusion: A Comparative Study of Three Communal Movements.* Liverpool: Liverpool University Press, 2003.

Vallier, Ivan. "Production imperatives and communal norms in the kibbutz." In *Communes: Creating and Managing the Collective Life,* edited by R.M. Kanter. New York: Harper and Row, 1973.

Ward, Colin. "Gustav Landauer." *Anarchy,* Vol.5 No. 1 (January 1965).

Warhurst, Christopher. *Between Market, State and Kibbutz: The Management and Transformation of Socialist Industry.* London: Mansell, 1999.

"Way of Life." *Kibbutz Degania Aleph* (http://www.degania.org.il/eng/life.htm).

Woodcock, George. *Anarchism: A History of Libertarian Ideas and Movements.* Aylesbury: Pelican Books, 1963.

———. *The Basis of Communal Living.* London: Freedom Press, 1947.

Yassour, Avraham. "Gustav Landauer: The Man, the Jew and the Anarchist." Ya'ad, n°2, 1989 (http://www.waste.org/~roadrunner/ScarletLetterArchives/Landauer/Yassour_Gustav_Landauer.htm).

———. ed. *Gustav Landauer on Communal Settlement: Exchange of Letters.* Haifa: University of Haifa.

———. ed. *The History of the Kibbutz a Selection of Sources—1905–1929.* Merhavia: 1995.

———. ed. *International Conference: Kibbutz and Communes, Past and Future, Abstracts of the Lectures.* Tel Aviv: Yad Tabenkin, 1985.

———. ed. *In a Kibbutz Commune (A Collection of Papers).* Haifa: University of Haifa.

———. ed. *Martin Buber's Social and Cultural Philosophy.* Indiana: New Harmony, 1993.

———. *The Withering Away Politics in Buber and Landauer's Utopianism.* (Prepared for the International conference *Utopia—Imagination and Reality*). Haifa, January 1990.

Z.H., "Collectives Voluntaires en Israel." *Noir et Rouge, cahiers d'études anarchistes communistes.* December 1962.

Index

Y

Z

Friends of AK Press

AK Press is a worker-run co-operative that publishes and distributes radical books, visual & audio media, and other mind-altering material. We're a dozen people who work long hours for short money, because we believe in what we do. We're anarchists, which is reflected both in the books we publish and in the way we organize our business. All decisions at AK Press are made collectively—from what we publish to what we carry for distribution. All the work, from sweeping the floors to answering the phones, is shared equally.

Currently, AK Press publishes about twenty titles per year. If we had the money, we would publish forty titles in the coming year—new works from new voices, as well as a growing mountain of classic titles that, unfortunately, are being left out of print.

All these projects can come out sooner with your help. With the Friends of AK Press program, you pay a minimum of $25 per month (of course, we welcome larger contributions), for a minimum three month period. All the money received goes directly into our publishing funds. In return, Friends automatically receive (for the duration of their membership), one FREE copy of every new AK Press title (books, dvds, and cds), as they appear. As well, Friends are entitled to a 20% discount on everything featured in the AK Press Distribution Catalog and on our website—thousands of titles from the hundreds of publishers we work with. We also have a program where groups or individuals can sponsor a whole book. Please contact us for details.

To become a Friend, go to: http://www.akpress.org.

ALSO AVAILABLE FROM AK PRESS

MARTHA ACKELSBERG—Free Women of Spain

KATHY ACKER—Pussycat Fever

LOUIS ADAMIC—Dynamite: The Story of Class Violence in America

MICHAEL ALBERT—Moving Forward: Program for a Participatory Economy

JOEL ANDREAS—Addicted to War: Why the U.S. Can't Kick Militarism

PAUL AVRICH—Anarchist Voices: An Oral History of Anarchism in America

PAUL AVRICH—The Modern School Movement

PAUL AVRICH—The Russian Anarchists

BRIAN AWEHALI—Tipping the Sacred Cow

DAN BERGER—Outlaws of America

ALEXANDER BERKMAN—What is Anarchism?

ALEXANDER BERKMAN—The Blast: The Complete Collection

DAVID BERRY—A History of the French Anarchist Movement, 1917–1945

STEVEN BEST & ANTHONY NOCELLA, II—Igniting a Revolution

HAKIM BEY—Immediatism

JANET BIEHL & PETER STAUDENMAIER—Ecofascism

BIOTIC BAKING BRIGADE—Pie Any Means Necessary

JACK BLACK—You Can't Win

DIANA BLOCK—Arm the Spirit: A Woman's Journey Underground and Back

MURRAY BOOKCHIN—Anarchism, Marxism, and the Future of the Left

MURRAY BOOKCHIN—The Ecology of Freedom

MURRAY BOOKCHIN—Post-Scarcity Anarchism

MURRAY BOOKCHIN—Social Anarchism or Lifestyle Anarchism

MURRAY BOOKCHIN (EIRIK EIGLAD, ED)—Social Ecology and Communalism

MURRAY BOOKCHIN—The Spanish Anarchists: The Heroic Years 1868–1936

MURRAY BOOKCHIN—To Remember Spain

MURRAY BOOKCHIN—Which Way for the Ecology Movement?

JULES BOYKOFF—Beyond Bullets: The Suppression of Dissent in the United States

MAURICE BRINTON—For Workers' Power

HARRY BROWNE—Hammered by the Irish

DANNY BURNS—Poll Tax Rebellion

MAT CALLAHAN—The Trouble With Music

CHRIS CARLSSON—Critical Mass: Bicycling's Defiant Celebration

CHRIS CARLSSON—Nowtopia

JAMES CARR—Bad

DANIEL CASSIDY—How the Irish Invented Slang

NOAM CHOMSKY—Chomsky on Anarchism

NOAM CHOMSKY—Language and Politics

NOAM CHOMSKY—Radical Priorities

TAUNTON
BRIDGWATER

www.philips-maps.co.uk

First published 2008 by

Philip's, a division of
Octopus Publishing Group Ltd
www.octopusbooks.co.uk
2–4 Heron Quays
London E14 4JP
An Hachette Livre UK Company
www.hachettelivre.co.uk

First edition 2008
First impression 2008

ISBN 978-0-540-09377-9

© Philip's 2008

This product includes mapping data licensed
from Ordnance Survey®, with the permission
of the Controller of Her Majesty's Stationery
Office.

© Crown copyright 2008. All rights reserved.
Licence number 100011710

Printed and bound in China by Toppan

Contents

Key to map symbols

Roads

12 (motorway symbol)	Motorway with junction number
A42	Primary route – dual/single carriageway
A42	A road – dual/single carriageway
B1289	B road – dual/single carriageway
	Through-route – dual/single carriageway
	Minor road – dual/single carriageway
	Rural track, private road or narrow road in urban area
	Path, bridleway, byway open to all traffic, restricted byway
	Road under construction
	Pedestrianised area
	Gate or obstruction to traffic restrictions may not apply at all times or to all vehicles
P P&R	Parking, Park and Ride

Railways

	Railway
	Miniature railway
	Metro station, private railway station

Emergency services

◆ ◆	Ambulance station, coastguard station
◆ ◆	Fire station, police station
H ✚	Hospital, Accident and Emergency entrance to hospital

General features

✚ PO	Place of worship, Post Office
i	Information centre (open all year)
	Bus or coach station, shopping centre
	Important buildings, schools, colleges, universities and hospitals
	Woods, built-up area
Tumulus FORT	Non-Roman antiquity, Roman antiquity

Leisure facilities

⚑ 🚐	Camping site, caravan site
⚑ ✕	Golf course, picnic site

Boundaries

• • • • • • • •	Postcode boundaries
▬▬ · ▬	County and unitary authority boundaries

Water features

River Ouse — Tidal water, water name

Non-tidal water – lake, river, canal or stream

〈 I — Lock, weir

Scales

Blue pages: 4½ inches to 1 mile 1:14 080

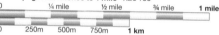

0	220 yds	¼ mile	660 yds	½ mile
0	125m 250m 375m	½ km		

Green pages: 2¼ inches to 1 mile 1:28 160

0	¼ mile	½ mile	¾ mile	1 mile
0	250m 500m 750m	1 km		

74 Adjoining page indicators The mapping continues on the page indicated by the arrow

Abbreviations

Acad	Academy	Mkt	Market
Allot Gdns	Allotments	Meml	Memorial
Cemy	Cemetery	Mon	Monument
C Ctr	Civic Centre	Mus	Museum
CH	Club House	Obsy	Observatory
Coll	College	Pal	Royal Palace
Crem	Crematorium	PH	Public House
Ent	Enterprise	Recn Gd	Recreation Ground
Ex H	Exhibition Hall	Resr	Reservoir
Ind Est	Industrial Estate	Ret Pk	Retail Park
IRB Sta	Inshore Rescue Boat Station	Sch	School
		Sh Ctr	Shopping Centre
Inst	Institute	TH	Town Hall/House
Ct	Law Court	Trad Est	Trading Estate
L Ctr	Leisure Centre	Univ	University
LC	Level Crossing	Wks	Works
Liby	Library	YH	Youth Hostel

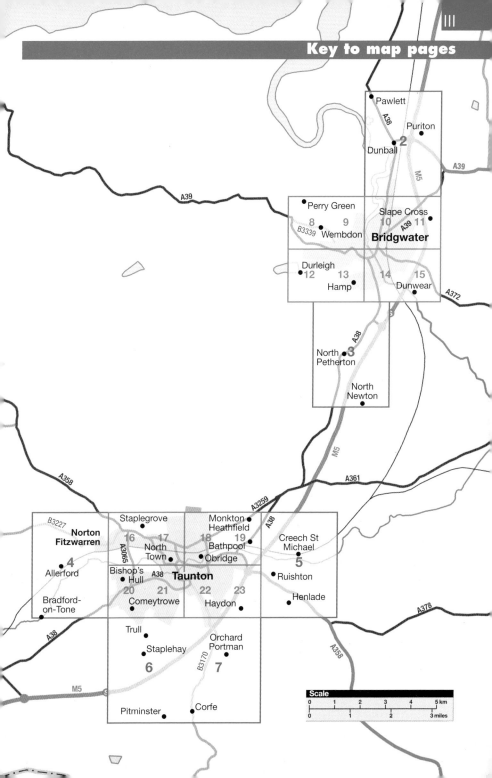

Pawlett

A38

Puriton

2

Dunball

A39

M5

Perry Green

Slape Cross

8   9

10   11

B3339   Wembdon

A39

Bridgwater

Durleigh

12   13

14   15

Hamp

Dunwear

A372

North
Petherton

A38

3

North
Newton

M5

A361

A358

A3259

Staplegrove

Monkton
Heathfield

A38

B3227

**Norton
Fitzwarren**

16   17

18   19

Creech St
Michael

North
Town

Bathpool

5

A3065

Obridge

4

Bishop's
Hull

A38

Taunton

Ruishton

Allerford

20   21

22   23

Bradford-
on-Tone

Comeytrowe

Haydon

Henlade

A38

A378

Trull

Orchard
Portman

A358

M5

6

Staplehay

B3170

7

Pitminster

Corfe

Scale

0   1   2   3   4   5 km

0   1   2   3 miles

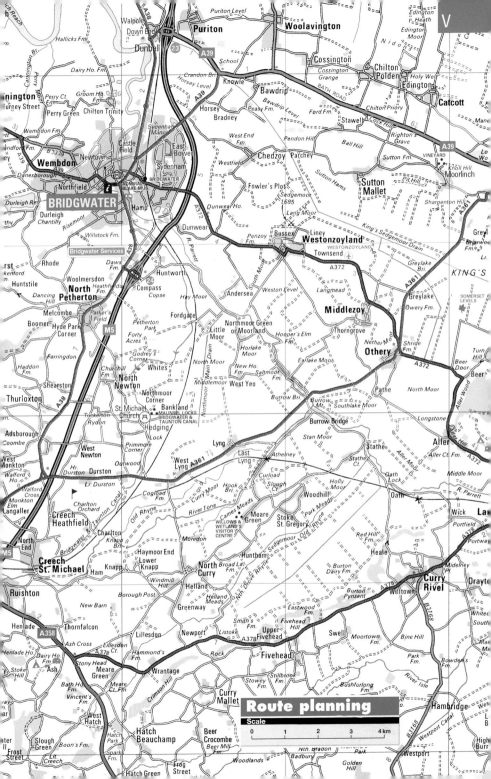

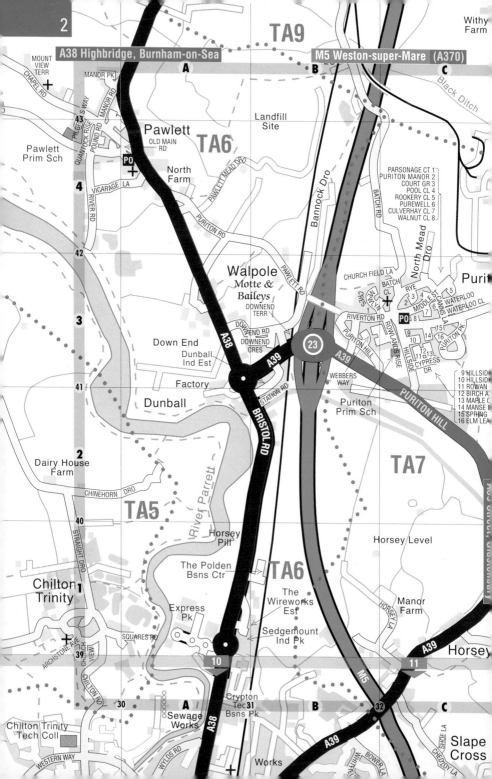

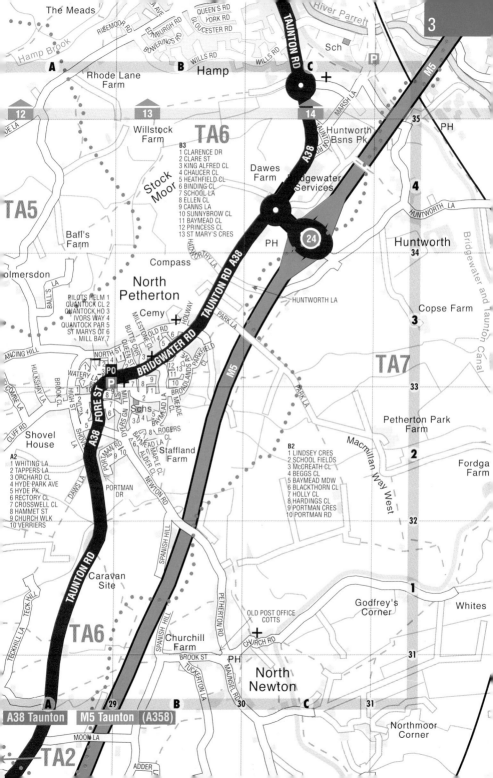

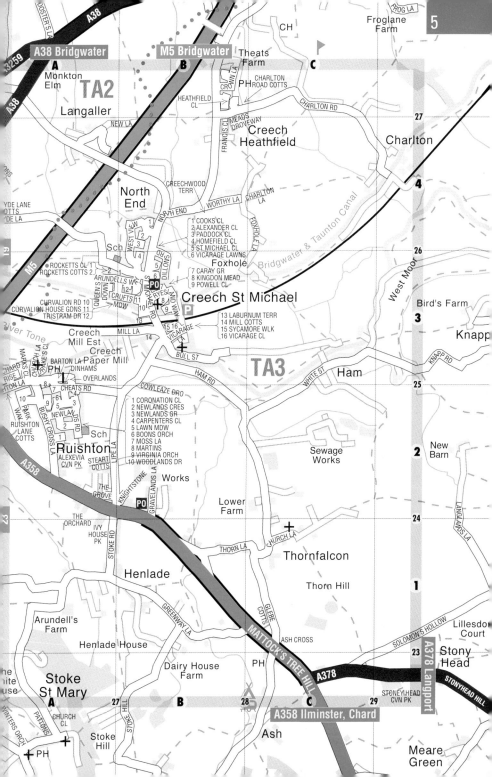

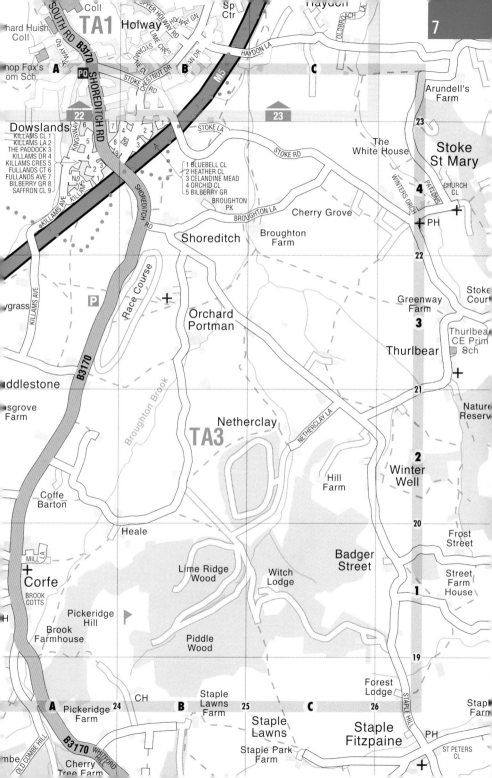

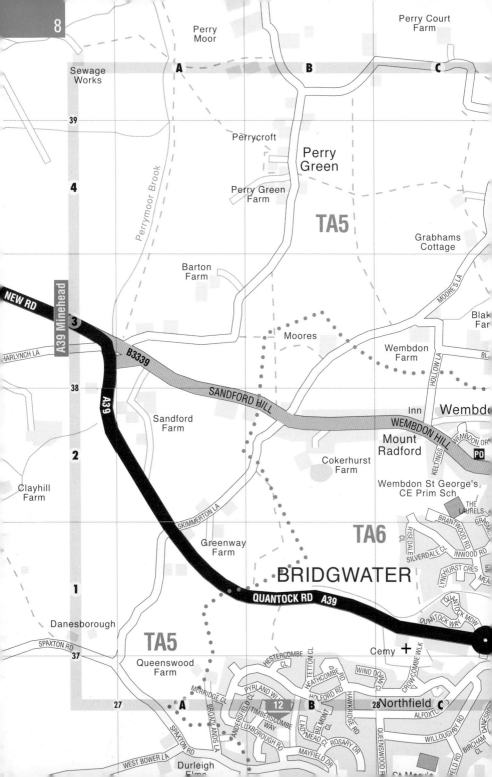

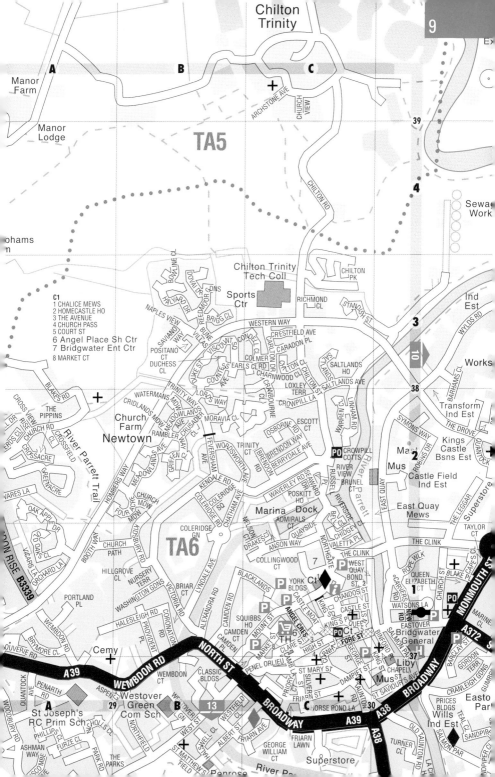

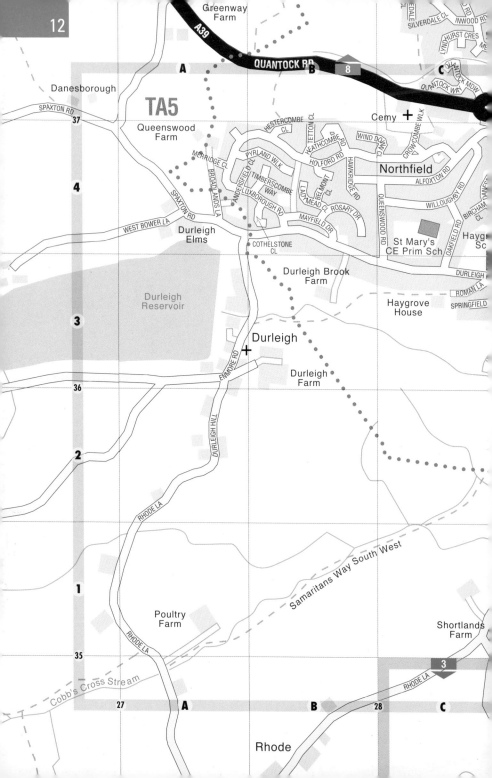

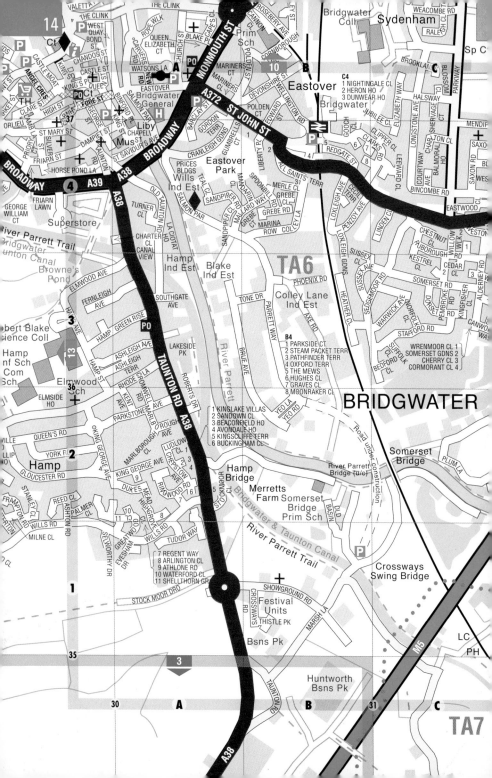

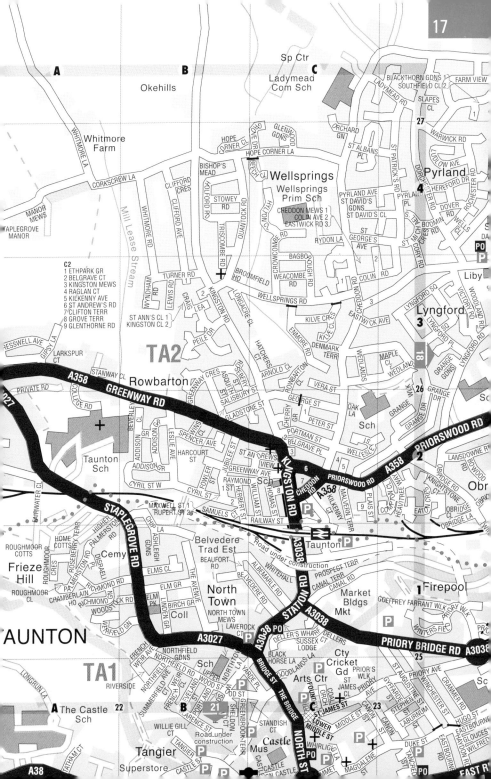

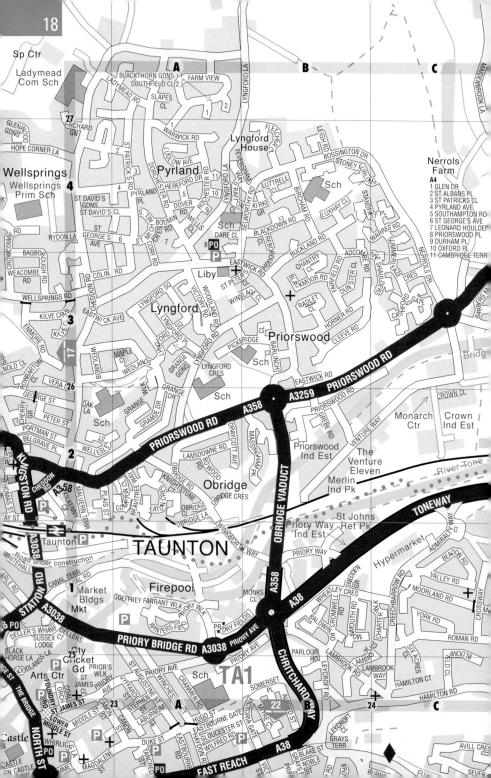

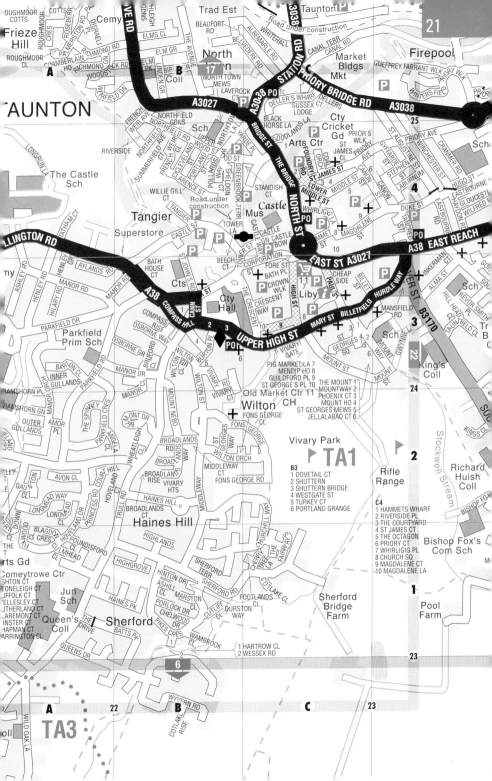

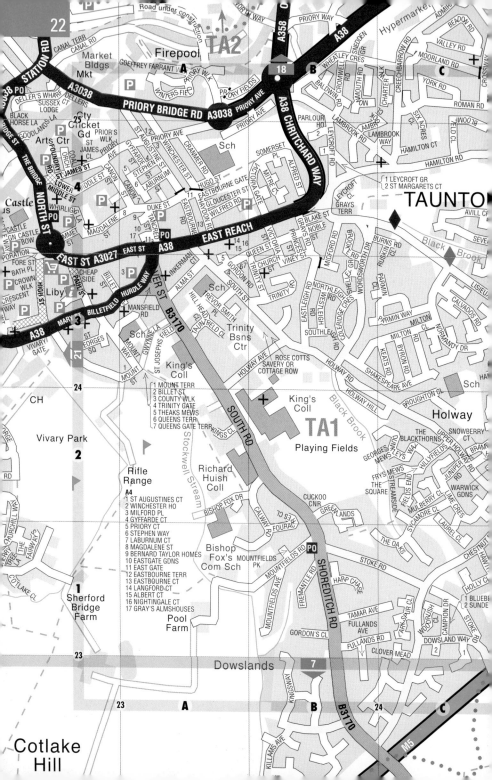

Index

Street names are listed alphabetically and show the locality, the Postcode district, the page number and a reference to the square in which the name falls on the map page

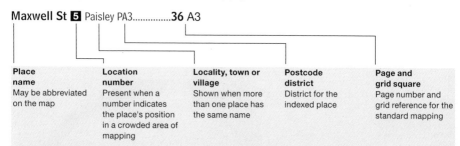

Maxwell St **5** Paisley PA3..............**36** A3

Place name	Location number	Locality, town or village	Postcode district	Page and grid square
May be abbreviated on the map	Present when a number indicates the place's position in a crowded area of mapping	Shown when more than one place has the same name	District for the indexed place	Page number and grid reference for the standard mapping

Towns and villages are listed in CAPITAL LETTERS
Public and commercial buildings are highlighted in magenta. **Places of interest** are highlighted in blue with a star *

Abbreviations used in the index

Acad	Academy	Ct	Court	Hts	Heights	Pl	Place
App	Approach	Ctr	Centre	Ind	Industrial	Prec	Precinct
Arc	Arcade	Ctry	Country	Inst	Institute	Prom	Promenade
Ave	Avenue	Cty	County	Int	International	Rd	Road
Bglw	Bungalow	Dr	Drive	Intc	Interchange	Recn	Recreation
Bldg	Building	Dro	Drove	Junc	Junction	Ret	Retail
Bsns, Bus	Business	Ed	Education	L	Leisure	Sh	Shopping
Bvd	Boulevard	Emb	Embankment	La	Lane	Sq	Square
Cath	Cathedral	Est	Estate	Liby	Library	St	Street
Cir	Circus	Ex	Exhibition	Mdw	Meadow	Sta	Station
Cl	Close	Gd	Ground	Meml	Memorial	Terr	Terrace
Cnr	Corner	Gdn	Garden	Mkt	Market	TH	Town Hall
Coll	College	Gn	Green	Mus	Museum	Univ	University
Com	Community	Gr	Grove	Orch	Orchard	Wk, Wlk	Walk
Comm	Common	H	Hall	Pal	Palace	Wr	Water
Cott	Cottage	Ho	House	Par	Parade	Yd	Yard
Cres	Crescent	Hospl	Hospital	Pas	Passage		
Cswy	Causeway	HQ	Headquarters	Pk	Park		

Index of towns, villages, streets, hospitals, industrial estates, railway stations, schools, shopping centres, universities and places of interest

Aca – Ayl

A

Acacia Gdns TA2 . . 19 B3
Adcombe Rd TA2 . . 18 B4
Addison Gr TA2 . . . 17 B2
Admiral Blake Mus *
TA6 . . . . 14 A4
Admirals Ct TA6 . . . 9 C1
Admiralty Way
TA1 . . . . 18 C1
Adscombe Ave
TA6 . . . . 10 C2
Albemarle Rd
TA1 . . . . 17 C1
Albert Ct
Bridgwater TA6 . . . 13 B4
15 Taunton TA1 . . . . 22 A4

Albert St TA6 . . . . . 13 B4
Albion Cl TA6 . . . . . 10 B1
Alder Cl
North Petherton
TA6 . . . . 3 B2
Taunton TA1 . . . . . . 23 A1
Alderney Rd TA6 . . 14 C3
Alexander Cl TA3 . . . 5 B4
Alexandra Rd TA6 . . 9 B1
Alexevia Cvn Pk
TA3 . . . . 5 A2
Alfoxton Rd TA6 . . . 12 C4
Alfred St TA1 . . . . . 22 B4
Allen Rd TA6 . . . . . 13 C1
ALLERFORD 4 A3
Allerton Rd TA6 . . . 10 B3
Allington Cl TA1 . . . 23 B4
All Saints' Terr
TA6 . . . . 14 B4
Alma St TA1 . . . . . . 22 A3

Almond Tree Cl
TA6 . . . . 15 A4
Alston Cl TA1 . . . . . 20 C1
Amberd La TA3 . . . . . 6 B3
Amber Mead TA1 . . 23 A3
Amor Pl TA1 . . . . . . 21 A2
Andersfield Cl
TA6 . . . . 12 A4
Angela Cl TA1 . . . . . 21 A2
Angel Cres TA6 . . . . 9 C1
Angel Place Sh Ctr
6 TA6 . . . . 9 C1
Anson Way TA6 . . . . 9 C1
Apple Bsns Ctr The
TA2 . . . . 16 B2
Apple Tree Cl
TA6 . . . . 15 A4
Apricot Tree Cl
TA6 . . . . 11 A1

Archbishop Cranmer
CE Com Prim Sch
TA1 . . . . 22 A4
Arlington Cl TA6 . . 14 A2
Arnold Cl TA2 . . . . . 17 C3
Arundells Way TA3 . 5 B3
Arun Gr TA1 . . . . . . 23 A4
Ashbourne Cres
TA1 . . . . 23 A3
Ash Cl TA6 . . . . 15 A4
Ash Cres TA1 . . . . . 20 B2
Ash Cross TA3 . . . . . 5 C1
Ashford Cl TA6 . . . . 13 B2
Ashford Rd TA1 . . . 20 C2
Ash Grove Way
TA6 . . . . 11 A3
Ashill Cl TA1 . . . . . . 21 B1
Ashleigh Ave TA6 . . 14 A3
Ashleigh Gdns
TA1 . . . . 17 B1

Ashleigh Terr
TA6 . . . . 14 A3
Ashley Rd TA1 . . . . 21 A3
Ashman Way TA6 . . 13 A4
Ashton Ct TA1 . . . . 20 C1
Ashton Rd TA6 . . . . 13 C2
Aspen Ct TA6 . . . . . 13 B4
Asquith St TA2 . . . . 17 B2
Athlone Rd TA6 . . . 14 A2
Avalon Rd TA6 . . . . 11 A1
Avebury Dr TA6 . . . 11 A1
Avenue The
3 Bridgwater
TA6 . . . . 9 C1
Taunton TA1 . . . . . . 17 B1
Avill Cres TA1 . . . . . 22 C4
Avon Cl TA1 . . . . . . 21 A2
Avondale Ho TA6 . . 14 A2
Axe Rd TA6 . . . . . . 14 B3
Aylands Rd TA1 . . . 21 A3

List of numbered locations

In some busy areas of the maps it is not always possible to show the name of every place.

Where not all names will fit, some smaller places are shown by a number. If you wish to find out the name associated with a number, use this listing.

The places in this list are also listed normally in the Index.

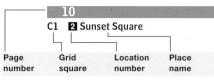

Page number	Grid square	Location number	Place name

10   C1 **2** Sunset Square

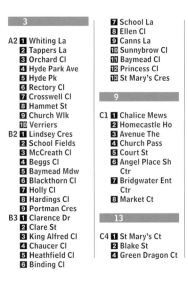

3

A2 **1** Whiting La
2 Tappers La
3 Orchard Cl
4 Hyde Park Ave
5 Hyde Pk
6 Rectory Cl
7 Crosswell Cl
8 Hammet St
9 Church Wlk
10 Verriers
B2 **1** Lindsey Cres
2 School Fields
3 McCreath Cl
4 Beggs Cl
5 Baymead Mdw
6 Blackthorn Cl
7 Holly Cl
8 Hardings Cl
9 Portman Cres
B3 **1** Clarence Dr
2 Clare St
3 King Alfred Cl
4 Chaucer Cl
5 Heathfield Cl
6 Binding Cl

7 School La
8 Ellen Cl
9 Canns La
10 Sunnybrow Cl
11 Baymead Cl
12 Princess Cl
13 St Mary's Cres

9

C1 **1** Chalice Mews
2 Homecastle Ho
3 Avenue The
4 Church Pass
5 Court St
6 Angel Place Sh Ctr
7 Bridgwater Ent Ctr
8 Market Ct

13

C4 **1** St Mary's Ct
2 Blake St
4 Green Dragon Ct

14

B4 **1** Parkside Ct
2 Steam Packet Terr
3 Pathfinder Terr
4 Oxford Terr
5 Mews The
6 Hughes Cl
7 Graves Cl
8 Moonraker Cl
C4 **1** Nightingale Cl
2 Heron Ho
3 Dunwear Ho

17

C2 **1** Ethpark Gr
2 Belgrave Ct
3 Kingston Mews
4 Raglan Ct
5 Kilkenny Ave
6 St Andrew's Rd
7 Clifton Terr
8 Grove Terr
9 Glenthorne Rd

18

A4 **3** St Patricks Cl
5 Southampton Row
7 Leonard Houlden Ct
8 Priorswood Pl
9 Durham Pl
10 Oxford Pl
11 Cambridge Terr
C4 **1** Glen Dr

21

B3 **1** Dovetail Ct
2 Shuttern
3 Shuttern Bridge
4 Westgate St
5 Turkey Ct
6 Portland Grange
C4 **1** Hammets Wharf
2 Riverside Pl
3 Courtyard The
4 St James Ct
5 Octagon The
7 Whirligig Pl

8 Church Sq
9 Magdalene Ct
10 Magdalene La

22

A4 **1** St Augustines Ct
2 Winchester Ho
3 Milford Pl
4 Gyffarde Ct
5 Priory Ct
6 Stephen Way
7 Laburnum Ct
8 Bernard Taylor Homes
10 Eastgate Gdns
11 East Gate
12 Eastbourne Terr
13 Eastbourne Ct
14 Langford Ct
15 Albert Ct
16 Nightingale Ct
17 Gray's Alm-shouses